One to One
B2B

One to One B2B

Customer Development Strategies
for the Business-to-Business World

Don Peppers and

Martha Rogers, Ph.D.

CURRENCY
DOUBLEDAY

New York   London   Toronto   Sydney   Auckland

A Currency Book

Published by Doubleday

a division of Random House, Inc.

1540 Broadway, New York, New York, 10036

Currency and Doubleday are
trademarks of Doubleday, a division of Random House, Inc.

Book design by Chris Welch

Library of Congress Cataloging-in-Publication Data

Peppers, Don.

One to one, B2B: customer development strategies for the business-to-
business world / Don Peppers and Martha Rogers.—1st ed.

p.   cm.

Includes bibliographical references and index.

1. Distributors (Commerce) 2. Customer relations. I. Rogers,
Martha, Ph.D. II. Title.

HF5422 .P38 2001

658.8'12—dc21

00-066022

ISBN 0-385-49409-2

10 9 8 7 6 5 4 3 2 1

This book is dedicated to our children—Tyson, Emmet, Tess, Margot, Bryce, Cameron, and Spencer—in the belief that theirs will be a more customer-friendly world than ours.

Contents

Acknowledgments

Over the course of researching and writing *One to One B2B*, we benefited greatly from the cooperation and assistance of many wonderful friends. We want to honor these friends now and express our gratitude for the support and insight they so willingly gave. We thank our agent, Rafe Sagalyn, and our publisher, Roger Scholl, for their belief in us and for their commitment to this project. We also thank our editor at Doubleday, Stephanie Land, for her patience and dedication.

Mike Barlow, our editorial director, kept the project moving forward, from its inception right through to its publication. He conducted the vast majority of the interviews with company officials that we relied on to write the case studies, and he provided well-researched, well-written first drafts of the cases themselves. Mike's steady hand on the tiller kept us from running aground more than once, and he was an invaluable resource during the process of putting *One to One B2B* together.

We were blessed with the advice and insight of our partners

and colleagues at Peppers and Rogers Group. We would be remiss if we didn't single out partners Lisa Hayford, Craig Johnson, and Paula Puleo, and consultants Ed Hrvatin and Tom Spitale, for going above and beyond the call of duty. Their suggestions and constructive criticism greatly improved the final draft. And for their guidance, wisdom, and generosity, we especially wish to thank Steve Skinner, Bob Dorf, Tom Shimko, Hershel Sarbin, Lane Michel, Tom Niehaus, Trish Watson, Valerie Peck, Bill Shulby, Jim Doucette, and Sophie Vlessing.

Geoffrey Moore, author of *Crossing the Chasm* and *Living on the Fault Line*, composed an exceptionally strong foreword to this book. Geoff's thoughts form a solid launching pad for the chapters that follow, and we are grateful for his insight.

Our editorial and research teams at Peppers and Rogers Group also provided valuable aid along the way. We owe special thanks to Bill Millar, Laura Cococcia, Tyson Peppers, John Courtmanche, Christine DiGrazia, Chris Helm, and Shaunee Cole; and to Vanguard Director Stacey Riordan. Their timely and significant contributions enhanced the overall quality of our effort. We also thank Josh Stailey, Ken Saunders, Ben Kunz, Tony Jaros, Jill Collins, Tracey Robinson, Julie Hollenberg, Tracy Reale, Rachel Mansfield, Monique Young, Janine DeMita, Emanuela Chiaranda, and Corliss Brown, for their support and assistance throughout the project.

Five carefully constructed case studies make up the essential core of *One to One B2B*. Building these case studies from the ground up required many hours of interviews with executives and managers at the organizations we profiled. For their time and attention, we thank Thomas Forsythe, Robert Langer, Kristena Bins-Turner, Penne Allen, Chris Halligan, Cliff Mountain,

Patrick Vogt, Andy North, Sarah Lavender, Yoav Etiel, Warren Winterbottom, Charles Ferrucci, Andy Smith, Paul DeStephano, Brad Workman, Frank Conforti, Huw Roberts, Pat Elnicki, Rachael Schroeder, Kristen Dorn, Joe Kirby, Kyle Talbott, Steve Speake, Bob Lento, Ronald Schultz, David Dougherty, Jay Halsted, Mike Serpan, Renea Morris, Matthew D. Conrad, Carlos Weiss, Newton Washington, Jan Martin Suter, Leopoldo Cid, Juan Cassagne, Daniel Altomonte, Jean Calembert, John Kramp, Gene Mims, Steve Blount, and John Cochran. Without *their* cooperation, there would be no *One to One B2B*.

Most of all, however, we thank our spouses, Pamela Devenney and Stuart Bertsch, for once again putting up with missed weekends, delayed holidays, and all-day editing sessions, and generally providing cheerful support for our quest to help every company become a successful one-to-one enterprise.

Don Peppers and Martha Rogers
November 2000

Foreword
Geoffrey Moore

Over the past several years the stock market has experienced unprecedented volatility, as investors seek to absorb the impact of technology shifts on the future performance of our publicly held companies. The volatility is based in part on the need to invest heavily in the present, typically taking on losses, in order to gain a sustainable competitive advantage to be exploited in the future. It is an inherently unnerving practice because one is not extending a proven trend but rather trying to invent future history.

One of the issues contributing to our case of collective nerves is how to appropriately value a customer base in terms of its expected contribution to future earnings, to assign a number to what some have called the *lifetime value of a customer*. With little data and no history to guide it, the market exhibits a kind of bipolar behavior, its mood swinging violently from intense optimism to profound pessimism, which in turn tempts companies to go on equally self-destructive binges at their end. Here's how it plays out.

In a mood of expansiveness, the market assumes disproportionately high rates of customer retention, and thereby bids up the lifetime value of the customer base. This, in turn, encourages companies to go on a *customer acquisition binge*—to go out and acquire customers at almost any cost—because every new load-in drives up their stock price further. Now this might be a good idea if only customers were a form of cordwood that could be stacked and stored for future use. Unfortunately, however, customers themselves tend to be volatile and don't normally take well to this stack-and-store approach. Instead they learn to equate *being acquired* with *being had* and defect in droves.

Once defections appear, the market shifts into a mood of depression. Now investors assume a disproportionately low rate of retention, drastically discounting the lifetime value of the customer base by assuming increasingly dire rates of erosion or churn. This, of course, drives down the valuation of the company, and that, in turn, motivates its management to go on a *customer retention binge*, blindly throwing resources at "doing whatever it takes" to keep existing customers happy. Customers, interestingly, don't take particularly well to this either. Sensing a transparent attempt to buy their loyalty, they accept the gifts but make no commitments, thus further eroding the economic viability of the new franchise.

It occurs to me, having now watched this behavior play out repeatedly, that we may have a problem of *root metaphor*. Metaphors, consciously or unconsciously, express our strategic approach toward the world we inhabit. Thus when we say we want to *acquire* or *retain* customers, we are implying a strategy of *ranching*: customers are a form of *cattle*, our customer base is a type of *herd*, and our *brand* is something that we might seriously consider searing into their flesh. In a similar vein, when we call our customers *consumers*, as Jerry Michalski, former editor of *Release 1.0*, likes to point out, we are implying that they have but two features worth attending to—a *mouth* and a *wallet*. The root metaphor is inherently *infantile*, implying large nurseries with chilling undertones of the "factory" scene in *The Matrix*. With implications like these, is it any wonder if customers do not cooperate fully in our plans for them?

I raise this issue here and now because you are about to read a very powerful book, *One to One B2B*, which is going to present to you a set of tools for creating deeper relationships with customers. From case studies of best practices you will learn both theory and practice for interacting with customers at a far more intimate level than you are able to today. This creates the opportunity to dramatically increase the returns from your existing customer base—*provided you can reshape the way you think of the people involved.*

Let me get you started on this journey. Begin with the notion of *putting the customer first*. An inspiring ideal, to be sure, but it embodies a deep flaw: there is no such thing as *the* customer. In the real world there is *a* customer, and there's another, and another, and at least in their own minds, they do not *add up*. This is individualism at work, and the power of one-to-one marketing demands that you never forget it. In other words, if you try to implement the techniques in this book homogeneously across an entire customer base—and that would be a very efficient thing to do—you will render them, and yourself, ineffective. You must continually perform, therefore, the mental disaggregation of the customer into many, many customers.

A second point along the same lines: The XYZ Corporation is *not* a customer. It is a collection of customers. In that collection, for example, are end users of your product or service who care deeply about its *features* and *benefits*. Those end users, however, report to managers, who are also your customers, and who do *not* care about features and benefits but rather about the *productivity* of the end users. And those managers in turn report to executives who, having delegated the productivity concerns, are concerned about the *strategic implications* of investing in your offerings.

Meanwhile, there is a support group somewhere, which is also made up of your customers, who don't really care about any of the foregoing since it is their job to maintain the *technical integrity* of your system as it interfaces with their company's systems. They are the only ones who will read your manuals. And there are financial professionals elsewhere in the organization, also your customers, who care about things like *account status* and the like—and are the only ones who will.

And so it goes. As Don and Martha argue persuasively, one-to-one marketing may have first arisen in the consumer space, but it is even more applicable in business-to-business relationships. And that leads me to a final term for rethinking—*relationship*. In recent years the world has received more than enough information on relationship marketing, to the point where the term is in danger of becoming meaningless. That would be a dire result indeed. To resurrect it, I think we need to drill down a level and think about a *series* of relationships, a progression of increasingly intimate interactions with a customer, each of which has progressively enhanced economic results, of which I will propose four, as follows:

1. *Maintenance.* This is a relationship of inertia and is the default performance of a customer base that is not actively being alienated. I am in a relationship of maintenance to my airline. It is not a pretty relationship, but its economic significance is huge because it represents that the cattle metaphor does work after a fashion. For matters where it is not worth changing, the herd stays in the pen, and thus every year corporations can forecast a substantial part of their upcoming revenues and earnings, with remarkably little investment to bring it off. On the other hand, while cost-effective, this is the relationship most vulnerable to defection and has little to no expansion possibilities.

2. *Referenceability.* This is a relationship of passive support, the default performance of a satisfied customer. I am a referenceable customer of my doctor, my dentist, my periodontist, my . . . but no, the list is too depressing to continue. If anyone asks me to recommend someone in one of these categories, I will recommend one of them. In business this too has huge economic ramifications, for pragmatic customers use word-of-mouth referrals as their primary influence in making buying decisions that have any appreciable amount of risk associated with them (as when, for example, you are trying to decide whom to allow to flay your gums). If your customer is referenceable, you have a rock upon which to build your church.

3. *Participation*. This is a relationship of active support, where customer and vendor become partners in a shared enterprise that involves them both. I am a participative customer of my accounting firm, Tiret and Company, in that I continually find new projects to engage them in as The Chasm Group expands its involvement in the world and as my personal interests become increasingly complex. They don't sell to me, in other words, I sell to them—and then pay for it to boot! This is *very* cost-effective marketing. It happens whenever your customer thinks of you as a trusted advisor, a partner rather than a vendor. You won't have the resources to support this relationship with many customers, so it is important that you target the opportunities that will be most mutually rewarding.

4. *Evangelism*. This is a relationship of hyperactive support, where a customer proactively markets your product or service without any urging on your part. I am an evangelist for Home Preservation Services, a company that performs all the maintenance services for our house. I mention them in my talks, I tell friends about them, I make jokes about how their service is a marriage preservation service, I even mention them in the forewords of books! I do this entirely voluntarily because I am so pleased with the outcome that I have to find ways to express it. As the term "evangelist" implies, this is the same energy that spreads religion, and of the four relationships it is the only one that can actually expand your market footprint. Not all businesses can generate an evangelistic response, but for those who can, the rewards are extraordinary.

In closing, I ask that you bring this vocabulary of relation-ship to your reading of this book and to your reflections upon that reading. The lifetime value of a customer base is a function of the quality of the relationships comprised within it. As Don and Martha have taught us before, the value of the base is typ-ically more a function of escalating the relationship with your current customers than running out to acquire more. To be sure, a balance is required, but few would debate that it is the post-sales relationship that needs the greatest attention in the vast majority of companies. That, I expect, is what has brought you to this book, to which I now commend you.

Geoffrey Moore
Partner, Mohr Davidow Ventures
Chairman, The Chasm Group
January 2001

Chapter
1

The once and future business strategy

In our first book, *The One to One Future*, we described a "future world" in which businesses would use interactive technologies and computer databases to compete for one customer at a time, constantly trying to strengthen their relationships with their most valuable customers. The world we described is one in which "share of customer" is considered a more relevant metric of success than market share, a world in which keeping and growing customers, over time, plays a more important role for a business than simply acquiring customers.

With the explosion of the World Wide Web and the Internet, this "one to one future" arrived sooner than anyone thought. So for most of the past decade we've been giving seminars and workshops all over the world on building one-to-one customer relationships. We've authored three more books, and dozens of articles, on various aspects of the subject. And we've built a global consulting business to help clients strategize and plan their own customer relationship programs.

Because *The One to One Future* examined the impact of interactive technologies primarily on the consumer space, many people assumed that the one-to-one customer relationship management revolution itself was primarily a business-to-consumer phenomenon. But the truth is just the opposite. The disciplines of building one-to-one customer relationships have always applied more naturally to business-to-business situations. In selling to other businesses, companies have *always* employed the principles of relationship building, feedback, and customization. And account management is directly analogous to the type of "customer portfolio management" we suggest for companies that sell to consumers.

In the past few years, however, new computer technologies and applications have been created to assist companies in managing their interactions with customers. These new technologies run the gamut from customer databases to contact management and sales force automation systems, from Web site operations to call center management systems. Increasingly, companies are also learning how to mass customize their products and services, literally delivering uniquely configured products to unique customers, in response to their individual interactions and specifications.

The availability of these new technologies has required companies to think much more carefully about the mechanics of developing and managing customer relationships, with the result that the theory and practice of one-to-one customer relationship management throughout an enterprise has been refined, enhanced, and built into a formidable body of knowledge.

Now we are coming full circle. It's time to take these principles, now that they have been developed, refined, and honed to a sharper competitive edge in the interactive consumer space, and apply them directly back to the B2B space. That's what this book, *One to One B2B*, is all about: applying one-to-one principles to the tasks businesses face when they are selling to other businesses, rather than to consumers.

The way we plan to do this is by examining in detail the customer relationship management efforts of five business-to-business organizations:

■ Dell Computer has an interactive Web program for its business customers that allows a business to streamline its purchase order requisition costs and better manage the "total cost of ownership" of its computers. The way Dell automates its relationships with these customers is genuinely enlightening. But often the real benefits of this kind of relationship are hidden from view. In Dell's case, one of the principal benefits of the program is that it gives Dell a one-to-one relationship not just with the purchasing and IT managers at client firms, but with the end users of Dell products within those firms.

■ Bentley Systems, a Pennsylvania company, sells its CAD-CAM software applications to architectural and engineering firms all over the world, largely through a network of value-added resellers. The companies that buy Bentley software manage large construction and engineering projects that require collaboration among many different vendors and suppliers, and Bentley has its eye on participating with its customers in the longer-term management of these projects. As a part of this initiative, Bentley is attempting to subscribe

its customers to its services, rather than simply selling periodic software licenses.

- Convergys, an outsourcer of both inbound and outbound
  call center services, found that its previous emphasis on
  client acquisition was yielding less and less. But pursuing an
  account development strategy—trying to sell more and better services to its existing clients—turned out to be a good
  deal more complicated than it had anticipated. Simply ranking clients by their value to Convergys was difficult enough,
  but then putting a new relationship-based sales and marketing strategy in place meant reengineering the structure and
  compensation of the sales force itself.

- Novartis CP, the Latin American agrochemical division of
  this global company, found its very existence threatened by
  the biotechnology revolution. However, by setting out to
  cultivate relationships with the end users of its products—
  the farm operators it was selling to—rather than its dealer
  network, the company has been able not just to stem the
  losses but turn a nice profit.

- LifeWay Christian Resources, a marketer of materials for
  churches across the United States, traditionally had defined
  success in terms of revenue growth. When top management
  decided to shift the company's strategic focus from selling
  more products to meeting customer needs more closely,
  LifeWay found that the only way to implement this strategy
  was to integrate it throughout the entire firm.

It's important to recognize that each of these case studies is
trying to capture what is essentially a "work in progress." That
is, the companies we're writing about are not resting on what

they've accomplished. They all have plans for leveraging their customer relationships much further. They are learning more and more as they make progress, and they are constantly adjusting their plans. We are catching them in mid-stride, documenting what they've done so far, and how this fits into their bigger plans.

As a result, there is an important element of transition planning that must be considered by each of these firms. They are not just setting up a new method for doing business; they are managing the change, from one method to another. Perhaps they are organizing their transition by emphasizing their relationships first with just a few top clients—the "picket fence" approach of Convergys, for instance. Or perhaps they are managing the transition by creating a function for facilitating change within their own organizations, as Novartis CP is doing, by tapping a senior executive to be the unofficial "culture change" agent for the firm's sales force. Or perhaps they've organized several dozen middle and top executives into teams to focus on customers, messages, and culture, the way LifeWay has done.

However this transition is managed, it points out an extremely important issue. Becoming a customer-focused, one-to-one enterprise is not something that will ever be fully "achieved." Being customer-focused is not a *destination* for a firm, but a *direction* in which to point the business. The day is never likely to come when an executive at one of these companies or any other company will be able to say, "Our customer relationships are now as strong and deep as they can ever be." Instead, even when the long-term strategic initiatives they are undertaking now have been largely accomplished, there will always be more to do, farther to go. Competitive success will come from being further along this never-ending path toward managing customer relationships than your rivals. And success will come one customer at a time, as you lock in the business of first one large customer, and then another, and another.

So each of these case studies we are presenting to you in this book should be viewed as a snapshot, capturing how a particular company looks as it is engaged in making progress, gradually but relentlessly, in a customer-focused direction. We gathered most of the material for our case studies the old-fashioned way: by talking with them directly. We interviewed executives, managers, distributors, front-line workers, and customers. We interviewed dozens of primary sources in person, over the telephone, and via email. We also relied on secondary sources, which are fully documented in the endnotes section. We relied on our collective business experience; and the advice, comments, and opinions of our colleagues at Peppers and Rogers Group. If the organization profiled in the case study is a former or current consulting client, we disclose this information in the endnotes. We applied the same research methodology to each of the organizations profiled in the book. None were granted editorial control or the right to veto content. We did, however, allow them to read early drafts of the chapters to confirm the accuracy of their statements and to correct factual errors.

And while the purpose of this book is to report on the achievements and successes of one-to-one B2Bs, we tried to be as objective and as thorough as possible in our reporting and analysis.

But before we dig into these case studies, which begin at

Chapter 3, we'll be discussing the basic theory of one-to-one marketing, or customer relationship management, and how this theory should be applied specifically in B2B situations.

B2B vs. B2C

Consumer marketers may have been first to launch a series of high-profile Web initiatives, but it may in fact be the B2B companies that have the most at stake, in the near term.

The interactive woods are full of dark and ominous implications for the competitive health of B2B firms in every industry. The rise of reverse auction markets and buyer cooperatives, for instance, threatens to drive margins in B2B situations down through the floor. Market-making Web sites of all types and varieties are springing up in every conceivable nook and cranny of B2B activity, from e-Steel and Water-Online to the automotive manufacturers' intranet-based buying cartel. They will have a potentially devastating effect on the financial well-being of many B2B suppliers.

There are several important ways in which a B2B situation differs considerably from a B2C situation, and most of these differences make it even more critical for the B2B organization to develop one-to-one customer relationships.

Relationships within relationships. The first and obvious difference between selling to an individual and selling to a business is that a consumer is a single decision-making unit, but a business is not. A business is composed of a number of distinct individuals. Many different people will likely have

an influence on the decision-making process. There are relationship dynamics on several levels. The B2B organization
must not only develop and cultivate its relationship with the
business customer, as an overall organization; it must also
develop relationships with the divisions, departments,
groups, and individuals within that organization. It must
learn what it can about the dynamics among all these sub-
sidiary entities, and it must engage in independent but coor-
dinated activities to strengthen its overall position.

So the B2B company is constantly trying to dig deeper, to
probe beneath the surface of its relationship with the organization, as a customer, in order to uncover its relationships
with the individual decision makers and influencers within
that organization. One of the secrets behind the success of
Dell's Web-based tool, for instance, is that Dell is now able
to identify and interact with the actual individual end users
of its products, wherever they are within a customer organization.

Just a few, large customers. While a B2C is likely to sell
to hundreds of thousands, or maybe tens of millions, of consumers, the B2B often sells to just a few dozen customers. So
a B2C company can usually rely on a statistical analysis of its
customer base to figure out what's going on at any point in
time with any particular "type" of customer, but it's often
much more difficult for a B2B company to generalize about
its clients in any way. Instead, the B2B must look at its customers individually and make what may amount to highly
subjective judgments about each one.

This was, for instance, the situation Convergys faced

when it tried to prioritize its own marketing and sales efforts in order to begin concentrating on its most important customers. It devised a "lifetime value" model that incorporated a number of subjectively ascribed attributes, such as the degree of technology entanglement or the "state of partnership" with a particular client. The attributes might be subjectively ascribed, but in order to gain any benefit from prioritizing its efforts, Convergys had to make these subjective judgments in a basically objective fashion, so that it could compare its client relationships across the whole customer base.

Account development selling. Because of the complex nature of organizations as customers, a B2B company is much more likely to view success not just in terms of how many new customers it can acquire but in terms of how deeply it can penetrate its current customer accounts. A B2B company will pay attention not just to the sales volume with a particular customer but also to the "development" variables, such as how many of the customer's divisions it does business with, or how many of the customer's executives it knows, and the importance of their influence within the customer organization. Account development strategies are a form of "share of customer" marketing, and this has always been a natural activity for B2B organizations. What has changed recently, however, is the sophistication with which a B2B company can pursue its account development strategy, because of the array of computer-based tools now available, including sales force automation systems, contact management software, and database analytics.

A B2B company may emphasize account development because it finds, as both Convergys and Bentley Systems did, that it can no longer get an acceptable level of traction in the marketplace just by trying to acquire new customers. Moreover, as both Bentley and Convergys discovered, account development is a particularly useful strategy whenever the product or service being sold is complex and difficult to use or implement, which is often the case in a B2B situation.

But Convergys also learned that because account development is an inherently longer-term strategy than customer acquisition, with results that are more difficult to measure immediately, it requires a sales force that is differently trained, structured, and compensated. Moreover, the sales force—and the entire B2B organization—must orient itself around a different overall goal. The principal goal of an account penetrating B2B organization is *finding products for its customers, not finding customers for its products.*

Channel complexity. Managing consumer relationships, for a B2C organization, often involves important channel issues, such as the company's relationship with its own dealers or with the independent retailers that sell its manufactured product. However, for the B2B enterprise, these same channel issues can be quite a bit more complex. Because the B2B product is often a more complicated and difficult product to install or use, the channel members in a B2B situation can often add a great deal of value to the overall process. Such is the case with Bentley's resellers, for instance. Bentley makes joint sales calls on its end-user customers with its resellers, and it has shared with selected resellers its various sales scenario "templates" for closing business. It has even taken an equity interest in certain of its resellers.

But in addition to the external selling channels, it is often the case that the "channel" organization is actually within the business customer itself. Because of the division of labor within any large business customer's own organization, purchasing agents and contract authorities often amount to nothing more than captive channel members, owned and operated by the business customers themselves. So a B2B company should want to create the same types of channel relationships with the members of a customer's "internal" channel as it would create with external channel members.

Knowledge-based selling. Precisely because the products and services sold in a B2B context are sometimes highly complex, it is often advantageous to base the sales process on educating and training the customers. Convergys' clients would make greater use of the company's services if they only knew better how to employ the phone to build relationships with their own customers. So one thing Convergys does is offer seminars and workshops to its clients, trying to educate them with respect to the benefits of phone interaction with consumers. And Bentley's "account use scenarios" represent the company's effort to win business by using the firm's deep and detailed knowledge of how its products can best be used in different client situations.

More than is the case in consumer marketing, because of the complex nature of its products a B2B enterprise must educate its customers. A B2B will often find itself in the position of having to teach business customers how to use its product or service more productively, and sometimes even having to teach customers *why* its product or service is beneficial at all. More than is the case in retail or consumer competition, therefore, B2B companies have always relied on printed publications, custom-published journals and magazines, seminars and other, similar, educational tools.

The truth is that relationships require both one-way and two-way communication. Interaction is communication, and the quality of that effort often separates winners from losers. Communication is the connective tissue of a relationship, so a B2B must skillfully and effectively communicate its product-educational message all down the demand chain, to end users, influencers, decision makers, and distributors—not to mention its other constituencies, such as employees, suppliers, and investors. Many firms custom-publish their own magazines, newsletters, or even journals, designed to continue the customer education process. Bentley Systems, for instance, authors and disseminates several publications to those customers who subscribe to certain services, and it disseminates other publications tailored to the needs of particular types of customers. These publications are designed to improve Bentley's ability to sell things to its customers, of course, but the only way Bentley can do this is by first improving its customers' knowledge of the issues being covered in the publications.

The companies portrayed in this book are finding that gaining their clients' trust must be the first step in communicating any new educational information or imparting any new expertise. A client is going to be suspicious of advice delivered by any party trying to sell something, unless that party has first gained the trust of the client. But how do you measure the benefit of all this? Acquiring some level of expertise, keeping it up to date, educating the people within your sales and service organizations—all these activities involve costs. And then in most cases, you just give the information away to clients for free. Where's the ROI in that? A B2B organization often has to make a great leap of faith before it can quantify the actual benefits of various aspects of the customer relationship management process.

Infrequent purchases. Moreover, because B2B products and services are often "big ticket" items, and this usually means the purchase cycle is long, there are sometimes lengthy periods of inactivity between actual purchase events. So, more than is the case in B2C, a B2B company must constantly be seeking to fill in these gaps, by selling services, or by subscribing its customers. Subscribing customers to your product (by turning the product at least partly into an ongoing service) is a good way to envision what Dell is trying to do with Premier Dell.com, and what Bentley is trying to do with its SELECT service.

In the "old" B2B process, you would spend years cultivating a relationship with a business customer and preparing to exploit a contract opportunity. When the opportunity finally arrived, you would compete for the multimillion-dollar, multiyear contract. Then, regardless of whether you won or lost the contract, the sales team would go on to the next "live" prospect situation, and you didn't need to bother with this client again until the contract came up for renewal.

B2B companies have always known that it makes sense to try to maintain relationships in the "dead periods" in between these very infrequent, large contracts, but in most cases the metrics and reward structures are not set up to encourage this, but to constantly produce new contracts, with new customers.

Helping clients manage themselves. Ultimately, the strongest and best type of relationship with a business customer will be one in which the seller is actually helping the buyer to manage its own business. Businesses are not usually simple operations. As customers, businesses often have problems that a selling organization can help with. So on one level, you have Dell helping its customers simply to manage their own purchasing and requisition processes for IT equipment, but on another level this could enable Dell to assist its corporate customers in managing their overall IT budgets and operations, including "TCO"—total cost of ownership.

Bentley Systems, for its part, is actively engaged in launching a series of services that will allow it to help a customer manage a construction project, and then to manage the ongoing maintenance, upkeep, and improvement of the structure throughout its life. This will involve not just archiving and indexing diagrams, but making information available on a real-time basis to all the various parties associated with a project.

It is our belief that in the broad arena of B2B commerce, organizations will rise or fall on the basis of their ability to cultivate one-to-one relationships with their customers.

One-to-one *is* CRM—defining the terms

You say po-tay-toe, and I say po-tah-toe. You say toe-may-toe, and I say toe-mah-toe.

The blizzard of new technology applications has generated a snowstorm of techno-terminology. There are literally dozens of abbreviations, anagrams, catchy names, sound bites, and buzzwords now being used by various companies to describe the same basic, technology-stimulated shift in the way businesses are doing business.

When we wrote our first book, we described this revolution using the words "one-to-one marketing." By our definition, one-to-one marketing occurs when you and your customer interact directly, the customer tells you something about how he or she wants to be served, and then you change your behavior with respect to this individual customer based on that interaction. This would be a "one-to-one" transaction. But note that "one-to-one" does *not* necessarily mean that every single unique customer will be treated uniquely. In almost every business situation except the Web, this is completely impractical. Instead, "one-to-one marketing" is a phrase that implies a specific, one-customer-to-one-marketer relationship, as is the case when the customer's input drives the marketer's output for that particular customer.

Nor does the word "marketing" capture the true nature of this new form of competition. To most minds the marketing function does not really involve customer service, complaint handling, finance, production and delivery, or even sales. But a "one-to-one marketing" program necessarily involves *all* those various business functions, and others. If you tell me what you want, and I change how I treat *you* based on *your input*, then the production "back end" of my company has to be capable of doing what the sales-and-marketing "front end" has learned you want. This requires a level of integrated activity on the enterprise's part that is beyond the ability of most businesses today. It is also the primary message in our second book, *Enterprise One to One*, so named precisely to drive the point home that no one-to-one "marketer" can possibly be successful without integrating the program throughout the entire enterprise.

In the meantime, every technology firm that can spell "PR" has been busy creating its own set of terms for this new type of competition. In addition, other business authors were making up their own labels. The situation is complicated by the fact that the technology companies are largely describing suites of applications or software programs, while the business authors are mostly trying to capture the essence of the new business processes. But whether we call this phenomenon Customer Relationship Management, or real-time marketing, or customer intimacy, or Learning Relationships, or continuous relationship management, or one-to-one marketing, the basic principles are the same. It really doesn't matter if your acronym is CRM, e-CRM, BRM (for "business"), e-BRM, ERM (for "enterprise"), e-ERM, TERM (technology-enabled relationship management), or just "one-to-one." We are all describing the same elephant.

For now, it is probably safe to say that one of the most widely used terms is "customer relationship management," or "CRM," and this is widely enough used so that in our own publications and in our own business *we use the terms "CRM" and "one-to-one" more or less interchangeably.* Note, however, that when we do employ the CRM acronym, or any other term describing this revolution, we aren't referring to a suite of front-end technology applications, but to the set of strategies and processes that make up this incredible revolution in the way businesses compete. And it is these strategies and processes, as they apply to the business-to-business space, that we will be examining in *One to One B2B*.

The great chain of B2B-ing

Because B2B competition is so different from B2C, there is an unfortunate tendency by some to consider these to be two completely unrelated types of business competition, but this is an oversimplification. One way to visualize the relationship between B2B and B2C is in terms of a continuum of business-to-customer practices, as they might exist at different locations along a classic "demand chain." A demand chain extends up from the ultimate end user of any product, the consumer, and all the way back to the original suppliers of the components of that product, the raw materials providers:

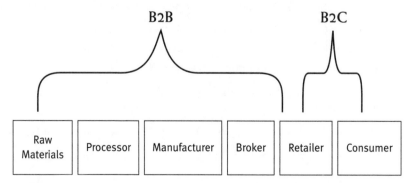

The reality, however, is that the boundaries are blurring along this continuum, not least because the Internet is making it possible to connect all sorts of previously unconnectable parties in a more and more cost-efficient way. So perhaps a better way to visualize today's demand chain would be as follows:

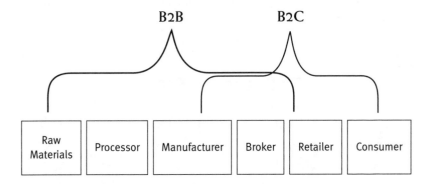

The overlap is where we find the most channel conflict, the difficulty most frequently encountered by any business that tries to create relationships with "customers" who are further down along its own demand chain than might have been possible before the Internet.

It's possible that eventually the question "Are you B2B *or* B2C?" will seem irrelevant. The proper question is likely to be "Where are you located on the B2B-B2C continuum?" If the concept of the traditional supply chain implies competition and exclusivity, the concept of the B2B-B2C continuum (or what many are simply calling the *value chain*) implies collaboration and inclusivity.

In Chapter 2 we'll recap the basic theory and application of one-to-one marketing and CRM in greater detail, and we'll note how it applies specifically to business-to-business organizations.

We will also discuss the relationship between customer relationship management and the broader economy. If you feel fully grounded in one-to-one or CRM principles, you are welcome to skip ahead to the case studies. But we urge you to review the basics before plunging forward. While there are many similarities between one-to-one B2C and one-to-one B2B, there also are some startling differences. If you haven't already read and absorbed the basic principles of customer relationship management, as documented in some of our previous books, we encourage you to do so before reading this one. We won't be repeating ourselves any more than absolutely necessary to set a level for our discussion. For a general introduction to these principles, we suggest reading *The One to One Fieldbook*, which we wrote with Bob Dorf. The *Fieldbook* is a virtual practice guide for professionals or companies engaged in implementing CRM programs.

One last note before moving on. We use the term "one-to-one" as an adjective to describe a general class of customer-centric strategies. The terms "1to1"® and "1:1"® are registered trademarks for our own specific brand of one-to-one marketing, in the consulting practice we run here at Peppers and Rogers Group. To avoid confusion, we'll stick to the term "one-to-one" throughout this book.

Chapter

2

The *real* economy

Much as today's historians regard the twentieth century as a volatile period of global reorganization following three centuries of European imperialism, future economic historians may look back at the current century as a time when culture and society adjusted to the emergence of a less cyclical, globally integrated world.

What exactly do we mean when we say "less cyclical"? Perhaps "less Keynesian" would be more appropriate. John Maynard Keynes saw the economy as an endless series of boom-and-bust cycles. Keynes believed that a subtle alchemy of analysis, planning, and careful fiscal tinkering by governments could mitigate these cycles, resulting in longer periods of prosperity and peace. Keynes wasn't such an optimist that he believed these cycles could be eliminated. He only proposed taking steps to make them less pronounced.

But what propels these cycles to begin with? Imperfect information, for one thing, and any other factors that inhibit a business from adjusting to changing circumstances. For most of the Industrial Age, businesses have based their manufacturing decisions on forecast demand. If you were manufacturing consumer items, you tried to predict how many individual cars or dishwashers or leather jackets people would buy at a price high enough for you to make a reasonable profit. As long as you guessed right, you had just enough inventory to meet demand. If everyone forecast correctly, then prices remained stable, supply met demand, and the economy ran smoothly.

If you underestimated, however, you had to scramble to find the resources to meet the unanticipated demand, bidding up the prices of all the components in your product, and fueling similar scrambles among your suppliers. You began retooling your plant to make more products—realizing, of course, that this effort would require an investment on your part and would take some time. But over a period of weeks or months, you ramped up your production to a rate more appropriate to meet the heavier demand. The whole manufacturing supply chain— not just you but all your various suppliers and customers up and down the chain—adjusted only gradually to such changes, as information about actual demand became more accurate and as production was increased. Soon everyone, including your competitors, produced at a higher capacity, which brought more and more of the demanded products to market.

Unfortunately, however, by the time the increased supply of products hit the market, demand might have fallen off. And even if demand did remain high, it was likely that more products would be hitting the market now than were ever actually demanded in the first place, since everyone would have increased production to meet this demand. So now you have to drop your prices and pull back. Again, it takes time to scale down your production. You cancel orders you had placed with suppliers, forcing them to take the same kinds of actions. Eventually you liquidate unsold products at lower prices, maybe you lay people off, and you hunker down to weather the slump. That's how the business cycle works.

In engineering terms, the business cycle is the predictable result of an insufficiently damped, oscillating system. Its raw intensity, however, has decreased significantly since the end of World War II. That doesn't mean the pace of the economy has slowed, it just means the wild and unpredictable swings of the past seem to have moderated.

Now, at the beginning of the twenty-first century, these oscillations have become even milder, perhaps permanently so. Two of the primary factors contributing to these gentler cycles have been the computer and the global telecommunications infrastructure. Both have greatly accelerated the speed at which the economy is capable of reacting to changed conditions. In a sense, they have given the economy the ability to accommodate a much higher degree of volatility than would have been deemed acceptable in the past. In the old days, the introduction of a new variable (say, a sudden shortage of rubber, or the introduction of a new manufacturing method) would have resulted in years of turbulence.

The point is that in the Age of Interactivity, the economy's self-correcting nature doesn't manifest itself over years or decades, but practically overnight.

The best metaphor for today's economy is the F-117A Nighthawk stealth fighter, which was designed to escape detection by enemy radar. Unfortunately, the shape required to

make the stealth fighter virtually invisible to radar also makes it aerodynamically unstable. It's impossible for a human pilot to keep it flying straight and level, because human beings cannot react quickly enough to detect and compensate for the aerodynamic oscillations that threaten to send the plane spinning wildly out of control.

So what keeps the stealth fighter flying? Its onboard computers continuously monitor the various forces acting on the aircraft and adjust its flight control surfaces from one microsecond to the next, much faster than any human being could manage. These extremely rapid corrections are what keep the plane flying.

No one seems capable of explaining precisely why the economy has more or less suddenly improved its overall performance, but the F-117A's computer-operated feedback mechanism is instructive. Some things should be obvious to anyone in business today. First, as digital technology speeds the flow of information, businesses are no longer forced to endure the inevitable "knowledge blackouts" that made it difficult to assess new levels of demand, or to keep track of the location and availability of supplies. Computers have automated more and more work processes, which means that today a business can often "retool" simply by throwing a switch, rather than having to restructure an assembly line.

In addition, as more and more of our economic activity is accounted for by the nonmanufacturing sector, a greater proportion of businesses don't have assembly lines at all, allowing them to adjust even more rapidly to changing situations. And of course, deregulation in a variety of industries has improved the efficiency with which businesses are able to respond to change. Whether we are talking about airlines changing their prices without waiting for government approval or an arbitrageur moving billions of dollars in foreign currency across a national boundary electronically, the fact that there are fewer regulatory obstacles means that businesses can act more quickly and efficiently.

What it all really adds up to is something we could think of as a dramatically increased *velocity* of business. Economists might still be having a problem explaining the precise source of the longest peacetime economic expansion in history, but one way to think about it has to do with the time it takes to make changes, to get things done, or to produce and measure results. To grasp the impact of this intuitively, think back to when your firm first installed a company-wide email system. Don't you remember having a feeling that suddenly, overnight, the *speed* of your business life had accelerated? Many of us may now consider ourselves email slaves, but can you imagine really getting *anything* done without email today?

The real secret of the mysterious productivity boom is probably quite simple: By compressing the time it takes to analyze a situation and make a decision, the computer has increased the number of things any business can get done in a finite period of time. And all time periods are indeed finite.

Each of these factors—rapid information access, growth of the service sector, deregulation, business velocity—have had the effect of reducing the amount of "friction" in the economy. And now, over just the next few years, as the Web is deployed as a business tool for more and more applications, the economy is about to get even more friction-free, almost unimaginably friction-free.

It's no secret that the World Wide Web already makes it possible for customers to "bid out" their business with unnerving efficiency. A consumer can get accurate, up-to-date comparisons of competitive pricing and product specifications with just a few mouse clicks. Unfortunately, the margins of those companies engaging in (or unwillingly engaged by) e-commerce initiatives are being hammered as a result. Operating on the Web, a company is likely to find it nearly impossible to command the kinds of margins that used to be possible, in the good old days of imperfect information.

The simple fact is that the Web has given the lie to that clothing retailer's famous advertising slogan, "An educated consumer is our best customer." Turns out that for the vast majority of marketers, an educated consumer is their worst nightmare. In the frictionless environment of the Internet, marketers find it's their profit margins that get no traction.

Multiply this problem many times over to get a feeling for its implications in the B2B sphere. Today, there are ways for every link in a supply chain to know what every other link is doing, more or less instantaneously. They're called B2B exchanges—virtual markets in cyberspace where buyers and suppliers meet to make deals. B2B exchanges act like automated auctioneers, flawlessly matching sellers to buyers at lightning speed. In 1999, $145 billion changed hands over such networks. By 2004, that figure is expected to reach into the trillions. In 2000, 31 percent of U.S. companies were using the Internet for B2B purchasing. By the end of 2001, 91 percent will be doing it. But, while a consumer might use the Web to effortlessly shop around for some big-ticket item like a car, PC, or washing machine, think carefully about the implications when a business uses the Web to offer a $20 million contract to the absolute lowest bidder anywhere in the world. In the B2B arena, we're talking about a very serious threat indeed.

Of course, in using the term "threat" we're viewing this solely from the seller's perspective. The fact that transaction costs and profit margins have both been squeezed out of supply chains in every industry the world over is also the proximate source of the marvelous, Web-spawned productivity boom. This "threat" is undoubtedly one big factor behind the unprecedented "new economy" prosperity we are all now enjoying.

Lower supply costs mean lower production costs for manufacturers, which mean lower prices for end users. Goldman

Sachs predicts that online B2B could reduce production costs by as much as 39 percent in the electronics industry, 20 percent in the communications industry, and 19 percent in the life sciences sector. Even traditional industries such as steel, freight transport, forest products, and fossil fuels could realize double-digit savings. The same Goldman Sachs report predicts that B2B e-commerce, all by itself, could raise the gross domestic product of industrialized nations by 5 percent over the next several years.

All of this means that suppliers will be forced to become more efficient and more adept at meeting the precise needs of their customers. Bayer AG hopes to trim 5 percent from its annual procurement costs by moving 75 percent of its transactions to the Internet. British Telecom aims to reduce its procurement budget by 10 percent through online B2B purchasing. Ford, GM, and DaimlerChrysler, coming together to create their own B2B purchasing network, are looking for procurement savings of up to 20 percent. GE has seen the cost of processing purchases drop from a high of $200 per transaction when using traditional methods to as little as $1 per transaction when using its own, homegrown B2B system.

As advantageous as this may be for the collective world economy, if you operate a business and are suddenly asked to contribute your own profit margin for the benefit of that economy, you are apt to have a contrary opinion.

There is only one viable defense in the face of this downward pressure on margins, and that is to build relationships with your customers, one customer at a time.

Old + new = *real*

General Mills stealthily uses its B2B e-commerce strategy to run rings around larger competitors. Despite their huge marketing budgets and higher gross revenues, some of these competitors have lower unit margins than General Mills, which has been quietly and effectively integrating e-commerce initiatives into its business plans for the past decade. When a tradition-steeped firm such as General Mills is revealed as a leader in the B2B field, the notion of the Old Economy versus the New Economy begins to seem a bit dated.

So let's agree that it's time to stop talking about the Old Economy and the New Economy. Let's start talking about what *The Wall Street Journal* and others have dubbed the Real Economy.

The Old Economy was born of bricks and mortar, a child of the Industrial Age. The goods and services it provides are largely material, visible, and inflexible. The New Economy is a child of the telecosm, ethereal and evanescent. The New Economy is a universe of information-based products and services, many of which are immaterial, invisible, and highly flexible.

The Real Economy is a fusion of these two economies, a serendipitous amalgam of opposites. Faster than anyone could have imagined, the Old and New economies have intertwined, creating an economic system whose scale and longevity we can only guess at. This is like witnessing the birth of a new star, only instead of watching from millions of light-years away, we are seeing the event unfolding right before our eyes. We feel the effect in our homes, offices, schools, shopping malls, and factories. As the waves of change ripple through us, it's only fair to ask, *what's next?*

Already, it's easy to see the emergence of two separate paths, one on which intermediaries create and manage exchange markets and another on which the buyers and sellers create their own exchange markets. At this juncture, it is still too early to predict which path will become the highway and which will become the byway. But it seems likely that both paths will exist for some time, and the most compelling business model may end up being some networked combination of the two. It's a sure bet that established players in the business-to-business space will resist sharing too much of their margins with intermediaries as long as the technologies and the infrastructure necessary to form their own exchanges are available.

This, of course, means that the intermediaries themselves are going to need CRM strategies if they plan to keep and grow the customers they accrue. David Alschuler, vice president of e-business at the Aberdeen Group in Boston, has commented that brand building can occur much more rapidly in a virtual environment than in a traditional bricks-and-mortar economy. On the surface, Alschuler's observation might seem like good news, especially for young firms pursuing market penetration strategies. But the flip side is that the customers you win quickly can be lost quickly. Indrajit Sinha makes this point nicely in his *Harvard Business Review* article "Cost Transparency: The Net's Real Threat to Prices and Brands." Sinha notes that cost transparency weakens brand loyalty and damages reputations by "creating perceptions of price unfairness."

We have seen in the B2C space how access to pricing information via the Internet has affected buyer-seller relationships.

But the impact of this access, while dramatic, is just a droplet compared to the impact such access is having, and will continue to have, in the B2B space.

Among Sinha's suggested remedies are tiered pricing or versioning. He also makes a case for dynamic or "smart" pricing tactics to vary prices with market conditions. While these might make excellent tactics, a broader and certainly more long-range strategy would involve taking steps to loyalize customers. That's where a carefully designed strategy to manage customer relationships, one at a time (a "one-to-one" strategy), becomes crucial. And nowhere will customer relationships be more critical to the survival of businesses than in the B2B domain.

Andy Zimmerman, global e-business leader of PricewaterhouseCoopers' Management Consulting Services practice, agrees: "Online commerce is about creating online customer relationships, a critical component in e-business strategy."

You can run, but you can't hide

When everyone in a particular market has access to the same information at the same time, when no information is hidden or delayed, when laws and custom demand full and honest accountability for all business and pricing decisions—that's transparency. Every first-year finance or economics class introduces students to the concept of the Efficient Market, a perfectly transparent transactional arena. The students are then taught that such markets don't exist, except in theory. That was indeed the case, until business-to-business met the Internet.

For thousands of years, sellers have enjoyed a natural advantage over buyers because only the seller knows the actual cost of what is being sold. It has always been easy for the seller to mask the cost in a variety of ways, and difficult for the buyer to see through the veil. In the business-to-business space, this inherent inequality was addressed by creating an "expert" buyer—the purchasing agent, who would act as an intermediary for the end users, wherever they were in the organization that was buying the supplies. This purchaser, however, has often been evaluated, not on how useful or effective the purchase turned out to be, but rather on how low a price was negotiated with the supplier.

Although the original purpose of the purchasing agent was to level the playing field, the purchasing agent quickly evolved into a screen between the seller and the actual customers. This added a new layer, another frictional component to be overcome before completing the transaction.

But the Internet is eliminating this boundary layer, too. In the old days, a good supplier would try to develop as many contacts as possible within each client organization, but the purchasing agent usually held the cards. With the arrival of the Internet, it became possible for suppliers to reach around the purchasing agent to form electronic relationships with end users throughout the organization.

In a B2B environment characterized by one-to-one customer relationships, a primary responsibility of the supplier is to avoid being slowed down by the friction of the purchasing agent. By considering the end users as individual customers, a supplier can develop relationships with individuals *within* the client organization. The supplier sees the client as a *set of cus-*

tomers, rather than as a single entity. Each customer within the client, of course, has a unique set of needs. The savvy business-to-business supplier understands that the real power of the Internet is its ability to assist the sales and marketing teams in identifying the customers within a client organization, ranking those customers according to their influence or authority, and then making it possible to approach each customer with a strategy designed to maximize his or her value over time.

Basically, what we're saying is this: Don't just treat different customers differently, *treat different contacts within your client organizations differently* as well.

All this requires a level of sophistication, planning, and organizational skill that is clearly beyond the capabilities of many traditional companies, and quite frankly, beyond the capabilities of most dot-coms. That's why we made the distinction earlier between the Old Economy, the New Economy, and the Real Economy. Organizations that embrace the Real Economy must develop the capabilities to survive and to succeed in the B2B space.

The best and brightest of these organizations are firmly, but politely, steering their customers online for faster access to account information, online placement of orders, and round-the-clock technical support. They make life easier for their customers by reducing the *time* it takes to place an order and the *cost* of the transaction. By eliminating the ritual paper trail, these organizations help their customers drive down procurement and allocation costs from hundreds of dollars per transaction to practically zero.

The one-to-one B2B enterprise is often an *Old* Economy firm using *New* Economy tools to compete in the *Real* Economy. It not only facilitates the order-taking process but remembers the needs and preferences of its customers. Then, when a customer returns to the Web site, the customer doesn't have to click through dozens or hundreds of choices to complete the order. Because the seller has electronically remembered not only what the customer ordered last time but also how the customer wanted it shipped, what pricing had been agreed to, and any special conditions, the seller can meet the customer's precise needs quickly and inexpensively.

The seller's "perfect memory" of the buyer's needs, preferences, and sales history cements the relationship. Now the seller is no longer merely an order taker. The seller is an agent for the customer.

Let's take this thinking a step further. What would happen if the seller began providing the customer with information about products and services offered by other vendors, so the customer could do comparison shopping on the seller's own Web site? What if the seller could add transactional data from other vendors to its "perfect memory" and display that data alongside its own transactional data, so the customer could readily see how much it was spending with *each* vendor? What if the seller equipped its sales force with the latest information about developments and advances in the customer's industry, even if the innovations were made by a competitor? And what if the seller knew not only how much it sells the customer, but exactly how much the buyer is purchasing from competitors?

Now the seller has moved beyond simply selling products and become a *trusted agent*. The trusted agent is the modern-day equivalent of the trusted servant, an aide whose competence,

wisdom, loyalty, and honesty are beyond question. Like the ar-
chetypes from ancient mythology, the trusted agent represents
a constellation of deeply held beliefs. Literature is replete with
examples of this archetype, revealing a profound and appar-
ently insatiable cultural hunger. Without putting too fine a
point on it, it seems obvious to us that any business trying to
build a one-to-one relationship with a customer is destined,
eventually, to try to become this customer's trusted agent.

But we're getting ahead of ourselves. Before taking another
step forward, let's take a couple of steps back to agree on the
fundamental rationale for building and managing one-to-one
customer relationships.

What is "one-to-one marketing" and why should anyone want to practice it?

As the terms "one-to-one" and "CRM" enter the popular lexi-
con, we hear more and more people saying, "I get it." When
gently pressed to explain exactly what it is about building one-
to-one customer relationships that they "get," however, these
folks often start talking about database marketing, call centers,
Web sites, or e-commerce. The fact is, a one-to-one customer
relationship program might include some, all, or none of those
features. And while one-to-one customer relationships are enabled by technology, the enabling technology should be
viewed as the means to an end, not the end itself.

So how do we define "one-to-one"? As we said briefly in
Chapter 1:

> You are engaged in a one-to-one customer relationship
> whenever the customer tells you something about how he or
> she wants to be served, and you change your behavior with
> respect to this individual customer based on that interaction.

This probably sounds like a commonplace business activity, especially for a B2B firm, and it is. But for most firms, including B2Bs, adjusting the company's customer-specific behavior to individual customer specifications is not a well-organized activity. It is carried out on an ad hoc basis, usually at the insistence of the account team or the sales organization, and the more specifications to be accommodated, the more cumbersome and manually patched together the whole process will be. So before you jump to the conclusion that "we already do this stuff," let's pursue the true implications of this kind of activity a bit further.

The idea of treating different customers differently implies that a longer-term relationship, based on previous interactions, is now possible. After all, if you treat every customer the same, then there is clearly no point to developing a relationship with any single customer. What can any customer possibly get out of uniform treatment that he couldn't also get *without* a relationship?

If, on the other hand, you have the capability to incorporate a customer's own input into how you treat that customer in today's transaction, then you can also *remember* that input for the future. And the more input the customer gives you, the more intricate a relationship you can develop.

The essence of any relationship is that it is an interactive, adaptive, ongoing process. The more the customer tells you, the more tailored your behavior can be toward that customer. Did you like it like that? You want it more this way next time? How about this, is that better? With every interaction you get more input from *this* customer, and you tailor your behavior a little more, and a little more, and a little more. With time, the customer will have invested some effort in teaching you how he wants to be treated. Now, *even if* your competitor is doing business the same way you are, your customer will want to remain loyal to you, because he won't want to go to the trouble of reteaching your competitor what he's already taught you. Because you know more about your customer than your competitor, you can serve your customer in ways that your competitor literally cannot, unless the customer starts the long process of teaching all over again.

When an architectural design firm gives Bentley Systems the information needed to manage its blueprints and diagrams, and to make them available securely to the vendors they've identified, they're not going to be eager to engage another firm to do this. When a multidivision corporation teaches Dell how to configure the hardware and software for its executives' computers, for various levels, departments, functions, and locations, they're not going to want to take the time and effort to teach someone else, unless they really have to. The more I teach you about my needs—provided that you continue to adapt your service or product to meet my evolving specifications—the less willing I will be to give up my relationship, at least partly because it will mean starting all over with someone else.

This is the essence of what we call a "Learning Relationship"—a relationship with a customer that gets "smarter and smarter" with every interaction. The Learning Relationship represents the central engine of a one-to-one enterprise strategy. A Learning Relationship *is* a one-to-one relationship. It is the single unique and distinct characteristic of any CRM program.

But now think about some of the implications of this:

- The traditional business organizes and measures itself on a "lateral" basis. The business goes from quarter to quarter, year to year, measuring sales revenue or profit *laterally* across different business units and the entire enterprise. But when we engage an individual customer in a relationship, the relationship develops *longitudinally*, through time, with respect to this single customer. It is characteristically different today than it was yesterday, and it evolves more as time goes on.

- The immediate financial goal of a traditional business is to maximize the value of a sales period, by generating more sales or profit during that period, across the whole enterprise. But the immediate financial goal for a relationship manager is to increase the long-term value of the *customer relationship*, through time—that is, to maximize the customer's expected lifetime value.

- The long-term financial goals of the traditional business and the one-to-one enterprise are identical—to maximize shareholder value. But shareholder value is a *future*-oriented variable. As such, it is much more closely related to the lifetime values of the customers being served than it is to this year's profit, or even next year's.

- A traditional business sees success in terms of market penetration, or market share, within each division or product category. A one-to-one enterprise will see success in terms of account development, or share of customer, across all divisions and product categories.

- A traditional marketing or sales professional will concentrate on finding more customers who want to buy his company's product. But a one-to-one customer relationship manager will ponder how to find more products and services for his customer.

These are just a few of the differences between a traditional marketing approach and a one-to-one Learning Relationship approach. To understand the benefits of such an approach for the business, let's turn first to the benefits for the customer.

Obviously, if the more I teach you the more you adapt your product or service to my needs, then with every interaction your product becomes more valuable—to me. The product has more economic value to me for two reasons: First, it fits my needs better and so therefore it requires less accommodation or compromise on my part. But second, my marginal cost of substitution continues to increase. The more I teach you, the more expensive it will be for me to substitute a competitor's product.

So the first benefit for the enterprise is that customer loyalty will improve. But the second benefit—really, the "flip side" of customer loyalty—is that unit margins are likely to improve as well. The principal reason your margins come under pressure in the first place, even when you keep costs under control, is that your competitors are pricing their products aggressively, in order to steal your customers. But if you could predispose a particular customer to *want* to stay loyal, because his switching cost is higher, then you won't necessarily have to match every last discount encountered in the marketplace. As your product continues to have more value for the customer, it may even be possible to *raise* your price, over time, to share the benefit of this increased product value.

And there are other benefits to the one-to-one approach that we haven't even factored in yet. First, obviously, there is the "human" factor—the probability that a customer will simply end up "liking" you more, as the relationship improves and customer satisfaction grows. This is indeed the factor that many CRM consultants focus on first—delighting the customer, exceeding the customer's expectations, and so forth. But, while likability is certainly something we should all work for, by itself it is neither a necessary nor a sufficient condition to generate loyalty. The world is full of customers who switch from one company they were happy with to another one they are equally happy with. And if you want an example of a company that customers remain loyal to in spite of the fact that they think the service is bad and don't even "like" dealing with them, you might not have to look further than the relationship you have with your own retail bank.

Another benefit of building one-to-one Learning Relationships is that it can improve the overall efficiency of a business. It can reduce costs, mostly by cutting out the wasted effort of producing products or services that no one wants. Mass customization works on the basic principle of modularizing the production or service delivery process, breaking the process into components, and then digitally combining these components to make a large variety of fully configured products. In this way, the mass customizer can cost-efficiently mass-produce goods and services in lot sizes of one. This means a product can be made to order, rather than built to forecast. So mass customization reduces inventory costs, and this single benefit is often enough to more than offset the cost of producing digitally combinable components. Indeed, cost reduction is one of the principal reasons manufacturing companies consider mass customization technologies in the first place.

To think it through intuitively, what the one-to-one enterprise is really doing is making a product only *after* a customer for that product has been signed. The company is not building some number of standard products in advance of their expected sales and hoping that its estimate of overall market demand is correct. Instead, *first* it has a customer, and *then* it makes the product for that customer. Once again, therefore, a significant element of friction is removed from the economic system, and in this case it is a cost reduction that can often be dropped directly to the manufacturer's bottom line.

In services, the principles of mass customization usually translate to greater asset productivity. If your company's Web site "remembers" individual customer preferences, then those customers will be able to get what they want more quickly. Ergo, your servers will be able to accommodate more visitors in any given time period.

In the chapter on Bentley Systems, we will see how the company saved millions in marketing expenses by simply not "broadcasting" its sales and marketing messages. Once Bentley decided to concentrate on growing the value of its existing customer base, it was easy to reduce media spending. And in the case of Dell, the development of the Web-based Premier Dell.com for corporate clients means that the company can book millions of dollars' worth of sales without the direct intervention of a sales rep. Not only does this allow Dell to save money, lowering its overall cost structure, but it allows the sales reps to spend more time on the phone or in the field meeting with clients.

While these benefits are in fact compelling, it is important to remember the magnitude of the "attitude change" inherent in adopting a one-to-one, customer-centric approach. What many executives fail to perceive is that CRM is neither a gimmick nor a technological solution. It doesn't exist in a vacuum and it can't be applied like a coat of fresh paint. It's true that CRM programs can generate impressive short-term gains, especially when the programs are designed to harvest low-hanging fruit. However, the real benefit of implementing a "one-to-one" strategy is over the long haul, especially in situations where competition is increasing and profits are endangered. The real benefit has to do with increasing the overall value of a company's customer base. But this benefit is likely to remain invisible to a corporation that continues to measure itself laterally, across an entire market, rather than longitudinally, one customer at a time.

The case studies in this book revolve around organizations whose executives and managers have made conscious decisions to change the way they do business, over the long term. None of them made these decisions lightly. No one woke up one morning and said, "Gee, it would be great if our company were to do some one-to-one marketing." More likely they woke up sweating in the middle of the night, thinking, "If I can't figure out a way to make my unit more profitable, I'm going to lose my job."

So while it would be nice to imagine a world in which organizations naturally follow CRM principles because they are logical, profitable, and humane to customers, the truth is that organizations often implement these programs primarily because they are forced into it. Novartis CP saw no alternative. Or rather, the alternative they glimpsed most clearly was extinction. As Dr. Samuel Johnson put it: "Depend upon it, sir, when a man knows he is to be hanged in a fortnight, it concentrates his mind wonderfully."

The companies we are writing about, for the most part, traded their product-focused traditions for customer-focused strategies because they were caught in a time warp. The velocity of business in their industry suddenly increased, the friction in their industry diminished, and the only way they could get any traction at all was to change the direction of the competitive struggle itself, by focusing on individual customer relationships rather than on individual products. The traditional methodology and all the infrastructure accompanying it had been designed to run at highway speed, rather than Internet speed.

> Highway speed: *65 miles per hour*
> Internet speed: *186,000 miles per second*

As the velocity of business has increased, the old model has not been agile, flexible, or fast enough to deliver the kind of results needed to sustain a profitable business. Managing individual customer relationships has emerged as the most viable strategy for many because it promises a hedge against margin erosion and customer disloyalty.

Nowhere has the rationale for CRM been more compelling

than in B2B competition. As valuable as customer relationship management can be in a B2C situation, it can be exponentially more valuable in B2B, where a single individual can be responsible for making multimillion-dollar decisions. As a B2B player, your ability to discover hidden information about this individual's needs—and your ability to act on this information at the right time—gives you a significant business advantage over a competitor who does not possess the same information or who is not in a position to act on it.

Our goal in this book is to take the intuition shared by good sales executives everywhere, and show how this intuition can be systematized into an enterprise-wide B2B strategy. This one-to-one B2B strategy, in turn, can be applied against front-burner issues such as channel conflict, margin erosion, global competition, and customer loyalty.

Four implementation steps

The simple truth is that most business-to-business organizations already practice some form of one-to-one customer relationship management. Mass marketing *never* made much sense in the B2B space, where the importance of managing and developing customer relationships on a one-to-one (or "belly-to-belly") basis is grasped intuitively. The fundamental notion that unique customers require unique business strategies has remained largely unchanged in the B2B space.

What has changed, however, is that technology now permits a company to develop and cultivate its customer relationships with a degree of intensity, forethought, and coordination that would have been totally unimaginable just a few years ago. We've developed a four-step methodology for thinking through the mechanics of creating, tracking, and growing a customer relationship. We first published this four-step method in *The One to One Fieldbook* in 1999, but we have been applying these same principles in our own global consulting practice since the mid-1990s. We know the method works, because we've applied it to more than a hundred client situations in all types of industries. Other consulting firms, of course, have other methodologies, but our process has stood the test of time, and you will probably find that it tracks well to your own intuitive understanding of what a relationship is made of.

Our four-step process for creating and cultivating better customer relationships is as follows:

1. *Identify* your customers. You can't have a relationship with an audience, or a market; you can have a relationship only with an individual. Therefore, the first step in CRM is to identify the individuals who make up your customer base.

2. *Differentiate* your customers, by value and needs. Treating different customers differently implies that you can tell them apart by their characteristics. Knowing which customers are the most valuable allows you to prioritize your sales and marketing efforts. Knowing what different customers need lets you cater to each customer's individual needs, and this is what will lock up their loyalty.

3. *Interact* with your customers. Interaction, dialogue, the exchange of information—this is the essence of any relationship. You want to be able to maximize interactions, so you want to interact cost-efficiently, driving more and more in-

teractions into the most cost-efficient channels, like the Internet. And what you want from the interaction is insight into the customer—insight that you can only get *from* the customer.

4. *Customize* for your customers. In the final analysis, extracting benefit for either party to a relationship will mean treating an individual customer differently based on what you now know about that particular customer. This is the "payoff step" for any relationship.

These are not completely sequential and orderly implementation steps. There will be a good deal of overlap among these four steps, which we often simply label the "I.D.I.C." process. Nevertheless, you can rely on I.D.I.C. to serve as a recipe for creating and managing customer relationships in any business situation. One of the primary benefits of using a structured methodology such as this is that it enables a company to better understand both the strategy and the relationship-building context of the various computer technologies now available to it. Rather than retrofitting a customer strategy to a technology, I.D.I.C. allows a firm to build the technology around its customer strategy.

In the old days—before computers, the Internet, and global competition—an organization could get by as long as a few of its best sales or marketing people had an intuitive grasp of the basic principles of building relationships with customers. Nowadays, a few bright people working independently and relying on brainpower alone just won't cut it. If your organization has a 200-person sales force that competes globally, the presence of three or four self-made "stars" on the sales team won't be enough. *Everyone* on the sales team now has to be a skilled relationship builder. *Everyone* on the sales team has to have the training and support necessary to function as a "trusted agent." And it's not just the sales force that has to be one-to-one-ready. The rest of the enterprise has to be brought up to speed as well, to ensure that all customer-facing departments have the support they need to succeed.

Let's now look at each of the individual steps within the I.D.I.C. framework and apply this framework to the specific issues faced in the B2B environment.

Identify your customers

You can't develop one-to-one relationships with your customers unless you know who your customers are—not necessarily by actual name and address, but with at least some form of reliable "addressability." Of course, there is knowing and there is *knowing*. In the B2B space, it might be tempting to say, "We *know* who our customers are: They're the businesses we sell to." The truth, of course, is that no one sells to "businesses." Organizations don't have brains and they don't make decisions. It is the people within these organizations who make and influence business decisions. *They* are your customers and *they* are the people you need to know. You can't have a relationship with a company unless you have relationships with the individual people within the company.

So the first piece of any one-to-one B2B strategy should involve collecting names, telephone numbers, email addresses, mailing addresses, and job responsibilities of key people within the customer's organization. Every reasonable attempt should be made to map the customer's table of organization with as much detail and accuracy as possible. You need to know who reports to whom, who is empowered to say "yes" and how far that empowerment extends.

You must also know how the individuals within a business organization get their information and make their decisions. Do they make decisions collegially? Is there a strict hierarchy? Is the decision-making process formal or informal? Who are the key influencers at each stage of the process, and what are their needs? Dell and Bentley, for example, commit significant resources and energy to identifying not only their customer organizations but the end users, decision makers, and key influencers within those organizations as well. They do this because they want to establish relationships with them.

In an interview in the CRM magazine *1to1*, Cyndi Greenglass, president of the consulting firm World Marketing Integrated Solutions, points out that it is important to know not only what a person *does* in an organization but who that person *is*, in a personal sense. She catalogues three different types of information that needs to be collected about the business and the individuals within it:

1. Firmagraphics. Information about the business itself, including things like SIC code, employee size, annual sales, and other specific business descriptors.
2. Demographics and psychographics. Information about the individual contacts within the business—their outward characteristics, like gender and age, as well as their psychologi-

cal makeup and needs. She cautions that this kind of information is much more difficult for a B2B to get than it is for a B2C. And it's highly perishable. But in situations where this type of information becomes available, a B2B marketer will have a genuine advantage in structuring a lasting set of individual relationships within the overall business relationship.

3. Infographics. How does the contact prefer to get his or her information? What type of communication is preferred? Knowing this allows a B2B marketer to structure more customized and persuasive interactions with each contact.

When you factor channel partners into the equation, the situation becomes even more complicated and exponentially more difficult to manage. Before launching any kind of CRM initiative, your B2B organization should take inventory of its entire range of relationships—from suppliers on one end to consumers on the other. You can begin by charting every possible interaction between your organization and your customers. We refer to this as the *customer touch map.*

In drawing a customer touch map, the important thing to remember is its purpose: to document and illustrate the interconnectedness of the relationships that keep your business running. On the next page, you'll see a "sanitized" version of a touch map we recently drew for a large client. The actual map covered half a wall and resembled the web of a very energetic spider. What *wasn't* surprising to the client was the complexity of the relationships. What *was* surprising to the client was the inescapable fact of all those separate databases storing valuable customer information and the almost total lack of communica-

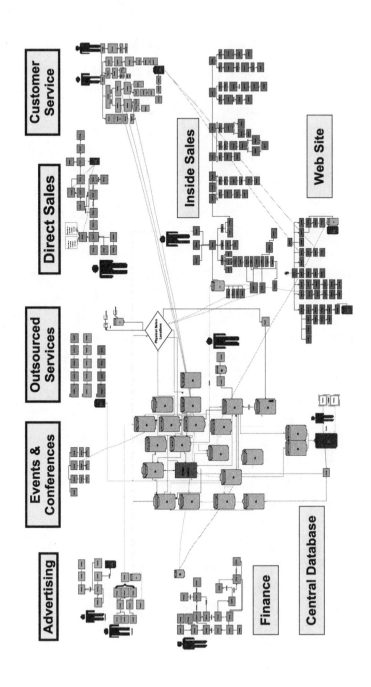

Customer Service

Direct Sales

Inside Sales

Web Site

Outsourced Services

Events & Conferences

Advertising

Finance

Central Database

Physical Sales Locations

tion among those databases. The map clearly illustrates the fact that this company had many different, isolated databases storing disconnected elements of customer information.

Differentiate your customers

Not all customers are created equal. In fact, no two are exactly alike. Customers are different in two principal ways: They represent different levels of value to you (some are very valuable, some not so valuable), and they need different things from you. So, after you have identified your customers, the next step is determining what they *want* from you and how much they're actually *worth* to you. Once you have differentiated your customers in this way, you can prioritize your efforts and tailor your firm's behavior toward each customer based on that customer's value and needs. Remember, the core principle of building one-to-one relationships is treating different customers differently. Until you've systematically determined how your customers differ from each other, you can't treat them differently.

We have found it useful to divide customers into distinct categories, based on their value:

MVCs: *Most Valuable Customers* represent the core of your current business. Your primary concern here is customer retention, because you don't want to lose these folks to your competitors.

MGCs: *Most Growable Customers* are those who would be significantly more valuable to your organization if you de-

veloped proactive strategies to increase the amount of
business they do with you.

BZs: *Below Zero* customers are those who in all likelihood will
never be profitable enough to justify the cost of serving
them. You should develop strategies to make them more
profitable or to encourage them to become one of your
competitor's customers.

While it's true that not all customers will drop neatly into
one of these three categories, dividing your customers into
value types such as these will make it easier for you to set objectives and develop strategies. Convergys realized major revenue gains by shifting from a gross revenue model for ranking
its clients to a value ranking system. The new ranking system
enabled them to allocate their sales and marketing resources
with far greater efficiency than in the past. Novartis CP increased its sales revenue and market share by implementing a
system that placed a great deal of emphasis on its MVCs, a
group it labeled PEP, for Primero el Productor.

Once you rank your customers by their value, you must differentiate them by what they need. Note that when we use the
term "need" in this context, we're talking generically about all
the customer's needs, desires, preferences, wants, wishes, and
motivations. As a consumer, if you prefer a dark-colored car
while your neighbor prefers a light-colored car, we call that a
difference in what you need.

It is often the case that a business customer's needs are related to its value to the seller. This is a happy coincidence, because it means that the selling company can cater to the

particular needs of its highest-value clients more efficiently. Dell differentiates its business customers by size, recognizing that the size of a firm often dictates the way it orders products and services. By understanding the varied purchasing habits of its individual clients, Dell knows not only what they need but also when and how they need it.

But while the size of a business might tell you something about what that business needs, and while the hierarchical position of a contact might tell you something about his or her needs within the organization, there is still no substitute for understanding the motivations, preferences, wants, and needs of the individual human beings within the business. Businesses don't make decisions. Only human beings make decisions. Business organizations, in the final analysis, are mere legal constructs to organize human activity.

In an era in which job titles have become nearly meaningless, the most important information to possess about someone in your customer's organization is not only what they actually need to get their job done properly but also what they need to feel happy, successful, secure, and fulfilled. People are persons. They not only have career needs; they also have personal needs. You'll find that it's important to keep track of both.

Often, all these various needs will not dovetail neatly with your organization's structure. But an organization that is committed to pursuing a CRM strategy will figure out the best way to match its resources with the needs of its customers.

One of the world's best-known multinational corporations currently requires its sales force to chart the individual players within its larger accounts. The sales force then sorts the indi-

vidual players by personality type, using a multipage questionnaire and a five-point rating system. Here is a sample page of
the questionnaire:

Open-minded, communicative	1	2	3	4	5	Reserved, uncommunicative
Analytic	1	2	3	4	5	Pragmatic, intuitive
Trustful	1	2	3	4	5	Skeptical, bureaucratic
Committed	1	2	3	4	5	Wavering
Straight shooter	1	2	3	4	5	Bargainer
Clearheaded, calm	1	2	3	4	5	Emotional
Tolerant, generous	1	2	3	4	5	Fussy, pedantic
Cool, formal	1	2	3	4	5	Warm, friendly
Persevering	1	2	3	4	5	Compromising
Optimistic	1	2	3	4	5	Pessimistic
Arrogant	1	2	3	4	5	Submissive
Planner	1	2	3	4	5	Improviser
Egocentric	1	2	3	4	5	Team player
Easy to understand	1	2	3	4	5	Puzzling

The completed questionnaires are scored, and the individual
players are sorted into a quadrant matrix of personality types.

Innovator Creative, open to new ideas, wants to improve processes, "do things better."	**Reviewer** Cautious, conservative, details-oriented, technical background.
Promoter Determined, activist, sees big picture, not overly concerned about details.	**Follower** Hesitant, risk-averse, worries about security, consequences.

A different version of this process is then applied to the sales force itself, whose members are sorted by personality and background. The goal at this stage is to identify good matches between reps and individual players within the account. After several iterations of internal polling, enough color-coded pairs will have been generated to create an account organization structure chart.

Part of the idea is to ensure maximum compatibility from the onset of the relationship, rather than discovering halfway through the sales process that the customer's vice president of operations isn't getting along with his sales rep because he's a Follower and she's used to dealing with Innovators. The overall value, however, is that it imposes a structure on the account management team that is based on customer needs, rather than company needs. The account team is *externally* focused (*What can I do to make my customer happy?*), instead of being *internally* focused (*How can I organize my geographic assignments to make my quota?*).

What's also useful about this kind of exercise is that it can be done entirely with existing internal resources. In fact, one of the primary advantages of a B2B over a B2C is that you already have access to most of the customer information you need to launch a vigorous one-to-one initiative. You don't need to conduct extensive external polls—most of your polling can be safely done in-house, by interviewing your own team of experts, the sales force. In other words, most of your time and energy at this stage should be spent using data you already have about the people you work with.

This, of course, raises the thorny issue of subjectivity. Unlike the relatively objective data generated by large-sample polling, the data you generate from your internal polls of sales reps or other executives will be highly subjective. Is this bad?

Not really. Often, the most reliable path to the truth is via subjective judgment. For example, one of the reasons we recommend differentiating contacts within accounts on the basis of their personalities is that personalities don't tend to change very much over time. Job title, level of authority, scope of responsibility—these "objective" aspects of a contact's professional life tend to change quickly. Psychological needs, on the other hand, tend to remain more constant. With relatively few exceptions, followers will remain followers and innovators will remain innovators. That's why it makes sense to establish a system for making subjective judgments and to sort your client contacts by personality type. Once you've done the basic work, you don't have to go back and do it again when the contact changes jobs, moves to another department, or even moves to a different firm.

When Novartis CP initiated a customer relationship management program to cope simultaneously with a rapid increase in competition and a shrinking market for its products, one of its priority tasks was grouping customers by personality type. This effort, which represented months of painstaking work, resulted in a color-coded, needs-based customer differentiation matrix that enabled Novartis to tailor sales and marketing strategies for each customer. The original matrix was developed by Jean Calembert of ASK, a Belgian market research firm that has done pioneering work in this field. Calembert shared a generic version of the matrix with us.

	Blue	**Gray**	**Purple**	**Green**	**Turquoise**	**Yellow**
Key personal needs	Help, support, encouragement	Fitting in, being sociable	Getting quality service, meeting challenges	Achieving success, winning recognition	Learning, improving, staying on top of latest technology	Maintaining a leadership position, increasing social status
Primary form of interaction	Tech manuals, telephone calls	Friendly visits, meals, ag fairs	Demos, trials, test markets	Internet, CD-ROM	Workshops, networking	Fax, cell phone, email
Tone of voice	Low-key, reassuring	Friendly, but firm	Technical, challenging	Scientific, neutral	Concrete, tangible	Forceful, financial
Role of sales rep	Guide, teacher	Best pal	Key advisor, problem solver	Peer, thinker	Partner, doer, facilitator	Interface, go-between
Customer's approach to innovation	Very slow	Slow, but wants to please	Very fast	Fast, but cautious	Fast, if justified by ROI	Slow, but concerned by "status"

Interact with your customers

Interaction is the basic stuff of a relationship, the defining element of it. But every interaction with a customer must take place within the context of all previous interactions with that customer. The dialogue between a customer and the organization should always pick up where it left off, whether it occurred recently or long ago, at the customer contact center or on the organization's Web site, in the customer's own office or in a restaurant. This is the only way a relationship can build a *context*, and the richer, more complex the context of a relationship is, the more advantageous it will become for the customer. The more you remember about me, the more I've taught you about myself, the more difficult it will be for me to start over again with someone else.

In times past, most interactions between a buyer and a seller were face-to-face. As society and technology advanced, more avenues of interaction opened, but they were usually slow and expensive. It wasn't until the advent of mass media that it became cost-efficient for sellers to reach large numbers of buyers—but mass media (in the form of print, radio, television, and outdoor advertising) is a one-way street. The Internet and the technologies surrounding it have reopened the dialogue between buyer and seller by making it possible for organizations to hold cost-efficient two-way discussions with hundreds, thousands, or even millions of customers simultaneously.

The impact of the Internet and the Web in the business-to-consumer space has been nothing short of revolutionary. The Web's influence on B2B has been perhaps less dramatic, but even more profound in terms of its effect on the global economy.

Smart B2B organizations discovered that when they migrated some of their customer interactions to the Web, they were able to expand greatly the range of customers under active management. Suddenly they were able to offer perks and services that previously had been reserved for their top clients to their small and medium-size clients as well. Why? The cost of Web-based interactions are infinitesimal compared to the cost of face-to-face interactions.

For a B2C, the Web's astoundingly low cost is interesting but largely irrelevant. B2Cs have never spent much on customer interactions, because customer interaction plays no role in a mass-marketing business model. For a B2C, taking advantage of the incredible cost-efficiency of the Web for interacting with individual consumers requires a revolutionary shift in the focus of the business itself. It requires the firm to adopt a completely different business model, which is exactly what one-to-one marketing represents, when it is compared to traditional consumer mass marketing.

For B2Bs, however, the Web has been immediately recognized as a major improvement in business efficiency, because B2Bs don't really do mass marketing anyway. B2Bs have always been interested in developing and strengthening individual customer relationships, and now the Web means they no longer will be required to spend enormous sums to do so, and can simultaneously get better at tracking and remembering across customer touch points.

Before the Web, when a B2B wanted to open a dialogue with its smaller customers, it probably couldn't afford to. A prime example of this is Dell, which uses its Web-based Dell.com pages to host a truly generous assortment of customer-friendly interactive tools. As a Dell manager succinctly put it: "Without our Premier Dell.com page, we would have to reserve these services for our largest customers. Now we have the potential to scale our services all the way down to the smallest customer."

No amount of automation, however, is likely to replace face-to-face communication between a sales rep and a large customer, and it would be self-defeating even to try. On the other hand, you can automate the way information is made available to the salesperson. You can make it easier for sales reps to access customer data when they're in the field. You can easily de-

velop a system that allows a rep to download customer transaction histories onto her laptop before making a sales call. You
can tinker with how the information is packaged and presented
on-screen to maximize its value to the rep. You can augment
the information with artificial intelligence, creating a virtual assistant for the rep. You can even include real-time cues to alert
her when opportunities arise for cross selling or up selling.

So one difference for the B2B, when applying the "interact"
principle, as compared to the B2C, is that in many B2B situations the technology should be used not to replace the human
beings who serve as the channels of interaction, but to empower them. By automating and improving the tools available
to the sales rep, you're pushing up the quality of the interaction. The interaction will still be on the human-to-human level,
but it will be enhanced by automated systems designed to sort
through the customer data and present it in a manner that's useful to the sales rep.

Customize for your customers

To develop a relationship with a customer you must be capable
of modifying your behavior to meet the expressed needs of that
individual customer. Customizing some aspect of your product
or service to meet the needs of a customer is the real-world
manifestation of *treating different customers differently*. It is proof positive that you are actually listening to your customer, learning,
and remembering what you've learned. Your ability to respond
to what you've learned makes it possible for you to deliver a

product or service your customer cannot get from your competitor, who hasn't learned what you know about *this* customer.

Changing your behavior could involve mass customizing a manufactured product, or it could involve tailoring the services surrounding a product. To become a true one-to-one enterprise, the production or service delivery end of your business must be able to treat a particular customer differently based on what *that customer* said during an interaction with your firm.

A one-to-one enterprise can also customize the interactions it has with its customers. Rules-based sales-call templates make it both practical and advantageous for a sales rep to develop unique proposals for each customer. The template should include basic information about the customer and about the customer's needs. It should include a list of products, services, or combinations of products and services that would likely appeal to that particular customer or type of customer, based on that customer's needs. It might also include information about recent purchases made by the customer's peers or competitors. It should include best practices and perhaps even a case study or two. If the template is Web-based, this kind of depth can be achieved with hyperlinks to related content.

The sales templates themselves can be composed of modules that can be mixed and matched. The more templates you create, the more mixing and matching you can do. Very soon you reach a point where you can effectively mass customize your face-to-face interactions. By mass customizing them, you make it far easier and much more cost-efficient to tailor unique proposals or presentations for each customer.

Bentley offers its sales reps the option of downloading customizable templates from the company intranet prior to a sales call. Sales reps who use the templates not only save time in putting together their proposals; they also make fewer mistakes because the templates include updated information on the price, availability, and capabilities of the products being offered.

Perhaps the single most important step in customizing your treatment of an individual customer is developing a "customer strategy" for that customer. What is it you want to accomplish, and how will you accomplish it? Importantly, different customer strategies are required for players within the customer organization as well. To be successful, a customer strategy should be developed by people who "know" the customer well, but this does not necessarily mean the people who actually interact with the customer on a regular basis.

If your own firm is primarily a sales-driven company—if generating sales is the primary activity of your business—then it probably makes sense to place the salespeople themselves at the helm of each customer relationship and to have them set the individual customer or account strategies. A stock brokerage, for instance, would be such a firm. But if your sales force is simply one of several channels for reaching and interacting with customers, then it can often be more effective to have the customer strategies set by someone else—someone with a broader view of the overall customer relationship. No matter how you set the account strategies, however, if you have a sales force at all, then the salesperson's interactions with the client should be motivated by the same strategy.

In Dell's case, for instance, the Premier Dell.com pages that are set up for any particular client are set up on the salesperson's own initiative, and the salesperson continues to play a key role in the ongoing business relationship. The main difference for the salesperson will be that he or she can now focus more exclusively on account development issues, and spend less time handling routine inquiries or tracking orders.

B2Bs: Partway there?

As we said earlier, relationship management, as a competitive strategy, is certainly not a new idea to most B2Bs. However, most B2Bs do not plan, develop, and execute CRM programs as methodically and scientifically as they would plan, develop, and execute, say, a product launch. Yes, a typical B2B's sales reps will record the comments and feedback of the customers they meet with, but the company may not do a good job of capturing and integrating its individual customers' interactions across all touch points, including the Web and the call center. Or the company may not systematically share the notes and insights of individual reps with others at the firm who also have a role in the customer relationship.

Yes, a typical B2B probably already prioritizes its marketing and sales effort so as to favor its largest customers, at least by revenue. But for the most part, B2B firms have not paid much attention to ranking customers in terms of a more scientific estimate of each customer's current and future value to the firm.

On the following page is a table, organized by I.D.I.C., which presents the current activity of a typical B2B firm for each of the four steps, and contrasts it with the desired tasks, for each step, that a B2B firm should be accomplishing.

	B2Bs typically *do:*	B2Bs typically *don't,* but should:
Identify	■ Identify MVCs by revenue. ■ Know key contacts within customer organizations.	■ Map all contacts within client organizations. ■ Assess and record each contact's level of purchasing influence. ■ Create programs specifically to identify end users.
Differentiate	■ Treat different customers differently. ■ Provide premium service levels for MVCs. ■ *Reactively* differentiate by customer's stated needs.	■ Rank customers by lifetime value (LV) and Strategic Value. ■ Develop strategies for BZs. ■ *Proactively* vary treatment of different needs-based categories of customers.
Interact	■ Capture interactions, through sales reps. ■ Assume that sales reps will resist sales force automation (SFA) or CRM initiatives because they find them threatening. ■ Reserve electronic data interchange (EDI) for largest customers.	■ Capture and "memorize" interactions across all touch points, including Web. ■ Compensate field sales force for providing details of customer interaction. ■ Promote the Web as an alternative to electronic data interchange (EDI).
Customize	■ Customize products and services when requested by largest customers, on an ad hoc basis. ■ Develop and execute account plans.	■ Mass customize products and services by modularizing the production or service process. ■ "Template" the treatment of individual customers according to needs-based categories, on a routine basis. ■ Develop and execute specific customer strategies, including strategies, including strategies for contacts within a customer organization.

In the case studies which follow, you'll see examples of organizations relying on CRM initiatives to battle margin erosion, global competition, and customer disloyalty. Each organization has developed a unique approach designed to suit its own needs. Each organization, however, is following the basic one-to-one game plan: *Identify* your customers, *Differentiate* your customers, *Interact* with your customers, and *Customize* for your customers.

Some of the organizations we profile in the chapters ahead are farther down the track than others. Some have made significant achievements in one or two areas of one-to-one strategy; others have made slower, but more consistent progress. As you would expect, there is no "one size fits all" prescription for success in the Real Economy.

Chapter

3

Dell
The automated relationship

Top line summary

Years ago, when a company such as Dell Computer Corporation approached a large client, its primary contact would have been the client's purchasing agent. The purchasing agent would say, "Here are the specs, give us your best price." All other things being equal, the lowest bidder would win the contract. If Dell, or any other vendor, had asked for a list of end users, the purchasing agent probably would have refused the request. And even if Dell had managed to obtain a list of end users and key contacts within the client's organization, it would not have had the resources or the capabilities to communicate individually with the people it needed to reach.

Then Dell developed a Web-based utility that helped its customers manage their own business information and IT purchasing function cost-efficiently. The same Web-based utility makes it possible for Dell to communicate directly with its end users, with the enthusiastic approval of the purchasing people themselves.

Now Dell routinely trades access to information for access to people. By making life easier for the managers and employees of its larger customers, Dell gets the opportunity to establish one-to-one relationships with the people who actually use the products and services it sells.

Information technology now makes it practical for many companies to follow Dell's example and to implement their own systems for developing and managing relationships on a one-to-one basis within a client's organization. Any B2B enterprise pursuing account development strategies must possess the ability to create and sustain customizable, one-to-one relationships with the decision makers, influencers, and end users working "inside" its clients.

If you're going to pursue pursue an account development strategy, you must be able to identify and interact in a cost-efficient manner with the actual people within the accounts who

a. use your products
b. make or influence the decision to purchase them.

Without the ability to identify and interact with individuals within the account, it will be extremely difficult, if not impossible, to develop and manage customer relationships on a one-to-one basis. That's why Dell's Premier Pages Service, recently renamed Premier Dell.com, is worth studying. It is a *system* for managing individual customers within an account.

Premier Dell.com is a brilliant yet largely unheralded initiative for managing B2B customer relationships via the World Wide Web. Premier Dell.com enables Dell to establish and manage Learning Relationships with millions of end users working at thousands of Dell's corporate customers around the globe. An end user can log onto his organization's Premier Dell.com site, shop for desktops, notebooks, servers, storage, and related services. The end user can also view his company's contracted prices for various Dell products, see a list of the preapproved compatible components and computer accessories for his company or even his own department or level, review past purchases, and find contact information for Dell sales and service reps.

To a greater extent than any other of Dell's impressive strategic initiatives, the Premier Dell.com reveals a customer-centric aspect of Dell's corporate culture that is rarely discussed. Premier Dell.com—which *could* be widely imitated but *isn't*—also raises fascinating questions about the roots of Dell's phenomenal growth and profitability. And it forces us to wonder: Why *isn't* every company doing something like this?

Sometimes a great notion

The idea that launched the Premier Pages Service came from one of Dell's large corporate clients in 1996. The client asked Dell to selectively aggregate some of the information available on Dell.com, the main Dell Web site, and present it in a way that made sense for the client and its workforce. At that time, Dell.com offered visitors simply too much information. Its home page was a crowded pastiche of products, services, deals, and company news. Basically, what this client told Dell was that it only wanted to see information related to its own specific needs.

So Dell built a unique, password-protected Web page for the client—and quickly realized that it could do the same for other large customers. From that simple beginning arose the Premier Pages Service, an extranet that could be mass customized easily for individual clients.

Dell now serves up more than 50,000 Premier Dell.com sites in fourteen languages. When the program began, the pages were essentially one-offs—hand-built, static HTML pages. Now they are Active Server Pages, which means they assemble dynamically, drawing on up-to-the-minute information stored in Dell's central database. In a sense, no Premier Page actually exists until someone types in the URL and enters the correct password. The newborn page then "vacuums" fresh data from the database, places it in the appropriate spot on the document, and presents it to the user.

When the database is updated, the page content changes dynamically, presenting new information seamlessly to the user. Dell customers find the Premier Dell.com convenient because it allows them to gather specific data without having to make phone calls, send faxes, or compose email. "For example, maybe someone at the customer organization needs to check the status of an order that was placed a couple of days ago," says Patrick Vogt, director of Dell's Relationship Online group. "In the absence of an online order status tool, there is a good chance that a game of phone tag will ensue between the customer and the sales rep."

Vogt says some of Dell's sharpest sales reps have programmed their voice mail messages to guide customers seeking order status information to the Web. Do the customers object? Not at all, according to Vogt. Dell customers who use the Internet to track down information or solve problems tend to be more satisfied than customers who don't. "They get the information they want, when they want it, from the Web, and they're happier," he says.

"The person calling us to check the status of an order isn't necessarily the end user. It could be someone from the user's purchasing department, an intermediary. That person needs the information immediately to get their task completed and go on with their day. Imagine how much easier that person's life becomes if all the information he needs is available on the Internet. Premier Dell.com can add value at every step in the supply process."

Vogt's observation takes on added meaning when you consider how much of that supply process occurs on Dell's side of the wall. For each and every benefit that Premier Dell.com generates for Dell customers, multiple benefits are generated for Dell itself. For the customer, Premier Dell.com primarily represents a convenience. For Dell, the Premier Dell.com is a strategic system that lowers the company's overall costs while simultaneously providing a relatively inexpensive platform for managing customer relationships at both corporate and end-user levels. Perhaps the clearest indication of Premier Dell.com's overall value to Dell is that Dell provides it to customers free of charge.

Not every Dell sales rep, of course, is capable of articulating the organizational value of Premier Dell.com. They don't have to. It's enough that they know Premier Dell.com frees up hours of their time each week—time they can spend pursuing new sales opportunities. "It's like having a sales assistant on call twenty-four hours a day," says Kristena Bins-Turner, business development manager of Premier Dell.com. Vogt agrees. "Take two sales reps. All things being equal, one personally answers every order status question from his customers. The other outsources all those questions to the Internet. The one who works smart and outsources the administrative tasks is going to wind up having thirty or forty minutes per day to sell. In the end, he will sell more because he has more time."

Taking it a step further, Vogt says that Dell sales reps who use the Internet-based services such as Premier Dell.com "as a group make more money than those who don't. The reason that happens is there's an enormous amount of operational goo that goes along with buying and selling computer systems. Our smartest sales reps leverage the Internet to handle as many of those tasks as possible."

As we're beginning to see, the phrase "automated relationship" is less of an oxymoron than it appears. Although it is technology that is enabling companies in every industry to begin implementing genuine customer relationship management programs, the relationships themselves can still be human-to-human. Indeed, the relationships *should* be human-to-human, wherever and to the extent this can be done cost-efficiently.

What's important is to use technology to empower the managers of the customer relationships, in essence supercharging their efforts. Technology can not only give managers the customer-specific information they need; it can also free them to concentrate on those activities that add the most value, rather than siphoning off their time doing administrative chores. It would be illogical to expect a Dell sales rep, who might be managing twenty or thirty accounts, to interact with each account in person, for every question, problem, and follow-up event. What makes more sense is giving the sales reps the tools to interact with customers efficiently and effectively, and Premier Dell.com accomplishes this. The fact that it's an "automated" form of relationship management does not detract from its value or quality, but adds to it.

Setting limits

Many users visit their company's Premier Dell.com site to shop for desktop equipment, initiate online purchases, and track the status of previous orders. In this respect, the service resembles Dell's regular online store, which offers a secure, robust transactional environment and reliable follow-through. What really differentiates the Premier Dell.com from the online store is its capability to help large corporate customers manage their ongoing relationships with Dell—and vice versa.

While the Dell online store offers visitors a broad range of general information and purchase options, a typical Premier Dell.com site displays a limited amount of highly specific information and a restricted menu of actions tailored to suit the user's needs and responsibilities. For example, not all users are likely to be granted direct purchase privileges. Some will be allowed to purchase a higher dollar volume of products, or different classes of products, than others. Some might be allowed only to select a workstation and generate a quote. The quote would be forwarded to the appropriate person in the organization with purchase approval privileges.

Bins-Turner explains the process: "You go online, build your dream system, and get a quote. Then you enter the email address of your CFO or purchasing agent and he gets a copy of the quote. He reviews it, and if it's OK, he authorizes the purchase."

Many of Dell's large corporate customers limit the variety of desktop configurations displayed on their Premier Dell.com sites. Typically, such customers will restrict choices to three or four combinations of components. This serves several purposes, chief among them being the enterprise-wide standardization of workstations and related equipment, allowing the customer to better manage its own complex environment.

Limiting the range of choices also allows a corporate client to manage its "Total Cost of Ownership," a metric routinely used by the Dell sales force to demonstrate the economic advantage of standardizing IT equipment. Basically, the TCO takes into account variables such as downtime caused by a lack of familiarity with nonstandard equipment, network glitches caused by mismatched components or unexpected bandwidth requirements, installation difficulties, ongoing maintenance, moves, and upgrades. Dell's premise is that in a typical open-architecture IT environment, the temptation to buy equipment based solely on price must be weighed against the TCO. An enterprise with standardized equipment, Dell argues, will enjoy a much lower TCO.

Though a Premier Dell.com site can function as a sort of virtual watchdog to prevent abuse of enterprise-wide standards, it still offers the end user a broad range of functionality. The fact that the end user has a choice—even if the choice is limited—is a significant part of Dell's relationship management strategy. What better way to begin instilling loyalty in a group of users than by granting them a degree of direct, unencumbered control over their own work environment?

What's important to note here is that *every company chooses its own purchasing criteria*, setting its own limits and restrictions and defining the functional differences among its own departments. So one thing that is absolutely critical to the success of Premier Dell.com is that each of Dell's customers must "teach" Dell how it manages its own IT purchasing and procurement process. Then, by enabling a customer to do a better, less costly job of managing itself, Dell is adding value that a competitor is incapable of adding at any price, until such time as the client chooses to teach the competitor what it has already taught Dell.

Launching a Premier Dell.com site

In the short time since its inception, Premier Dell.com has evolved from clunky, labor-intensive perks for large clients into sleek, low-maintenance CRM tools. It now takes Dell only two days to set up a new Premier Dell.com site. The process has been streamlined and stripped of red tape. A Dell sales rep nominates an account and contacts his or her account segment administrator. A team of Online Services specialists swings into action and has a working model ready within twenty-four hours. The account team reviews the model, adds or subtracts information and capabilities, and sends approval back to the Online Services crew for launch. By the next day, the new Premier Dell.com site is ready to go live.

Premier Dell.com has proven so versatile that some sales reps rely on the sites to help them acquire new customers. Let's say a rep is scheduled to visit a prospect. The rep is fairly certain that the prospect will become a customer who would benefit from having a Premier Page at some point in the future. Instead of waiting for that indefinite future to arrive, the rep arranges for a Premier Dell.com site to be created for the prospect. The rep arrives at the appointment, opens his laptop, dials in to Dell's site on the Internet, and runs a quick demo of the prospect's live Premier Dell.com site—complete with suggested equipment configurations, pricing, and support options.

Robert Langer, who led the Dell Online group before launching his own dot.com company, confirms that talented sales reps use Premier Dell.com for acquiring customers, as well as keeping and growing them. "It can be quite an impressive tool, even in a cold-call scenario where the sales rep is saying, 'Look what I can do for you if you give me the opportunity.' Premier Dell.com sites demonstrate the kind of relationship they *could* have with Dell if they become a customer."

The sales reps also like the Premier Dell.com because it requires very little maintenance or oversight, says Langer. "Once the client has been trained to use it, the system runs by itself."

Dell also knows that Premier Dell.com is not meant to serve

as a permanent, full-time substitute for the relationship between a client and its account management team. "A Premier Dell.com site doesn't replace the account team—it automates the process of gathering information and relaying it to the client," says Bins-Turner. "It frees up the account team to answer the more complicated questions, to serve more accounts, and to get more personal with the customer."

Dell is also smart enough to know that not every business customer will want to use Premier Dell.com to make online purchases. Some will use the service primarily to track orders, others will use it to enforce standards. Many, according to Bins-Turner, use their Premier Dell.com sites to access HelpTech, a free, online support service designed for business and institutional customers. It is available only through a customer's Premier Dell.com site.

"HelpTech is an application that ties together a lot of the regular service and support functions that are available on Dell.com but adds features that are necessary if you're supporting an entire organization," says Bins-Turner. "It tracks the status of service calls and provides tools that help you troubleshoot and diagnose various problems. It has all the technical specs for all the Dell systems. You can even use HelpTech to see how much time is left on your warranty. We've got customers who only use their Premier Pages to access HelpTech."

HelpTech also is a good example of how an organization can expand or enhance a set of existing customer needs, and then deliver a service based on this enhanced set of needs.

Future plans for the pages include a redesign that will improve user-level customization, Bins-Turner said. "The end users today don't have any control over what they see and what they get. The new site will let them customize their pages. They'll be able to hide certain features, throw things under a 'favorites' tab, customize greetings, colors, and other features like that."

Whatever bells and whistles are added, however, Dell managers and executives are satisfied, for the moment, to view Premier Dell.com as a highly elegant solution to one of the challenges facing its sales force: maintaining customer relationships in an increasingly complex environment.

"Instead of having to call their sales rep and say, 'Give me the purchase history on all the systems I bought for this location in the last forty-two days because my boss needs it,' our customers can go to their Premier Dell.com site, get the information they want, save it into a spreadsheet, and go," says Bins-Turner.

Use of the Premier Dell.com is strictly voluntary. Dell customers aren't required to have Premier Dell.com sites and those that have them aren't required to use them. Customers who feel more comfortable interacting exclusively with a human being retain the option of bypassing all the automated systems. It just takes longer.

And there's no question that Dell would still be Dell even without Premier Dell.com. But it would be a less profitable Dell, with higher per-customer servicing costs and a substantially higher head count, particularly in the areas of sales and sales support.

A Dell without Premier Dell.com would also be a less user-friendly Dell—at least for its smaller business customers. Services such as instant order status and purchase history would only be available to the largest clients. "Premier Dell.com allows us to offer the same services to small and large firms," says Bins-Turner. "Without Premier Dell.com, we would have to reserve these services for our largest customers. Now we have the potential to scale our services all the way down to the smallest customer."

By developing new services for its very largest customers and then rolling these services out more broadly, Dell has struck on a formula that works. The Learning Relationships Dell forms with end users not only grow revenues but also expand the set of possible needs Dell can meet in the future.

The loyalty channel

As vice president and general manager of Dell's Large Corporate Accounts Division, Cliff Mountain leads the sales teams responsible for acquiring and growing clients with 3,500 to 18,000 employees. He sees a bright future for Premier Dell.com in Dell's ongoing sales and retention efforts. "Remember, the customer works with us to set up the page," he says. By investing time and energy, the customer helps Dell create a barrier against defection. Every time the customer uses Premier Dell.com, the barrier gets a little higher. Eventually, even if one of Dell's competitors launches a similar—or even a *better*—system, the customer's switching costs would provide a significant incentive to remain loyal. In other words, it becomes more convenient for the customer to stay than to go.

What Cliff Mountain is describing, of course, is a Learning Relationship in action. You tell us something about yourself and we act upon what you just told us. You teach us more about your needs. We respond by meeting them even more particularly. You critique our performance and tell us where we need to improve. Over time, we get better and better at meeting—and anticipating—your needs.

Mountain has it exactly right when he describes Premier Dell.com as a two-way channel. "It offers our customers a tremendous amount of information about us. And it offers us a tremendous amount of information about our customers. We can 'see' where they've been on the site and where they're going. We can 'see' what they've picked up in the online store, what they've put back, and what they've actually bought."

From this feedback, Dell can assemble detailed portraits of its ongoing customer relationships. "We can see how we're progressing against particular goals and objectives," says Mountain. Analyzing the click streams reveals which products and services are considered useful by the end users—and which aren't.

This sort of nitty-gritty customer knowledge is what fuels the relationship management process. It is an essential component of any one-to-one strategy. It would, however, be a gross exaggeration to suggest that Dell uses every piece of data it collects to enhance existing customer relationships. Dell faces the same dilemma faced by most other large organizations: Too much data, not enough time. It's like that famous scene in *I Love Lucy* where Lucy and Ethel try to keep up with the candies on the moving conveyor belt. As soon as they catch up, the conveyor belt begins moving faster.

The data, of course, isn't falling on the floor. It just isn't being fully utilized. The real problem is that customer data becomes stale even faster than candy. Remember in Finance 101 when you learned that "a dollar today is worth more than a dollar tomorrow?" The same reasoning can be applied to customer data. The only way it will grow in value is if you put it to work for you.

It's fair to say that if you're relying on customer knowledge as a competitive edge, maximizing the value of the data you collect should be considered a prime directive. But what are the best ways to make sure this happens?

For the time being, Dell is comfortable using the knowledge it gathers within each business segment to improve its chances of closing sales with prospects whose needs are similar to those of existing clients within the segment. Dell's sales entry system makes it difficult to view customer activity across multiple segments, so it's almost impossible to assemble a complete picture of any individual customer's entire sales history with the company.

Let's say, for example, you're a sales rep in Dell's Global business segment and you're preparing a sales proposal for a very large, U.S.-based multinational organization. Under the existing system, it will be difficult for you to obtain information quickly about similar customers in Dell's Enterprise segment or Dell's Large Corporate Accounts segment.

Dell won't say for the record how much sales revenue currently flows through its 50,000 Premier Dell.com sites. But consider this:

- Every day, online sales generate $50 million in revenue for Dell.
- Online sales now represent approximately 40–50 percent of Dell's annual revenue.

- The bulk of Dell's sales revenues are generated by its large business customers.
- Almost all of those large business customers have Premier Dell.com and use it to make online purchases.
- Each online purchase or transaction saves Dell money.
- Each online purchase increases Dell's store of customer information.

So far, we've built a pretty strong case to show how Premier Dell.com helps Dell keep its costs down and how it improves the efficiency of the Dell sales force. Now let's look at how Premier Dell.com is increasing the dollar value of Dell's customer base. In the long run, this is how Premier Dell.com will benefit Dell—by developing its worldwide "share of desktop."

Share of customer strategy

Dell offers Premier Dell.com customers the option of allowing their employees to buy Dell equipment for personal use. "They might not be able to buy at the corporate contract price, but they can go into a separate online store and purchase a system at a special discount, using their own credit card," says Bins-Turner.

In a very real sense, Dell turns the client into a channel to reach new customers. Dell's ability to accomplish this feat is an inspired example of how a nimble organization can use technology to grow the value of its customer base. Dell, like Bentley (see Chapter 4), has made a conscious choice to pursue *customer* development strategies over *market* development strategies. Dell was not content to achieve a dominant position in the PC marketplace by simply winning the world's premier corporate accounts. What makes Dell a role model is that it pushed the envelope and discovered there were plenty of customers it could still get, keep, and grow *within* those accounts.

In some instances, Dell has teamed up with large clients to provide the client's own customers with Dell equipment. When Eastman Chemical Co. launched a major e-business initiative, it realized that many of its customers didn't have the IT infrastructure necessary to participate. As one of Dell's earliest Premier Dell.com customers, Eastman had learned the strategic value of this sort of technology entanglement and was more than willing to offer itself as a "virtual" sales channel.

Eastman recently forged an alliance with Dell and UUNET, an MCI/World Com company, to create what it calls the Customer Enabling Program. The program basically makes it easier for clients to purchase computer hardware and access the Internet. Dell provides discount pricing on hardware for Eastman customers, as well as a special toll-free telephone number to place orders. Dell also has dedicated an inside sales rep to manage Eastman customers.

UUNET, which was already providing Internet service for Eastman's global network, was designated as the program's official ISP. Eastman reimburses customers through a purchase credit for the cost of the connection fee and the first six months of Internet service. Additionally, UUNET has set up a dedicated, toll-free telephone number for Eastman customers seeking Internet access.

Eastman itself has created a special help desk for customers who participate in the program. The help desk is staffed by

Eastman employees who understand the purpose of the Enabling Program and who are familiar with the hardware, software, and telecommunications services customers need to make the most of Eastman's online business services.

It's not entirely surprising that Eastman, a Tennessee-based chemical manufacturer with $4.5 billion in annual revenues, would enter into such an arrangement with Dell. Everyone at Eastman—from the top of the organization to the bottom—has been a Dell user since 1997, when Eastman agreed to let Dell "bulldoze" its varied inventory of PCs. Since then, every PC at Eastman has been a Dell PC. Eastman executives still refer to the "bulldoze" operation with awe, saying it lowered the company's overall computing costs and created easily manageable standards for desktop equipment throughout the organization. It wasn't long before the Eastman executives discovered the benefits of their Premier Dell.com site—and then adopted the idea for their own customers. The result was Eastman.com, which offers online ordering, order tracking, transaction histories, and an online product catalogue to Eastman customers who register for the service.

"We hold Dell.com up as our benchmark in terms of what we'd like to become through Eastman.com," says Fred Buehler, director of e-business at Eastman. Buehler was among ten Eastman executives who studied Dell's approach to e-commerce over the course of several years. One of the primary lessons they learned was that many customers prefer a tightly integrated relationship with a vendor if the relationship offers solutions to the right set of problems, and this can easily be applied in a variety of categories outside of IT.

In Eastman's own principal industry, for example—chemicals—various documents and certificates are required to ensure quality and content of a shipment. Sometimes, a buyer receives a batch of chemicals before receiving the required documentation. Since the buyer can't legally begin processing the chemicals until the documents arrive, production can grind to a halt, resulting in downtime, missed deadlines and occasionally a spoiled batch of chemicals. Eastman customers who register for the company's online service, however, can access their accounts via Eastman.com and download the various certificates or approvals in real time. They don't have to wait for the physical documents to show up, which means they're never in a panic, trying to figure out how to contact someone at Eastman who can arrange a midnight fax. It's simply easier and more economical for the customer—and for Eastman—to have the required document posted on a secure, password-protected Web page, available day or night to authorized users.

It's not hard to see how Eastman's business vision benefits Dell. Eastman wants to make sure its customers have the technology to do business over the Internet. Dell wants to sell Eastman's customers the PCs they need to get started. No doubt some of those customers will wind up having Premier Dell.com sites themselves. Who knows how many of *them* will then also look to Dell as a benchmark, as did Eastman, and create their own "premier" type of service with their own clients?

The Eastman story also reveals an interesting aspect of Dell's rapid growth. Many people assume Dell's success is based on having a direct sales model that eliminates channel costs. But selling direct isn't the only factor behind Dell's rise. A large portion of Dell's success can be traced to its ability to forge long-term relationships with its end users. Selling direct is just one element of this type of relationship, which depends primarily on acquiring more and more information from a specific customer, and then putting that information to use in adding value for that customer. Thus, even if Dell decided tomorrow to sell its products or services through a channel, which it already does for some types of accounts in a number of countries, it would still retain this formidable advantage over any competitors. Moreover, the advantage applies to its position with respect to its business with each of its clients, one client at a time.

As yet another example of Dell's ability to grow the value of a market segment, one customer at a time, Dell has set up Premier Dell.com sites for more than 150 colleges and universities, and is using those pages to begin relationships with a new spectrum of individual users—the "next generation" of Dell customers.

Many of these schools want to standardize the computer equipment used by their students. The easiest way to achieve this is by offering the students the same corporate discount the school gets from Dell. The school then guides the students to its Premier Dell.com site, where the discount provides the necessary incentive for them to purchase from a list of standardized items. Dell benefits from this in two significant ways: First, it offers Dell a new stream of revenue from within the original customer. Second, it offers Dell the chance to begin customer relationships with the students.

"One of our large accounts is Northwestern University. Thanks to Premier Dell.com, we're now selling laptops and peripherals to Northwestern's law school students," says Bins-Turner. "When those students go off into the business world, they'll say, 'I had a Dell notebook in college and it was great, it worked really well. And Dell will remember me.' That's the beginning of a great new relationship."

Virtual integration

One of the lessons we have learned over the years is the value of technology entanglement as a strategy for enhancing customer loyalty. Dell has a similar strategy, which Michael Dell calls "virtual integration." His book, *Direct from Dell* (Harper Business, 1999), does an excellent job of demonstrating the practical worth and merit of such one-to-one strategies. Here's how he describes his version of technology entanglement:

> The whole concept behind virtual integration is to use direct connections, enhanced by technologies like the Internet, to bring your customers virtually inside your business so you can meet their needs faster and more efficiently than anyone else.
>
> Many companies focus on partnering with their customers from a single dimension—say, from a marketing perspective or as a sales requirement. We partner with them in every way we can, as our direct relationships with our customers enable us to be simultaneously cost-efficient and customer-responsive. Those relationships have proven to be one of our greatest competitive strengths.

Because Eastman Chemical Co. deploys an unusual variety of specialized software packages—from licensed applications to homegrown programs—each new PC required several hours of attention from the Eastman IT department before it could be placed on a user's desk. When Eastman decided to standardize the software on its PCs, it asked Dell, its hardware vendor, to solve the problem. Through its DellPlus Service, Dell responded by creating a high-speed network that loads software directly onto Eastman's PCs while they are still on the assembly line—at any Dell manufacturing facility worldwide.

For Dell, the primary benefit of this type of service isn't the increase of revenue it generates. The primary benefit is that it makes it extremely difficult for the customer to even consider defecting to a competitor or reseller. Like the Premier Dell.com, the software standardization service creates strategic value for Dell that is hard to quantify. This is clearly an instance in which Dell is more than willing to trade a few dollars today for the promise of many dollars tomorrow. Or as Michael Dell explains it: "We're not just going to be their PC vendor anymore. We're part of our customer's own information technology group."

Dell has also created Valuechain, a sort of mirror-world version of Premier Dell.com, for its top suppliers. Each participating supplier gets a password-protected page at Valuechain.Dell.com, where they can review Dell's specs and standards, view a list of orders they've received from Dell, and monitor the shipping status of those orders. Dell plans to connect Valuechain to Premier Dell.com, so suppliers can judge customer-specific demand in real-time and react accordingly. When this linkage is achieved, both Dell *and* its suppliers will be able to reduce their inventories to the absolute barest minimums with complete confidence.

Let's take a moment here to consider why Dell chose the

name Valuechain and why a "value chain" is different from a supply chain. The concept of the value chain was introduced in the mid-1980s by Michael Porter, the Harvard professor and author. The idea was expanded by John Dobbs in a 1998 white paper he wrote for Cambridge Technology Partners. In his paper, "Competition's New Battleground: The Integrated Value Chain," Dobbs argues that while business has traditionally viewed the supply chain in terms of purchasing, transportation, warehousing, and logistics, the new "chain" is something much wider and much deeper. Dobbs defines the integrated value chain as a collaborative, customer-centric process that acts as an extended enterprise or "virtual" corporation to create competitive advantages for every link in the chain. Dobbs crowns Wal-Mart as the king of value chain integration, noting that Wal-Mart's strength derives from a strong corporate belief that it is "buying *for* rather than selling *to* its customers." Dell certainly is a contender for this throne, especially in the B2B space. Like Wal-Mart, it leverages its customer-centric business model to respond with lightning speed to changing conditions.

As more and more B2B organizations confront the demands of the Real Economy, value chain management will emerge as a critical business ability.

Account management strategies

Even if Premier Dell.com disappeared tomorrow and even if Dell abandoned its direct sales model, it would still possess a unique advantage over its rivals. What is this competitive edge that has kept Dell in the lead? It is simply this: Dell's sales and marketing processes are organized around its individual customers, not around its products.

As of this writing, Dell organizes its U.S. customer base into eleven separate "business segments," and it is constantly reevaluating this alignment to make it more and more useful for managing its customer relationships.

Business segment	Criteria
Global	Companies with 18,000 employees or more that have headquarters outside the U.S. and operations in the U.S., or have headquarters in the U.S. and significant operations in other countries
Enterprise Accounts	Companies in the U.S. with 18,000 or more employees
Large Corporate Accounts	Companies with 3,500 to 18,000 employees
Preferred Accounts Division	Companies with 400 to 3,500 employees
Internet Partner Division	Internet Service Providers, Application Service Providers, and Web-Hosting companies
Healthcare	Hospitals, HMOs, medical provider groups, medical laboratories
Federal Government	Federal agencies, federal employees and APO/FPO orders
State and Local Government	State, county, and municipal agencies and organizations
Education	Students, faculty, and staff, as well as K–12 and Higher Education institutional purchases
Small Business Center	Companies based in the U.S. with fewer than 400 employees
Consumer (Home and Home Office)	Home users, both professional and recreational

Relationship Group (Global through Healthcare); Public (Federal Government through Education); Home and Small Business (Small Business Center and Consumer)

"A few years ago, Large Corporate Accounts, Enterprise, and Global were all together in one segment," recalls Mountain. "So you would have accounts with $15 million PC budgets competing for attention with accounts that had $150 million PC budgets. When we divided it up into three segments, the smallest customers of the original group became the largest customers of a new group and, as a result, they got a whole lot more attention."

The top five of the eleven business segments compose what Dell calls its Relationship Group. The accounts within this group are assigned dedicated sales reps who are responsible for managing and growing existing accounts, as well as acquiring new ones. Dedicated sales reps are also allocated to accounts in the Healthcare segment. Some, but not all, of the Higher Education accounts have dedicated reps. Similarly, some of the government accounts have dedicated reps, depending on their complexity and size. These are reps who are rewarded not just for products sold, but for increases in share of wallet for a customer account.

While it might appear that Dell has simply arranged its account management organization in a tiered fashion to allocate relatively greater priority to larger firms, appearances can be deceiving. Dell's sales organization structure is designed to ensure that it can adapt its services to meet the different needs of different types of customers. Dell has resisted the impulse to group accounts by industry, based on its fundamental understanding that IT products are, and probably always will be, perceived as commodities. As a result, what most distinguishes one company's IT needs from another's is not the industry in which the company competes, but the nature of the company's procurement and IT management function. And with few exceptions (healthcare being the most obvious), these procurement and management processes are almost always directly related to an enterprise's actual size, rather than its industry. Dell makes a fetish out of understanding how its customers make purchase and procurement decisions. The company is capable of applying its understanding not just in one or two types of business situations, but across a wide range of situations.

Only one segment, Healthcare, could be considered a true industry "vertical." Dell created a unique segment for the healthcare industry because the IT needs of customers in that segment are markedly different from the IT needs of most other Dell customers. Those needs, in turn, require a highly specialized style of sales and marketing management. But even accounting for this one vertical segment, Dell's whole organizational purpose is to adapt itself to the manner in which its customers obtain, install, and manage their IT assets.

"If you look closely at the segments, you'll see different procurement processes," says Mountain. "That's really what we're thinking about. For instance, when you're dealing with the federal government, it's more important to know how the contract process works than it is to know whether the PCs will be used for email or word processing."

Early on, Dell discovered that by adopting a more granular approach to customer grouping, it could respond faster to the needs of individual customers within any particular group. This granular approach also made it relatively easy for Dell to devise specific sales, marketing, and account management processes for each group. Although most Dell customers are assigned to a business segment by virtue of size, the finely drawn groupings actually serve to differentiate the customers by their general, if not specific, sets of needs. This kind of happy accident is possible because IT needs still tend to depend more on an organization's size than on any other factors. In other words, a large global organization, no matter what business it is in, will have vastly different IT requirements than a smaller, regional organization.

Whether by accident or design, Dell's account management strategy has made it possible to manage accounts much more carefully and with a higher degree of specialization than could be achieved by any of its competitors. "Fortune 500 companies have very specific global needs. Our smaller customers have different needs. By breaking it down to a very granular level, we can come up with solutions that fit the particular needs of each customer set," says Mountain. "And because we're direct, we can provide those solutions faster and better."

Hunters and developers

Within the five segments of the Relationship Group, Dell differentiates customers based on where they are in the account management process. Dell understands that the "vintage" or relative maturity of a particular customer matters and that different vintages of customers require different approaches. Dell also understands that human psychology plays a role in deciding who handles which account. Some people are better at winning new accounts than managing existing accounts. So the sales force is differentiated into "hunters" and "developers."

Account management phase	Status	Goals	Account manager type
Acquisition	Dell has done little or no business with the organization, but has identified it as a prospect.	Establish relationship with potential client; close initial sale.	Hunter
Development	Dell is on client's approved vendor list; client buys at least one Dell product line.	Sell multiple product lines; sell into different departments.	Developer
Retention	Client buys frequently; uses Premier Dell.com to compile reports, track history, and make online purchases.	Extend reach into client's organization; increase client's LTV to Dell.	Developer

At Dell, the first phase normally is handled by a hunter. The second and third phases are handled by a developer. Mountain explains the difference: "A hunter is typically really good at convincing people to do something. They're wonderful for the customer and wonderful for Dell. They're fast movers, they're fast thinkers and they do a phenomenal job of explaining the Dell model. But they might not be quite as adept at the day-to-day management of an account."

Dell has tweaked its sales force compensation plan to ensure that hunters aren't penalized for turning over their best accounts. And the hunters are encouraged to prepare the customer for the handoff. "We make sure there's some overlap between the hunter and the developer," Mountain explains. "The handoff is absolutely critical. We suggest introducing the concept of the development and retention piece on the hunter's second or third call. The customer gets comfortable with the idea and understands that the developer is going to be someone who can help move things forward. We also stress to the customer that there's a psychological difference between a hunter and a developer, so everyone knows what to expect."

Developers are not only responsible for managing accounts—they are required to grow them. "We measure the developers on pure share of wallet metrics by account," says Mountain. "We have a very targeted program where we put your account on a thermometer and if it's a three, we say, 'How can you get it to a four?' If it's a three, it's because today they're buying desktops, notebooks, and workstations. To get it to a four, you need to sell servers, DellPlus, DellWare, and associated services. We even put in special incentives to encourage the developers to sell these products."

Because the developers are required to sell more complicated systems, Dell provides them with additional training opportunities. They are also encouraged to rely on in-house specialists called "subject matter experts," who are trained to support Dell's sales development and retention efforts.

Single point of contact

When Mountain spoke about the importance of managing the "handoff" from hunter to developer, he hit upon an interesting point. No matter how complex the sales organization becomes, the sales process must continue to appear "simple" to the customer. To that end, Dell makes sure that each account in the

Relationship Group has a single point of contact—one dedicated account manager. For the customer, the advantages are less uncertainty, higher confidence, and probably better service. For Dell, the advantages are better customer communications, lower cost of sales, and less confusion over who is responsible for the customer.

Additionally, the account managers have emerged within the Dell organization as trusted, reliable sources of insight into customer needs. When a new product line is under development, the opinions of the account managers weigh heavily in the process. This is another instance in which having a customer-centric philosophy works in Dell's favor. "If you have a product-centric model, typically the folks who have all the resources and decision-making power are over in engineering," says Mountain. "At Dell we have phenomenal engineers and a huge R&D budget, but fundamentally the customer business segments tell the product groups what to build, based on the feedback we receive from our customers. I'm not very good at engineering products, but I have a lot of input—more than my counterparts at the organizations competing with us."

This customer-centric approach is the key to Dell's ability to develop and sell products and services that people actually need. The opposite philosophy is to develop products and services based on internal needs, and then struggle to create demand through traditional marketing techniques, in essence hiring nothing but hunters. Build-to-forecast models made sense before there was any other way to find out what people really needed. Now that it's possible to know and remember what customers want—and when they want it—it seems illogical for organizations to pursue product-centric business strategies.

Smart manufacturing

It would be impossible to write about Dell without including at least a brief overview of its mass customization capabilities. There is little argument that Dell has been, and continues to be, a leader in this area. After spending years putting together computers in his dormitory bedroom, Michael Dell knew that it would be relatively easy to devise a system for assembling desktop systems out of standard modules. He also knew how easy it would be to vary the finished product by substituting one standard module for another. Because he had started out building custom systems for individual clients, he was entirely comfortable with the idea of just-in-time manufacturing and limited inventories. After all, who wants a bunch of unused components cluttering up the bedroom?

Most of Dell's competitors had superimposed traditional business methodologies onto their PC product lines, not fully grasping that the PC was an entirely different animal from its ancestors. The advent and acceptance of the PC as a common appliance gave rise to a phenomenon that would change all of society. The mainframe had been an extension of the existing social order. But the PC was the catalyst for a new social order, a social order in which information and computing power were to be distributed and shared, rather than rationed and hoarded. By the time Dell emerged as a significant player, people were no longer debating whether or not everyone should have a PC. People expected to have PCs on their desks, both at work and at home. And once the PC became standard issue, the new question for users became: How can I get a PC that does what I want it to do?

Dell was the only PC maker to recognize this opportunity and seize the moment. The achievement was made possible by Dell's direct sales model, its customer segmentation system, and its mass customization capability. The direct sales model guaranteed a reliable stream of fresh, accurate customer information. The segmentation system ensured a customer-centric approach to the development of sales and marketing strategies. Mass customization made it possible for Dell to deliver products that matched the needs of its customers far more closely than any competitor could, and to lock its customers into ever tighter relationships, one customer at a time. Dell currently assembles its PCs from hundreds of standardized modules, creating a huge number of possible combinations. How many exactly? Tens of thousands, probably, but "we've never actually figured out how many combinations there really are," says a Dell spokesman.

Navigating the course

It would be inaccurate to suggest that Dell is at some sort of crossroads, even though it's difficult to predict whether its future growth will depend largely on business-to-business, business-to-consumer, or some mix of both. Indeed, Dell has recently sent mixed signals about its intentions, indicating one month that it plans to deepen its penetration of the consumer market and vowing another month to concentrate on the business market. Some of Dell's public statements no doubt reflect a degree of uncertainty within the company, which is entirely natural when you consider that Dell is going where no PC maker has gone before, literally inventing or pioneering new markets with each passing financial quarter. Dell performs more like an inspired virtuoso in a jam session, rather than a ponderous, predictable corporate entity, and this makes it hard to say with authority exactly where it is heading next.

In any case, Dell recently created a new business segment, the Internet Partner Division, for Internet Service Providers, Application Service Providers, and dot-coms; and has expanded the capabilities of its DellHost service to include next-business-day setup for small and medium-size businesses. These types of initiatives are aimed at growing Dell's presence in the high-margin market for Internet servers. Kevin Rollins, Dell vice-chairman, compared the push to capture a larger chunk of the Internet-related hardware market to the company's decision to focus on direct sales back in 1993. That might be an overstatement, but it demonstrates Dell's refusal to be held captive by any single strategy or formula, no matter how successful it may have been in the past.

What Dell is unlikely to jettison, however, is the belief that its success is based on delivering value beyond mere price. Surveys have certainly shown that price was not the primary driver in customer decisions to purchase Dell computer products.

Every quarter, Dell sets a new record for consumer sales. The consumer space is both profitable and strategic, says Langer. "The vast majority of those consumers also work. If

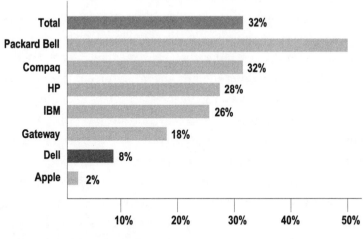

Price as primary motivation in purchasing a PC

Source: 1999 Sanford C. Berstein Consumer PC Survey

they have a positive experience with Dell at home, they're probably going to recommend Dell machines at work. There's a clear hand-in-glove synergy here that we want to cultivate. Because if we're known as a business supplier only, then we might not be thought of as a potential supplier for the home. If we're known only as a consumer company, then we might lose opportunities in the business-to-business space. So it's critical for Dell to be heavily, aggressively cross calling into both markets."

The challenge, Langer says, is for Dell to remain actively engaged in each customer's computing experience—even when those customers are not in an active buying mode. "Dell recognizes there will be gulfs between major purchases," he says. "But there are significant profit pools in between those purchases."

This is a serious, and perhaps critical, issue for Dell. How far will Dell go to become actively involved in the day-to-day activities of its customers?

Perhaps Dell will create mass customized packages of computer-related services that could be sold on a subscription basis, across all its markets, to ensure a steady, predictable revenue stream from each customer. Dell had taken several steps in this direction, offering inventory management and logistics services to business customers, but it later retrenched, licensing its consulting products instead to Andersen Consulting. It also agreed to market e-commerce consulting services delivered by third-party vendors such as Andersen Consulting (now Accenture) and Gen3.

Looking ahead, it seems that Dell's biggest challenge will come not from its competitors but from its customers. Dell is already way out in front of its competitors, and there's nothing wrong with that. What will happen to Dell if it gets too far ahead of its customers?

As Dell relies more heavily on the expansion of business-to-business e-commerce, it runs the risk of entering a market where it is one of the few players with any real experience. Michael Dell's brother, Adam, painted a vivid picture of the future in an article he wrote for *Business* 2.0 in 1999. A New York-based venture capitalist, Adam Dell accurately describes the Internet as "one big value chain" composed of infinite subsets of value chains:

> Within each chain exist multiple parties and competitors, complex overlapping partnerships ... On the Internet, where companies are driven to razor-thin margins, it is im-

perative to understand how these value chains fit together and how the transaction revenue generated from them is sliced up among the players.

It should surprise no one that Dell is among the vanguard of organizations wrestling with this prime dilemma of the Real Economy.

Tasks ahead for Dell

Dell clearly "leads the league" in deploying technology to forge tighter bonds with its corporate customers and end users. The company's Premier Dell.com remains a benchmark for using the power of technology to reduce the costs of interactivity and to make life easier for customers. Premier Dell.com also frees up time for the sales force to pursue new accounts and cultivate existing accounts. Most important, Premier Dell.com makes it possible for Dell to form one-to-one relationships with the business executives at client companies who actually use its products.

What should Dell be doing now? For one thing, Dell should invest more time and effort in the area of needs-based customer differentiation. Yes, the procurement and purchasing processes at a large enterprise are likely to differ significantly from those at a smaller firm, but why stop there? What about the fact that some companies are characterized by a high degree of central control over their IT spending and management, while other companies are not? Or what about companies that embrace outsourcing on a regular basis versus those that don't? Some companies have well-developed IT help desks with very competent internal IT expertise, and others do not.

But in addition to differentiating corporate customers themselves, Dell should think about differentiating different types of end users, influencers, and decision makers within these corporate clients. Now that Premier Dell.com can let Dell peek into the actual workings of an individual corporate client, shouldn't the company try to deduce how different players within a client make decisions, and which players influence which others? What about the differing levels of computer skills among all these players? All by itself, the fact that different corporate executives will have different computer skill levels should be more than enough for Dell to offer much more highly customized services to lock in the loyalties of these executives.

Dell also needs to develop a system that will allow it to gauge customer value more accurately. Currently, Dell measures the value of its corporate clients by looking at how many people a client employs, using the same measuring stick of enterprise size that they rely on for assessing the company's procurement processes and methods. But as relationship building becomes more expensive, as more services are added into the mix, Dell will find it necessary to have a more accurate picture of which customers to give priority attention to, and soon ranking by last year's employee count won't be good enough.

We already know that Dell is comfortable providing Premier Dell.com free for its large corporate customers, not only because of the relationships it cements but also because it reduces Dell's own internal costs. Perhaps Dell should follow the lead of its own customer, Eastman Chemical, and subsidize the IT efforts of some corporate clients. The problem is, with little formal knowledge about how to rank its corporate clients by their long-term value to Dell, it's going to be quite difficult to determine which clients are worth subsidizing to guarantee their loyalty.

Dell should apply what they've learned from the success of Premier Dell.com to visualize the future of their entire business. If computer hardware is increasingly commodity-like, and there are very few industry analysts who would disagree with that, then Dell's direction for the future should be to find more services to add, on top of Premier Dell.com.

In the B2C space, for instance, it's obvious that Dell should roll out a version of Premier Dell.com to its retail consumer customers. Imagine Dell using its Premier Dell.com system to strengthen its relationships with millions of these individual decision makers. Ideally, such a plan would allow Dell to plant seeds that could grow, in time, into a significant crop of consumers whose loyalty is based not just on Dell's quality in a commodity environment but on their own individual relationships with the firm.

In the B2B space, however, Dell should look carefully at expanding the scope and benefits of the services it provides to its corporate customers, going beyond the services now offered in the Premier Dell.com program. Managing IT procurement and configuration is one thing, and it is a very big thing. But without minimizing the success of this service, are there other ways Dell could offer even more detailed and useful help to its corporate clients? Some things Dell might want to consider include:

- Taking over more of the responsibility for providing "IT availability" at a client.
- Providing various software and applications on an ASP (Application Service Provider) basis.
- Getting into the business of managing corporate databases, backup databases, server farms, email, and Web site reliability.
- Offering comprehensive computer applications training.
- Helping companies prepare their wireless-migration plans, moving from today's PC-dominant world to tomorrow's world of ubiquitously available wireless Web accessibility.
- Providing tools to enable its clients to help their own business customers better deal with IT, interactivity, and business processes.

Like many companies struggling to break free of the commoditization trap of the Real Economy, Dell is indeed in the process of redefining the business it's in. By focusing on the customer, rather than just its products, Dell has already built a powerful platform for launching any or all of these new services. In doing so, the company will be ensuring a strong financial future, even as the PC itself is gradually reduced to commodity status, destined to be manufactured and sold by low-cost producers.

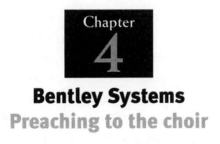

Chapter

4

Bentley Systems
Preaching to the choir

Top line summary

Software developer Bentley Systems faced an agonizing dilemma: It already owned a huge share of its market, and yet still needed to grow annual sales revenues at a respectable pace. A strategy that focused primarily on market development would not deliver the kind of results sought by Bentley management. So Bentley turned to a strategy that emphasized account development. But first, Bentley's management team had to confront an internal culture that was strongly product-centric and nudge it carefully toward a more customer-centric approach. They accomplished this in a series of initiatives designed to prove how one-to-one marketing programs could succeed in real-world situations.

Imagine a market in which virtually all of your potential customers already own one or more of your products. Imagine further that most of these customers have plenty of cash to spend and a demonstrable need for many of the other products you manufacture but they don't already own.

In that kind of situation, wouldn't it make sense to have a sales strategy focused on customer development instead of market development? And if you manage a business that sells indirectly, wouldn't it make sense to develop well-defined relationships with your channel partners? After all, they often serve as the front line of your sales effort and, more likely than not, believe they "own" the relationship with the end user.

You don't have to look far to find examples of organizations with broad share of market but modest share of customer. The banking, telecom, and travel verticals are replete with firms struggling to prevent their margins from dropping even as their market penetration continues to grow.

More and more organizations are discovering the value of strategies designed to increase margins by developing deeper relationships with their customers and their channel partners. One such organization is Bentley Systems Incorporated, one of the world's leading providers of software for the engineering, construction, and operation (E/C/O) market. Bentley now has annual revenues of $200 million, but it began as a small software development firm in Exton, a Pennsylvania community north of the Brandywine Valley and west of the Main Line. Although Bentley's reputation was built on its pioneering work in software, the company is also a pioneer in the area of account management strategy. This is important to recognize because account management is a prerequisite for account development. You can't develop an account without first devising a strategy for managing it.

"Our account management strategy is invaluable to us," says Warren Winterbottom, Bentley's senior vice president of Americas sales. "It's the only way to establish ourselves in the customer's eyes as more than just a series of transactions. Account management allows us to establish long-term relationships with our customers. In fact, our account management strategy actually requires us to perform all the activities necessary for building customer relationships. Without it, all you have at the end of the day is a bunch of orders."

The Bentley story divides neatly into three distinct stages of evolution:

1. Market development (customer acquisition) 1984–1993
2. Channel development (distribution infrastructure) 1993–1998
3. Account development (one-to-one marketing) 1999–present

Bentley's history is somewhat unique. It's important to note that in its early days Bentley operated primarily as a software developer for Intergraph Corp., a global vendor of business software and a major stakeholder in the young company. Bentley Software was sold direct by Intergraph. It was also distributed through a network of resellers set up by Intergraph.

So while most firms initially face the task of setting up a reliable distribution network and then scrambling for customers to build market share, Bentley began with a distribution system already in place, thanks to its relationship with Intergraph.

Free to concentrate its resources on market development, Bentley grew rapidly. It wasn't long, however, before Bentley found itself needing to consider a challenge familiar to many young technology firms: If the firm is successful, imitators will attempt to steal its customers, usually by initiating some form of price war. Then the firm will have to make a difficult choice: It can compete on price and watch its margins erode, or it can stick to its guns and watch its market share drop. Either way, it loses.

There is a path around this lose-lose scenario. The firm could implement a one-to-one marketing strategy that focuses on building customer relationships and increasing its share of each customer's business. This is the path Bentley chose to follow. It has proven a good choice. Bentley's CRM programs have enabled it to reduce the size of its marketing budget by one-third. The millions of dollars Bentley saved was invested in developing a fully functional one-to-one Web site. The Web site, in turn, now helps Bentley save additional millions of dollars in software distribution costs because it allows users to download products directly from the Web.

Due to the success of these initiatives, the one-to-one marketing philosophy is spreading throughout Bentley. Each day, Bentley becomes more of a one-to-one enterprise, an organization where customer-focused activities are the norm instead of the exception.

Ask any Bentley sales or marketing executive and they'll tell you unequivocally that their energies and resources are spent on growing existing accounts—not on beating the bushes for new ones. They'll also tell you honestly that while they've taken some tremendous leaps in the direction of customer-focused sales and marketing strategies, they still have a long way to go. It's worth remembering that becoming a one-to-one organization can be a difficult and time-consuming process. Each of the four basic implementation steps—Identify, Differentiate, Interact, and Customize—requires the organization to change certain aspects of its operations, ranging from the way it manages customer data to the way it manufactures and delivers products or services.

Every step taken toward the goal can be seen as a victory, even if some steps are skipped or delayed. For example, as we shall see later, Bentley does a solid job of differentiating its customers by needs. But it is less advanced in its ability to differentiate customers by their value to the organization.

Does this mean Bentley isn't a good one-to-one role model? Quite the contrary. Like the other organizations we examine in this book, Bentley is far enough down the one-to-one marketing path for us to predict the outcome of its efforts with a reasonable degree of confidence. Certainly it's true that if Bentley knew the lifetime value of its individual customers, it could prioritize its efforts more cost-effectively. Until Bentley has the systems in place to accomplish this, however, it makes exemplary use of the data it already has to anticipate the needs of its customers and to customize their experiences with the company as much as possible.

It will be easier to understand the challenges confronting Bentley—and to fully appreciate the depth of the company's commitment to one-to-one strategies—if we begin by examining the market for its products and services.

Now, where did I put that door?

When we look up at a tall office tower, most of us are blissfully unaware of the huge amount of paperwork generated by the small army of architects, designers, engineers, developers, builders, contractors, government officials, and managers involved in the construction and maintenance of the structure. The drafting of plans, elevations and blueprints—along with the inevitable revisions and re-revisions—consume thousands of working hours. Each time a change is made, there is a chance that some sort of error will be introduced. Sometimes the error is minor enough to be corrected without tearing down a wall or ripping up a floor. Occasionally the error is serious enough to require demolishing the work in progress and starting over.

It is because of this innate potential for disaster that fastidious documentation and accurate record-keeping have been considered essential to the success of every large-scale construction effort since the days of the pharaohs and their pyramids. Over the centuries, however, this necessity has become the bane of almost every architect's professional life. Managing the ever-complicated "paper trail" came to be seen as a necessary evil, a burdensome task that required great care but little creativity.

In the 1970s and early 1980s, companies such as Computervision and Prime Computer began automating pieces of the drafting and documentation processes. The development of computer-aided design (CAD) technology helped shift some of the most tedious work from the drafting table to the computer—invariably a "heavy iron" mainframe that was hardwired to dumb terminals in the drafting room. Early CAD tools were a step up from T squares and straightedges, but their functionality was limited. Most of the early tools were not designed to interface with other data systems, which severely restricted their utility and practicality.

It wasn't until the mid-1980s, when computation began migrating from the mainframe to the desktop, that it became possible to consider fully automating the paper trail. Once the potential existed, it wasn't long before everyone involved in the construction industry expected—or demanded—some degree of automation.

This led to a rapid surge in demand for software that would enable architectural firms to begin sharing data files not only among internal work groups but also with clients, contractors, lenders, building managers, government agencies, and tenants—everyone involved in the project from inception to demolition.

Bentley Systems was perfectly poised to benefit from this new market. Two brothers, Keith and Barry Bentley, had formed the company in 1984. Three more Bentley brothers, Greg, Ray, and Scott, would join the firm later. Bentley's core product was MicroStation, an innovative CAD program that ran on a PC. As the market for desktop engineering software grew, it seemed natural that sales of MicroStation would grow along with it. By the end of 1990, Bentley had an installed base of 100,000 MicroStation users. By 1995, that base had grown to 200,000 users. Among large firms and government agencies, MicroStation had emerged as the most popular desktop CAD solution. Among all users, it was second only to Autodesk's AutoCAD system.

Inspired by the popularity of MicroStation, the Bentley brothers felt they were ready to exert a greater degree of control over the sales and marketing of their products. They began by renegotiating their agreement with Intergraph and assuming responsibility for managing the distribution channel, which was composed mostly of independent systems integrators. While this action brought Bentley a step closer to its end users, the integrators continued to manage the customer relationships.

Bentley embarked on a global initiative to tighten its relationships with the integrators. These integrators, which Bentley calls MicroStation Value Added Resellers (MVARs) to emphasize the Bentley connection, would form the backbone of a hybrid sales infrastructure, in combination with Bentley's own account managers. The infrastructure would support sales efforts at the corporate and the dealer level. This hybrid infrastructure had several immediate benefits, among them:

1. allowing Bentley to exercise greater control over the tone and consistency of the corporate message it wanted to send end users;
2. giving the customers an added sense of confidence because they knew the integrator was backed by Bentley's reputation and experience;
3. affording small and medium-size integrators access to the marketing resources of a major company;
4. creating opportunities for Bentley to become more involved in the front-line sales process.

CEO Greg Bentley compares the hybrid sales channel to similar arrangements employed widely in the insurance industry. "The large underwriter provides longevity, continuity, reliability, and stability. The independent agents provide the local service component. In our model, we're the large underwriter and our channel partners are the agents," he says. "Technically speaking, we haven't sold direct. Nonetheless, our account managers keep very much involved when our products and services sell through intermediaries."

Working closely with channel partners emerged as a keystone of the Bentley corporate strategy. In some instances, Bentley would take an equity position in a reseller, naming it a *Bentley Integrator.* This had two positive effects. First, it created an even tighter bond between Bentley and the reseller, which sent a strong signal to potential clients. Second, it eliminated the reseller's natural anxiety about eventual competition from Bentley itself. "Instead of an 'us against them' environment, it's a 'we together' team environment, which I have to believe is going to result in more lucrative wins and more profitable sales," says Greg Bentley.

One such channel partner is ModernTech SI, a Knoxville, Tennessee-based systems integrator with annual revenues of about $6 million. Joe Kirby, ModernTech's CEO, explains the benefits of the relationship: "When I tell a prospect we're partly owned by Bentley, that helps us exponentially. And there's another advantage: We get terrific résumés now from people all over the world, people I never guessed we would have gotten résumés from. Why? Because they like the idea of working for a small company that's got a big company behind it."

During Bentley's period of channel development, sales of MicroStation continued briskly. Despite this, the Bentley brothers knew they were now racing with the clock. If they continued to view revenue from MicroStation as the company's primary engine of growth, they would soon find themselves at the mercy of forces beyond their control. They could easily imagine a number of "downside" scenarios:

■ The market would stop expanding and sales revenue from MicroStation would flatten. Bentley would face a choice of accepting stagnant margins or reducing operating costs.

■ The market would shrink and sales revenue from MicroStation would decrease. Bentley would be forced to cut spending, curtail growth, and reduce expectations.

■ The market would keep growing, but a competitor would introduce a product that would supersede MicroStation. Revenue would flatten or fall, profits would stagnate or drop. Regaining the competitive advantage would require a significant investment in R&D.

■ The distribution channel, made up of independent resellers, would change in some unforeseen way that would negatively affect sales of Bentley products.

Greg Bentley compares the situation to a checkerboard on which every square is already occupied by a checker piece. "Our job is to put as many checker pieces on those squares as possible—not to look for empty squares, since (at least in most parts of the world) there aren't any!" he says.

Expect the best, prepare for the worst

Bentley Systems formulated a two-part strategy to ensure continued growth regardless of market conditions. The first part involved broadening the product line. Bentley would rely on the talent and experience of its staff to develop a multitude of new applications and services. Diversifying the product line would reduce the firm's reliance on MicroStation to generate income. The new offerings would be developed in concert with end users, assuring a market for them when they were released. Bentley established a series of industry user councils at which the best minds from the various disciplines of construction engineering were gathered under one roof to brainstorm about new products and services. From these sources, Bentley collected a wealth of valuable information it could put to immediate use in the design, development, and implementation of new technology. Significant improvements emerged from these sessions and were incorporated into Bentley's ProjectBank and TriForma product lines.

The second part of the strategy was more complex, less intuitive, and potentially riskier. It also offered the best hope for long-term profitability. Bentley would transform its traditional culture of pursuing market share into a culture of developing share of customer. Several factors helped speed this decision. Over time, it had become apparent that within the distribution channel there were varying degrees of commitment to selling the new fuller line of Bentley products. The channel, Bentley concluded, was acting as a partial brake on revenue growth.

Focusing on the end user, however, seemed a more promising overall strategy than reengineering the distribution channel from the ground up. Replacing the existing channel model with a direct sales strategy would have been impractical since Bentley had neither the means nor the organization in place to sustain such a radical transformation. While a cynic might argue that Bentley turned to an account management system out of necessity rather than choice, it's clear that Bentley made the best of an existing situation. Like any organism, Bentley adapted to its surroundings.

"In the Americas, we have thirty full-time account managers and eight sales directors," explains Winterbottom. "There are more than 240 salespeople in our network of resellers. It makes sense for us to utilize this reseller network. And it makes sense for us to include our resellers as much as possible in the account management process."

Another determining factor in Bentley's evolution was the inception of multitiered technologies that relied on distributed servers to manage information. This changed the dynamics of the desktop software market. Without server-level integration, MicroStation would be at a disadvantage, as would many other programs designed primarily to function in loosely networked environments. Despite advances in desktop and Web-based information technologies, the premise of multitiered systems would be especially appealing to architects and engineers who needed fast, secure access to complex data files.

In an application-server environment, data files can be "checked out" by authorized users, modified, and synchronized with the system without disrupting the workflow. Changes made on a document in San Francisco would be instantly available to a field office in Athens or Beijing. All files, as well as attachments, can be tracked by attributes such as time, date, location, most recent user, file type, file size, title, or keyword. From the standpoint of an architect or engineer, this was the Holy Grail of automation since it allowed every document associated with a project to be stored and accessed electronically—in real time, with ironclad security and revision tracking.

Bentley was the first software firm to realize fully how this evolution in computing would affect the construction industry. For the first time since the invention of the plumb line, construction projects could be tracked from cradle to grave. Part of Bentley's prescience no doubt resulted from the company's informal policy of hiring experienced architects, designers, and engineers to fill key sales, marketing, and support positions throughout the organization. They knew firsthand that buildings aren't built just once—they tend to be refitted, remodeled, and redesigned several times over a lifetime of many decades. They knew that manufacturing plants, highways, and airports aren't one-time construction events, but usually a series of multiple projects over time. And they were bright enough to see how each of those multiple projects could offer profitable opportunities—for Bentley, for its channel partners, and for the end users. (This ability to see around the corner—that is, to see opportunities in evolving technologies that might better meet the needs of end users—would again prove critically useful to Bentley when information management systems began migrating to the World Wide Web in the late 1990s. In the E/C/O sphere, Bentley products helped pioneer this migration.)

Clearly, Bentley had the vision. Now it needed a detailed game plan to transform the vision into a sustainable stream of revenue and profit.

Enter the SELECT program

Keith Bentley is one of the few top corporate executives who can write software *and* run a business. Despite his accomplishments, he had enough humility to realize that even with all the talent and information available to him, he was unlikely to create another program that could fundamentally change the market the way MicroStation had. He also knew that even though the firm's most recently developed software packages had been welcomed warmly by the E/C/O market, his customers would be sated after purchasing, at most, two or three different products. Then it might be years before they were ready to purchase again. Keith Bentley's challenge was to figure out the best way to use these "quiet intervals" between sales. This is the same problem articulated by Robert Langer in the preceding chapter about Dell. What is the best way for an organization to remain actively involved with each of its customers—even when those customers aren't ready to make a major purchase? This is a key question for any one-to-one enterprise, and especially for a B2B.

The fact is that most B2B organizations don't have a strategy or system in place to take advantage of the quiet intervals between sales. It's not that they're unaware of these intervals. More likely they've been trained or acculturated to see them as lost time, as dead zones in the purchase cycle. Sometimes these quiet times represent opportunities simply to deploy their customer acquisition resources elsewhere.

Or perhaps they're looking at the problem backward. Most enterprises believe it's important to know the purchase cycles of their customers: If you know the moment when your customer is ready to buy, you will be in a better position to sell your customer something—at that moment.

This type of reasoning works if you're in a business where you get to see your customers relatively often. Some B2C businesses—such as supermarkets, drugstores, and other retailers—can count on seeing their customers at least once or twice a week. But organizations that sell products such as boats, cars, refrigerators, manufacturing tools, real property, or high-end business equipment have customers who purchase much less frequently. If you have customers who buy from you only every few years, how can you establish and cultivate customer relationships?

In the E/C/O marketplace, a three-year software solutions contract worth $1 million might take as long as eighteen months to close. At any given moment, Bentley might have dozens of such deals in the works, all in various stages of development. Once a deal has been inked, it might be four or five years before the customer is ready for another purchase of similar magnitude. If nothing else, this makes it exceptionally difficult to project revenue very far into the future.

There are two basic ways to address this type of challenge. You could sell or give away a range of additional services related to your product—cleaning, adjusting, calibrating, refilling, repairing it under a warranty's terms, configuring other products and services to go with your product, and so forth. Or you could alter your business model to "subscribe" customers to your product, rather than selling it to them.

Greg Bentley, the oldest of the five Bentley brothers and the last to join the firm, is the one who spearheaded the company's evolution beyond product sales. His choice was to wrap a wide array of ancillary services and perks into a single, all-encompassing subscription plan called SELECT.

SELECT provides subscribing customers with literally dozens of benefits such as 24/7 technical support, discounts on Bentley products, free platform swaps, and free software upgrades. SELECT customers are allowed concurrent licensing of their Bentley software, which essentially means the licenses are transferable from moment to moment within the company. This benefits the customers by giving them greater flexibility to redeploy expensive software applications among their users. And it benefits Bentley by expanding usage and creating demand for more software products.

The beauty of SELECT is that it functions as both a dependable income stream and a robust customer retention tool. When a customer signs up for the subscription plan, Bentley can bank on that customer's loyalty. For the duration, Bentley and its MVARs have a generous window of opportunity to sell more products to a customer who already has declared his or her allegiance.

For example, a large architectural firm with an installed base of 200 MicroStation users might be a good prospect for an upgrade to TriForma, Bentley's 3-D modeling application. Or an electric utility with 100 seats of MicroStation might be a prime candidate for other Bentley products such as GeoOutlook, which can be interfaced with truck-mounted Global Positioning System (GPS) equipment.

The important idea here is that it's not only possible but essential to create a practical system for bridging the gap between infrequent sales, if you plan to build your business success around customer relationships. SELECT is an example of a system designed to bridge this gap. It helps Bentley stay involved with its customers. It makes it easier for Bentley to cross-sell a variety of its products. And it allows Bentley to focus on growing the firm's share of customer instead of just its share of market.

Custom publications

SELECT subscribers also receive complimentary subscriptions to the company's custom publications, important tools for strengthening the company-customer relationship. Bentley's publications aimed at its most valuable users include:

- *MSM* (*MicroStation Manager*) is a glossy magazine with a circulation of 82,000. *MSM*'s editorial coverage offers technical information and feature stories on major engineering projects and is targeted at Bentley's enterprise clients such as Jacobs Engineering, Bechtel Engineering, Fluor Daniel, and Sverdrup. The articles are shaped in part with input from Bentley's account managers, who have the most personal relationships with customers and who tip off the editors with story ideas.
- *SELECT ONLINE* offers online access to the company's custom publications, including *MSM*.
- *SELECTIONS* is a weekly HTML email newsletter featuring product updates and promotions and mailed to SELECT subscribers on an opt-in basis.

Bentley also produces other publications in various formats targeted to specific customer segments:

- *ControlAltDelete*—published quarterly by Bentley's Australian office and aimed at MicroStation users in that country.
- *Bentley Case Studies*—success stories from eight industries that are sent to targeted users within each industry.
- *MicroStation NewsGroup*—an online service that allows Micro-Station users to communicate with each other in a shared forum.

In addition to its custom publications, Bentley posts daily news affecting customers on its Web-site home page, and also allows customers to sign up to receive Bentley corporate press releases via email on the day they're issued. To the surprise of Bentley executives, more than 2,500 customers opted to receive these releases.

A new revenue model

In the final analysis, the most enduring legacy of SELECT may be how it changed fundamentally the way Bentley Systems measures success and allocates resources for the future. Under the old model, Bentley set annual goals for increasing its sales revenue, and it measured its own performance against these goals. This essentially kept the company locked into a customer acquisition mode, no matter how many innovative programs or initiatives it designed to break free. The launch of SELECT, and its rapid acceptance by customers, liberated

Bentley to measure its performance with a refreshingly simple set of metrics tied to customer development.

"We actually now measure our success by 'reinvestment' [in products beyond MicroStation] dollars per existing MicroStation license," explains Greg Bentley. For example, Bentley Systems had 300,000 users in 1999 and total revenues of $190 million. About 200,000 users were SELECT subscribers. Their combined annual subscription fees generate $100 million in revenue.

Now let's say Bentley sets $200 million as its next goal for annual sales. Achieving this goal would require selling another $500 worth of new products or services to each SELECT subscriber. This is a situation in which "preaching to the choir" is truly an advantage. Not only does Bentley save millions of dollars by not marketing to the masses; it makes the most of its marketing dollars by spending them on its most loyal customers.

For example, when Bentley releases a new software product, it emails the announcement to its SELECT subscribers and directs them to a special Web site where they can download the software. In addition to the money Bentley saves by not printing and mailing brochures, the company realizes substantial savings by not having to burn, package, and mail thousands of CD-ROMs. While the cost to Bentley of distributing its software hasn't quite dropped to zero, it has been significantly lowered—thanks to creative use of email and the World Wide Web.

Freeing itself from the customer acquisition game doesn't mean Bentley can relax, however. In the subscription model, customer retention becomes absolutely critical. Or putting it another way, if you can't hang on to a customer, you certainly won't be in a position to increase your share of that customer's spending. In a very real sense, Bentley has redefined its universe of customers. Bentley's market is no longer every possible user. Bentley is intentionally narrowing the focus of its account management efforts to concentrate more on its best customers. To someone who isn't familiar with one-to-one marketing, this must seem awfully risky, sort of like a tightrope walker purposely choosing a slender thread to balance on.

In fact, Bentley's strategy is perfectly suited to the realities of its marketplace, one in which customers make large purchases infrequently and tend to stick with a vendor for several years before switching. Bentley's most formidable challenge, therefore, is to keep its customers from switching.

"The great thing about our model is that it creates the potential to increase revenue without greatly increasing the number of users," says Greg Bentley. "Even if new license sales don't increase, you would still have the opportunity to increase your subscription revenue in the ever-growing installed base." On the other hand, if Bentley loses a SELECT customer, then it stands to lose revenue. In this kind of situation, attrition is the most dangerous foe.

Self-differentiation

From the viewpoint of Bentley's account managers, SELECT is more than a source of contractual revenue. It's an extremely effective tool for differentiating accounts on the basis of their value to the organization. Paul DeStephano, a Bentley sales director, explains why. "It tells us who our best clients are. It tells us they're committed, that they've already decided to make a long-term investment in Bentley products. SELECT is a great identifier of these strategic customers."

DeStephano supervises seven account managers in the company's ModelEngineering Business Group. Collectively, they are responsible for about $20 million in annual sales revenue. Of that revenue, slightly more than half is generated by what Bentley calls its Tier 1 accounts. The remainder is generated by Tier 2 accounts. In the ModelEngineering group, any client with 24 MicroStation seats or more is designated as a Tier 1 account and is assigned a Bentley account manager, although each site also works with a local MVAR. Clients with fewer than 24 seats, the Tier 2 accounts, are managed by MVARs. DeStephano additionally is responsible for making sure the MVARs in his region get the support they need from Bentley to remain competitive in their markets.

Each of DeStephano's seven account managers is assigned 20 to 30 Tier 1 accounts. On first glance, this seems a relatively straightforward approach to differentiating and managing customers according to their dollar value to the organization. But in reality the process is more complicated. Many of Bentley's Tier 1 customers have multiple offices in several different regions of the U.S. An increasing number of Bentley customers have offices or installations on several continents. Overseeing 20 or 30 such clients can prove an overwhelming task for even the most dedicated account manager. So two of DeStephano's primary tasks are matching his account managers with the right accounts and then helping them determine which of those accounts have the most strategic value (i.e., growth potential) to the organization. Matching is the easier of his tasks. He considers geographic location and industry experience when assigning accounts, ensuring that the account manager won't be far from his customers and will possess the requisite degree of familiarity with each customer's problems.

Helping the account manager select the top four or five accounts, from among the 20 or 30 he has been assigned, is a more difficult matter. SELECT certainly plays a role as an indicator of high potential value. In the absence of a formal set of customer valuation criteria, however, DeStephano relies mostly on instinct and experience to guide his choices. "At this point, we've been around long enough to know who the big players are. If you have a Bechtel or a Fluor Daniel among your accounts, they're going to get lots of your attention."

Bentley does not currently have a system for quantifying the actual value or the strategic value of its accounts, although it is now in the process of developing a value ranking system that will better enable it to focus its sales and marketing efforts on accounts with the most growth potential.

Mapping the relationship

Once these top accounts have been identified and assigned, it's critical for DeStephano and his team to identify the key decision makers within each account and build relationships with them. These relationships form an informal road map that helps guide the team as it pursues its mission of customer development. This road map of relationships also keeps the account managers from losing their way within an account. Most sales organizations discover that their largest accounts often speak with many voices, all vying for attention and each convinced that he or she speaks for the crowd. A relationship map, even if it's only a rough sketch, can lower the volume of this cacophony by serving as a "who's who" of contacts. In the case of Bentley, having the relationships spelled out clearly prevents the account managers from wasting precious time and energy dealing with issues that could be handled more efficiently by one of Bentley's internal support groups or by an MVAR.

In other words, Bentley does not expect its account managers to be all things to all people. In a very real sense, they are sales specialists tasked with the responsibility of growing customers. Their mission is strategic, not tactical.

DeStephano explains the difference: "I don't sell features. That's not my strength and it's not my job. My job is selling a vision, selling a business solution to senior management. Most of the people I talk to at an account are VP level or above. If we need to go above that, if we need to talk to the board of directors, then we bring in Greg Bentley. You have to make sure the levels match up."

Mismatched efforts can result in lost time and lost revenue. "When we get beat, it's usually because we've tried to manage the customer at the opportunity level instead of at the enterprise level," says DeStephano. "The account managers can't afford to spend their time in the trenches. They have to manage their customers at a higher level."

Knowledge-based account management

Bentley's strategy holds the account managers responsible for growing the value of their assigned accounts. Because they focus on large accounts, they are expected to close large deals. In this regard, they aren't fundamentally different from top salespeople at many large corporations. What sets Bentley account managers apart from traditional salespeople, however, is not the *size* of the deals they arrange. What sets them fundamentally apart is the *complexity* of these deals.

Indeed, complexity is a primary difference between B2B relationships and B2C relationships. B2C organizations with customer development strategies must have the ability to manage hundreds, thousands, or even millions of similar relationships with individual customers. B2B organizations pursuing customer development strategies must develop systems to manage not just relationships, but *relationships within relationships*. It's useful to think of these intertwined, interlocking interactions as *complexes of relationship* or *systems of relationship*—sort of like a medieval model of the universe with its multiplicity of wheels spinning within wheels.

"This is a *much* more complicated selling environment," says Winterbottom. "If you're a Bentley account manager selling an engineering database software solution to the IT director of a global enterprise, you're going to have a lot of issues to resolve before you close. You're going to be answering a lot of questions and spending lots of time with the product manager to make sure you get everything right. You've got to have the training and the expertise to give a final presentation to the customer that covers all the bases."

For an account manager, training and education are the keys to success. As we will see in the Novartis CP case study (Chapter 6), knowledge-based selling requires a very different approach and a very different level of commitment than product-based selling. This is another key point of difference between B2B and B2C strategies. In addition to contending with a more complex set of relationships than a B2C, a B2B organization is likely to be selling a more complex set of products and services.

For organizations selling a wide range of complicated goods and services, the salesperson must be as knowledgeable as the customer. Ideally, the knowledge-based salesperson should possess *more* information than the customer, or at least know where to find critical information quickly. Companies such as Bentley and Novartis CP simply can't afford to deploy salespeople who can't provide accurate answers to the difficult technical questions posed by their customers. In the case of Novartis, a wrong answer could result in a ruined field of crops. In the case of Bentley, a wrong answer could jeopardize the schedule of a multibillion-dollar oil pipeline project or require the demolition of a partially constructed hospital.

As the executive in charge of sales, Winterbottom is keenly aware of his team's need for formal "knowledge support." That kind of support can come in many forms. It can include improved sales collateral, faster access to business-critical information, more in-house professional training, and tuition grants for postgraduate study. "Not only do we plan to deepen our knowledge and training programs; we plan to expand them horizontally to include our resellers. Remember, they have 242 salespeople working for them. It's clearly a benefit to all parties if we can help those salespeople achieve the same level of training and education as our account managers."

High-quality training programs are invariably costly and time-intensive. In today's high-velocity, supercompetitive environment, it's difficult for even the most enlightened organization to spare the time and expense necessary to propel its sales force ahead of the "knowledge curve."

And yet staying ahead of the curve is essential. This is where sales force automation tools prove their worth. Many elements of the knowledge support function required in a B2B situation can be automated and digitally stored so they can be accessed on demand by authorized members of the sales team. Bentley has devised an ingenious system for helping its account managers keep pace with their technology-savvy clients.

Scenario-based selling

Just a few years ago, Bentley was a company offering a handful of products to a hungry, immature market. Like any aggressive young firm, Bentley strove to increase its market share. Now the situation is different. Bentley ships 85 products, and its U.S. market penetration is greater than 70 percent among major E/C/O organizations. Or as one Bentley executive puts it: "There aren't many first-time users out there anymore." Bentley isn't desperately seeking customers—it's seeking bigger and more profitable deals with the customers it has.

But with so many products, so few account managers, and such a large market, how can Bentley credibly offer tailored solutions based on the needs of its customers? To put it another

way, how can Bentley—or any organization, for that matter—
function as a one-to-one enterprise under such circumstances?

Bentley's response to this challenge was the Account Scenario. Every one of Bentley's 85 products is mapped to eleven
scenarios that have been carefully formulated to match up with
the needs of specific sets of users. Ninety percent of Bentley
sales now map to these scenarios.

Account Scenarios

1. Architectural Firm
2. Architectural/Engineering Firm
3. Engineer Consultant
4. Facility Information Manager
5. Gas/Electric Utility
6. Manufacturing Company
7. Municipality
8. Operating Plant
9. Telecommunications
10. Transportation Design and Engineering
11. Transportation Management

A three- to five-page document is created for each of the
eleven scenarios. Each document begins with a brief description of the environment, needs, and objectives of the customers within the particular scenario. At a minimum, these
capsule descriptions can keep an account manager from con-
fusing the precise needs of an architectural firm with the su-
perficially similar but profoundly different needs of an
architectural/engineering firm or an engineering firm. While a
faux pas might seem forgivable to someone outside the archi-

tectural/engineering community, it could easily taint, or even doom, a sales proposal. As Winterbottom observed earlier, it's a complex selling environment. Any hint of ignorance, no matter how benign, could be the kiss of death.

Following the capsule description is a more detailed overview that includes job titles of decision makers, primary as well as secondary business objectives of the customers, and a menu of specific challenges facing the customers in that scenario. Each document includes a portfolio of products matching the needs of users within the scenario. There is also a list of likely follow-up projects and tasks that are sometimes overlooked by the client, but may require additional software or services from Bentley. The scenario documents also include lists of similar accounts that can be used as references and recommendations for the most effective way to present a sales proposal to the client.

"It's a great road map for the account manager to follow," says Winterbottom. "Before going on a sales call the account manager fires up his laptop and reviews the scenario. Then when he sits down with the customer, he's confident that he's presenting the most accurate and most relevant information."

Bentley has taken the extra step of assigning eleven "scenario managers" to be responsible for creating and maintaining the knowledge base associated with each scenario. "The role of the scenario manager is to provide the account managers with all the information they need to close deals," explains Winterbottom. "The scenario manager is a person who understands the user's processes and understands how our technology provides benefits for the users within his or her scenario. The scenario manager is an evangelist, a source of expertise, and a compendium of up-to-the minute knowledge."

The scenario managers also are responsible for understanding how Bentley products interact with each other and how they interact with products made by the firm's competitors, since many Bentley customers have "legacy ware" or mongrel systems that were stitched together over time from bits and pieces provided by several vendors.

A portion of the scenario manager's compensation package includes a commission on sales of products from his or her scenario. "If the account manager uses the scenario to close a deal, the scenario manager gets credit for it," says Winterbottom. "So our scenario managers are out there pumping as hard as they can to help the account managers."

We'll return to the issue of compensation later. Before leaving the topic of account scenarios, it's important to discuss another benefit they represent. By organizing and systematizing its sales processes around customer needs, Bentley has constructed a solid platform from which to launch all of its future customer-centric programs. Bentley has surmounted some of the most difficult challenges facing any traditional company striving to become a one-to-one enterprise.

The automated pitch

Grouping product and service offerings by sets of user needs—instead of simply by product lines—makes it far easier to create a highly tailored sales presentation. The account managers can dial into the Bentley intranet to access richly detailed sales templates, enabling them to generate customized—and highly accurate—proposals for clients on the spot.

These templates serve as mass customization tools for the account managers. Without them, they would have to either handcraft each proposal from scratch or rely on "one size fits all" contracts. The templates allow for a high degree of customization—while actually reducing the account manager's workload. That's the beauty of mass customization. It increases productivity and diminishes effort.

Bentley works with a system of about twenty sales templates, but each contains a wealth of highly specific information that can easily be customized by the account manager. The templates are stored as Microsoft Word documents and are accessible to authorized users of the Bentley intranet. The information-rich templates are also an essential piece of Bentley's overall strategy to put greater emphasis on knowledge-based selling.

"You get on the intranet and there they are," says Pat Elnicki, Bentley's proposal manager and a creator of the template system. "You click on the document, save it to your laptop, and start working. There are prompts throughout, so you can enter client-specific information to customize the proposal. You can even put your client's logo on the proposal. What you *can't* do is change the pricing or alter basic terms and conditions we write into all our contracts." In this aspect, Bentley's templates are similar to Dell's Premier Dell.com Web pages—both represent an effort to standardize, automate, and facilitate critical business processes.

The primary purpose of the template system, however, is to

make it as easy as possible for the account managers to generate customized, written proposals. The alternative would be to rely on either boilerplate or "back of the envelope" proposals.

"The prewritten templates allow account managers to create proposals on demand," says Elnicki. "Because all the language and pricing have been preapproved, the account manager needs only to customize the document and it's good to go. You literally can have a customized proposal on a client's desk in minutes, instead of days."

Bentley's channel partners also have access privileges to the templates, and this greatly reduces the chances for errors or misunderstandings that could derail a sales opportunity. The idea of making the templates available to intermediaries—as well as to the account managers—might seem risky at first glance, but it's a risk that Bentley has grown comfortable with.

Winterbottom says he wants to continue pushing Bentley's account management strategy, along with all its programs and benefits, as far down the distribution chain as possible. "We want to move our account management strategy closer to the end users. That's how we'll build the deepest, long-term relationships."

Winterbottom plans to accomplish this in two ways. First, he's made the sales directors responsible for supporting the sales teams of the MVARs in their region. Second, he's making advanced sales and technical training available to the MVARs so they can bring the same level of expertise to a sales presentation as the Bentley account managers. "That's the best way to move this concept forward," he says.

Nurturing the relationship

We've now seen how Bentley divides the labor among its sales and sales support teams. But in the final analysis, who is directly responsible for nurturing Bentley's relationships with its end users—the architects, draftspersons, and designers sitting at their workstations cranking out plans, elevations, and blueprints for tomorrow's constructed infrastructures?

If the account managers are the hunters and the MVARs are the gatherers, who tends the hearth and keeps the fires burning? Who are the cultivators, the growers? At Bentley, project managers carry out many of the nurturing duties. Imagine them occupying a space between account managers and product managers. They are the ones who make sure all the applications are still running smoothly after the implementation team has packed up and gone home. They are the ones who get to know the users by name and will sit beside them, listening to their gripes and hearing their suggestions.

"My job is building confidence and trust," says Andy Smith, a former architect who now leads Bentley's project managers in the United States. "My presence lets the customer know that Bentley is committed to a partnering relationship, that we will follow through on our promises and that we'll get it done—whatever it is."

The project manager also serves as a highly visible reminder to the customer of Bentley's commitment to maintaining a long-term relationship. Smith has become so effective at projecting a sense of duty that account managers frequently ask him to visit with potential customers or sit in on sales presentations.

"As a project manager, I have the ability to reach deep into Bentley resources to fix a problem. The customer knows this and values this, because it means he won't have to outsource a solution to a third party. Because I bring a certain level of experience to the table, I can pretty much guarantee a successful resolution to most problems. That's good for the client *and* good for us," says Smith.

Sometimes an account manager will ask Smith to follow up on a hunch. After meeting with a client, one account manager sent Smith a one-sentence note saying, "They're ready to do more." Smith hopped on a plane, met with the clients, and carefully listened to their needs. On the trip back home, he identified a Bentley consulting service that would help the clients overcome the particular challenge they faced. Because the clients regard their project manager as a *trusted agent,* they agreed to contract with Bentley for tens of thousands of dollars' worth of consulting—a purchase they had not even considered prior to their meeting with Smith.

Here again, we see the value of the trusted agent concept. In a world of increasingly commoditized products and services, a relationship founded on trust is the only genuinely sustainable competitive edge. Without trust, you're back to square one— competing on price. Especially in the Age of Interactivity, and especially in B2B, where both products and relationships tend to be complex, it is trust that is the true currency of commerce.

Any enterprise that wants to implement a one-to-one strategy will quickly discover that establishing trust is absolutely essential. None of the four basic implementation steps—Identify, Differentiate, Interact, and Customize—can be achieved without a reliable flow of accurate information between the buyer and the seller. Only in a trusting relationship can information pass back and forth freely. That's why it is imperative to earn the customer's trust as early as possible in the relationship and to create a system that will support and validate that trusting relationship over time.

Smith has become such a welcome figure that many of his clients regard him as more of a colleague than a vendor. This is especially true in the case of NBBJ, one of the largest architectural firms in the United States and one of Bentley's most important accounts. Like many large architectural firms, NBBJ is spread out all over the country. It has two separate divisions, each operating with a certain degree of autonomy—one for the eastern United States and the other for the western United States. While this affords NBBJ many benefits, such as quicker reaction time and better regional coverage, it also hampers internal communications. "We have a real tendency to go in two different directions and not tell each other," says one NBBJ manager.

NBBJ recently upgraded many of its users to TriForma. Kyle Talbott, an NBBJ architect, was put in charge of the implementation. He quickly became one of Smith's biggest fans.

"He's absolutely essential," says Talbott. "Andy has just really helped to keep the whole thing together. He understands our issues, he's our advocate within the Bentley organization. He's the guy that gets things done, that makes things happen for us at Bentley. In addition to that, he helps keep *us* organized. He manages us as a client exactly the way he should. He tells us very frankly when we're going in a direction that's going to lead to trouble down the line and he helps us to keep communicating from coast to coast. So he's vital to the process."

From Smith's own perspective, the relationship is held together by hard-earned trust. "I've been involved with NBBJ for more than a year and they recognize that I have the ability to deliver on the promise that there should be a partnership between us and them as end users," says Smith. For example, NBBJ wanted a voice in Bentley's product development process. They wanted to be sure Bentley's product developers were listening to their suggestions and incorporating them into future releases. "So I've become their spokesman inside our organization at Bentley," says Smith. "I look out for their needs. If they say, 'Andy, we want these widgets to turn blue this week,' then I'll go find the right people in our organization, get in their face, and tell them why we've got to make these widgets turn blue this week."

Smith also functions as an internal communications agent for the client, explaining to users and line managers why top management decided to upgrade an existing application or switch to a different platform. "I will help educate the users so they understand why a change is being made. It's all part of the process."

Here again, Smith is helping the client manage its own business, in much the same way that Premier Dell.com allows Dell to help its clients manage their purchasing and order tracking processes.

The project manager also keeps track of how the client spends its money with Bentley over the course of a project. "If a customer commits to spending X number of dollars, I monitor the spending and the rate of spending to make sure everything is going smoothly. I almost become like a partner with the CIO," says Smith.

According to Smith, the project manager's job is composed of four basic tasks:

1. Carefully defining the customer's specific needs and understanding the customer's problems. "You have to listen to staff at all levels to find out what's really going on, or you risk seeing everything through one person's rose-colored glasses."
2. Identifying the real leaders and decision makers on the client side. "You need to know who you can count on to make things happen." This gets back to the idea of "relationships within relationships"—Smith not only knows the account, he knows the key people within it.
3. Opening up a process that encourages regular communication between the project manager and the client.
4. Clearly identifying the "finish line," making sure everyone knows where the finish line is and then reaching it. "The best way to win confidence is getting the job done."

Earlier in this case study, Greg Bentley used the image of a fully occupied checkerboard to describe one of the challenges facing the company. Smith uses the image of a multidimensional chessboard to illustrate his piece of the Bentley mission. "I have pawns, knights, rooks, and queens—all the people with all the talents and skills necessary to solve a client's problems. Some of these talented people might work at Bentley, some of them might work for the client, and some of them might be outside consultants. My role is to align them, to get them into position, and then to deploy them at the right moment to get the job done."

The year of the account

Bentley formally launched its account management strategy in 1999. Its executives invariably describe the strategy as a work in progress. Some aspects of the strategy are sharply defined and fully developed, while some are still coming into focus. As mentioned earlier, the lack of a fleshed-out customer valuation formula makes it difficult for the company to rank customers by value and assign resources accordingly. In the next chapter we'll demonstrate how Convergys uses a relatively simple set of customer valuation criteria, which they call their "lifetime value model," to prioritize the sales and marketing effort expended toward different customers.

On the other hand, Bentley has developed an ingenious method for grouping its customers by needs—the eleven account scenarios—and organizing its sales efforts around these scenarios. This is a key indicator of a one-to-one enterprise, and it rightfully deserves praise. A more traditional company would have its sales efforts marching in lockstep with its product lines.

Not surprisingly, Bentley is still in the process of evolving a compensation plan for all the players involved in its one-to-one marketing efforts. The account managers, who stand at the front lines of the new strategy, are compensated much like the salespeople at traditional companies. About half their annual income is salary. The other half is commission. They can draw on 25 percent of their target. Commissions are paid on a year-to-date basis, which means the account manager must keep busy. "If you have one bad quarter, you're playing catch up for the rest of the year," says DeStephano. "And remember, the account manager is only driving revenue out of those twenty or thirty assigned accounts."

While this might seem the antithesis of one-to-one marketing, it serves the purpose of focusing Bentley's sales efforts on its Tier 1 customers—those with the highest potential value. One might even argue that because the commissions earned by the account managers all come from sales to strategic accounts, the compensation plan encourages the cultivation of long-term customer relationships.

Charles Ferrucci, Bentley's vice president of account marketing, compares traditional sales and marketing strategies to broadcasting and the new customer-focused strategy to narrowcasting. In his own area, he's seen remarkable benefits from the change in philosophy. "We are blessed by knowing who our customers are," says Ferrucci. "Instead of advertising in trade journals, we publish our own magazines for our customers, with articles about our products and the people who use them. Instead of printing thousands of brochures, we use our Web site and email to communicate with our customers. When you add it all up, it's a significant advantage."

As a result of these efficiencies, Bentley's marketing costs have dropped dramatically. The savings are being invested in the company's Web site to transform the site into a powerful strategic tool for interacting with customers. As more customer interactions migrate to the Web, Bentley is likely to see further savings in its distribution costs. Bentley executives emphasize that there are no plans to eliminate the existing distribution channel, only plans to make it more customer-focused, more efficient, and more profitable.

And they emphasize that their goal is not to overtake

Autodesk as the leading supplier of CAD software. Bentley is more than willing to let its competitors fight over market share while it concentrates on growing more profitable relationships with its existing customers. "Our objective is to have our customers outsource a hundred percent of their technology requirements to Bentley and our integrator network. We'd like our customers to think of us as their IT department," says Winterbottom. "The way we're going to accomplish this is by developing long-term relationships with our customers, by proving to them we're in it for the long haul, not just for the transaction. That's what account management is all about."

Tasks ahead for Bentley

While Bentley has taken many significant strides toward becoming a customer-centric enterprise, several key tasks remain. For instance, Bentley has begun differentiating accounts by need, but it really doesn't systematically differentiate them by their value to Bentley. Without having a reliable way to predict the value of an account over time, Bentley can't genuinely prioritize the resources of its sales, marketing, or customer service functions.

And though Bentley has mapped its 85 products into eleven account scenarios, the scenario development process needs further refinement. Ideally, the account scenarios should describe customer needs, not product sets. At a minimum, however, the scenarios should be more finely granulated, so the product sets match the real-world needs of the customer groups more closely. Eleven scenarios are certainly better than one, but fifty "subscenarios" would be even better.

Bentley, like Dell, has found it advantageous to move "up the food chain" to deliver more comprehensive service packages to its clients. For now, SELECT can be used to provide seamless document management, including filing, archiving, and transmittal to involved third parties. And the right way for Bentley to gain the most leverage out of SELECT is for the company to reorient its thinking about the nature of its customer base to begin with. With SELECT, rather than selling products to customers Bentley is *subscribing* customers to an ongoing stream of products and services. Running a subscription business is very different from running a product marketing business.

In addition, many of Bentley's customers almost certainly want to develop their own "value streams" of services to transcend the periodic projects they do for their own clients. SELECT provides Bentley with an ideal opportunity to begin helping them in this task.

SELECT is a program that should be configured in such a way as to allow an architectural firm to go into not just the "project" business of designing and constructing a building, but also into the "long-term management" business of taking care of the building, maintaining it, and upgrading it even after it has been built. Because Bentley's program can provide continual, updated documentation of a project's design, it can also help the architectural firm do a lot more than just creative work. A building is a complex system of pipes, wires, ducts, heating and cooling elements, and lighting treatments, not to mention the surrounding landscaping, lawn maintenance, irrigation, and gardening care, as well as driveway and parking lot construction and maintenance. The more of this comprehensive system that SELECT can accommodate, the more it will be relied on by Bentley's clients to drive their own profitability.

When Bentley looks for additional ways to strengthen its relationships with its customers, the company might want to consider services that aren't tied directly to SELECT. It's not hard to imagine Bentley helping its customer firms with the preparation and financing of the bid they tender for a project. Or instituting training classes for a client's engineers or architects—not just in the use of Bentley's software, but in the nuances of design. Or hosting Web sites and other IT infrastructure for a client, allowing the client to manage its own far-flung collection of independent architects and engineers more efficiently.

Bentley has come a long way. But as far as they have come to date, there is always more they can do. Making the transition to a one-to-one strategy should be viewed as a continuous journey, not a destination that can be achieved in some finite time. Here are some suggestions:

- By adding more services to its collection of offerings—customer-specific services tailored to the individual needs of each client—not only would Bentley be able to increase its share of customer, it would also be locking in its customers' loyalty for longer and longer periods, with tighter and tighter bonds. Some of these services could be provided by partner companies, albeit with Bentley vouching for the quality and offering the service within the context of its own customer relationship.

- Consider creating a "Bentley Barometer" to help customers

with ongoing projects, tracking key metrics such as maintenance costs, materials costs, or energy costs at a glance. This would help Bentley move "up the food chain" by providing critical management-level data in a format that doesn't require an engineering degree to comprehend.

- Help clients develop Lifetime Value models for specific constructed assets such as bridges, highways, hospitals, and airports. By providing this type of service, Bentley moves beyond the role of technology vendor and into the role of strategic consultant.

- Provide incentives and compensation for channel partners who bring new customers into the pipeline. Over time, such a program could be expanded to provide rewards for keeping and growing customers.

Chapter 5

Convergys
Racing for the best clients

Top line summary

One key measure of any one-to-one enterprise is its ability to plan and execute different strategies for different customers. By this measure Convergys, the leading provider of outsourced customer care services, has clearly taken some giant steps. The company's motive, as with many other firms pursuing this type of competitive strategy, was simply to deal with what it saw as a persistent and significant decline in the productivity of its client-acquisition sales approach. By focusing instead on individual client development, Convergys hoped to produce more reliable and effective business growth.

Account development strategies such as those pursued by Convergys are expensive, labor-intensive, and time-consuming. Any B2B pursuing an account development strategy has to know which of its accounts are worth penetrating. A B2B that tries to penetrate all of its accounts equally is simply setting itself up for failure.

So when the company shifted its attention from market penetration to customer development, it needed first to devise a system for ranking clients according to their true value to the firm, including their growth potential. Without such a system, Convergys would be flying blind. It would be unable to prioritize its efforts and would be incapable of focusing its resources on those clients that would yield the highest ROI on its sales and marketing expenditure. But calculating customer value accurately in a B2B scenario can be an extremely difficult task. Usually, there are fewer customers than in a typical B2C scenario, there is less hard data, and there are longer gaps between sales. Faced with the absence of quantifiable, objective information, Convergys was forced to make do with what it had: a wealth of subjective information about its clients.

But once it had prioritized its customers by their current and potential future value, the firm then had to reconfigure its own service offerings in order to align itself with the different needs of its different types of clients. And it had to offer its services within a context of providing integrated, well-developed business solutions for its clients' various problems. This required the company in turn to improve the technical and business competence of its sales force, and to align its sales compensation structure with the new measure of customer valuation it had devised.

How do you grow a multimillion-dollar account by 60 percent in twelve months? Ask Bob Lento's sales team at Convergys, the world's largest provider of billing and customer management services, and they'll tell you the "secret" to their success had two parts:

1. Pick the right account to begin with, by recognizing which of the firm's many clients have the greatest potential for growth.
2. Dedicate a different type of sales resource in order to nurture this account over a longer period of time.

In many ways, Lento's team was grappling with the same issues confronting Bentley. Both firms chose to pursue account development strategies. For Bentley, account development meant gaining access to its end users and putting more software on their computers. In the case of Convergys, however, account development meant figuring out precisely who its most *growable* clients were, and then developing specific, proactive strategies that would increase the amount of business those clients were doing with Convergys.

For Convergys, one of the more difficult parts of the development strategy was devising a reliable system for ranking accounts not just by their actual, current value but by their strategic value, or growth potential, as well. This is an effort that is usually far more difficult to accomplish than it looks.

The true value of any customer can be thought of as the net present value of the future stream of profits from the customer. But this value is a function not only of the customer's "inertia" (i.e., what the customer is currently spending and intends to continue spending) but also of whatever changes in the customer's future purchasing behavior can be brought about through the marketer's own initiative. We call the customer's inertia its "actual value," which consists of the value a company will realize on a customer based on that customer's currently expected behavior. Then, over and above a customer's actual value, we define "strategic value" as the customer's growth potential. It is the additional benefit a company might be able to realize from changing a customer's future behavior by applying a proactive strategy (taking over business the customer was giving to a competitor, for instance, or introducing and selling a completely new service that the customer has never before considered purchasing). For a B2B firm trying to execute an account development strategy, the entire point of the strategy is to maximize a client's strategic value—to realize the most possible growth potential.

To a far greater degree than most other firms, Convergys has taken the many difficult steps necessary to devise a formal mechanism for ranking its clients by strategic value. Because of this, Convergys is now in a far better position to apply its resources where they are most likely to generate the greatest ROI. In other words, they have established a formal, measurable, and repeatable process for treating different customers differently.

You might ask yourself, "Why don't *all* companies approach their customers in this manner?" You'll discover that while many would like to, they are hamstrung by traditional methods of determining customer value. And in some instances, while they might pay lip service to the idea of differentiating customers according to their potential for growth, they are really still more interested in the customer's current value. Many companies might ask, "As long as total revenues are climbing, why should we worry too much about which accounts are more *valuable* than others?"

This might even describe the attitude at Convergys a few years ago. What motivated the company to change its world-view? What prompted it to replace its product-centric sales strategy with a client-centric model? To understand the company's trajectory, let's quickly review its recent past.

Acquired habits

Sometimes success can be the enemy of innovation. But the fact that a business model works today doesn't guarantee that it will work tomorrow. For example, MATRIXX Marketing, a former division of Cincinnati Bell, had developed a highly successful strategy for growing revenue through corporate acquisition. Many of the new clients acquired by MATRIXX had been the clients of other companies—until those companies were acquired by MATRIXX during the late 1980s and early 1990s. When Cincinnati Bell spun off MATRIXX and another division to create Convergys in 1998, the newborn company naturally adopted many of the strategies that had served MATRIXX so well. (Cincinnati Bell is now BroadWing Inc., a nationwide provider of voice, data, wireless, and Internet services.)

Like MATRIXX, Convergys cherished the belief that more clients inevitably resulted in more revenue. Indeed, the growth-through-acquisition strategy had resulted in a dramatic surge of revenue for MATRIXX. But it soon became apparent that Convergys would not have the luxury of following the same path. Thanks largely to acquisitions made the previous year by MATRIXX, Convergys saw its revenues leap from $988 million to $1.4 billion in its first year as an independent company. But organic growth—that is, growth from ongoing operations at Convergys—was in the modest single digits.

This was the situation facing Bob Lento when he joined Convergys in 1998. Lento was hired as senior vice president of sales and marketing for the company's Customer Management Group (CMG), which provides a variety of specialized corporate services, such as business-to-business telesales, technical support, and customer service. Typically, CMG draws its clients from several industries, including communications, technology, financial services, consumer products, and direct response marketing. For example, if you can't figure out how to turn on your new PC and you call the manufacturer's technical support desk, your plea for help might be handled by a contact center staffed and operated by CMG. Additionally, CMG might be hired by that same computer manufacturer to organize the information collected from callers, analyze it, and present it in such a way that it can be used by the manufacturer to improve its products or services in the future.

In this type of market, the quality of service provided by a vendor is more important than its ability to "put butts in seats," which had until then been considered the primary role of the traditional call center outsourcer.

Lento quickly realized that in such an environment, chasing market share alone would not guarantee higher margins. With the help of David Dougherty, then CMG's president, and Ronald Schultz, then CMG's chief operating officer, Lento's team began outlining a "less is more" vision for the future. CMG would ask its top salespeople to take on fewer clients. Instead of emphasizing the acquisition of new clients alone, CMG would identify its best clients, develop Learning Relationships with them, grow their value, and retain them for as long as possible. CMG executives describe it as the difference between dating around and raising a family. That captures the essence of the strategy. Stripped of its details, one-to-one marketing is basically a process for creating and nurturing long-term, profitable business relationships.

Lento and his team intuitively understood the advantage of taking the long view. Henceforth, CMG's strategy for growth would be to focus on client development. This strategy would require the company to organize its sales and marketing efforts around the needs of its most important clients—the ones with the highest actual *and* strategic value to Convergys.

It was a bold strategy and marked a sharp departure from the traditions of the past. Initially, the management team faced resistance from some employees who were unwilling to exchange their old habits for new ones. Some employees left. Those who stayed, however, were quickly won over by CMG's client-driven, client-centric philosophy. "The people who thrive and prosper here are the people who can put up with change, who enjoy it, and who don't get knocked off course," observes Schultz. "They are the survivors."

Putting the new strategy in place would involve:

1. Setting up a methodology so the company could begin differentiating clients first by value, then by needs.

2. Establishing a systematic issue discovery process to determine the precise needs of each client. This is an absolutely essential component of any one-to-one B2B program.
3. Developing an information system capable of providing client data, on demand, to authorized Convergys users.
4. Reorganizing and redefining existing products and services so they could be more easily tailored to serve the needs of individual clients.
5. Revamping compensation plans to provide incentives for client-focused behaviors throughout the organization.

Hurdles to clear

The challenge of transforming a product-driven company into a one-to-one enterprise can be hampered by internal obstacles, such as independently functioning business lines. Most companies can only grow by decentralizing a number of their business functions, establishing different business units and giving them both the responsibility and the authority to make their own decisions.

But there is a downside to decentralization. Businesses overwhelmingly choose to align their organizations based on the products and services being sold, rather than basing the firm's organization on the particular customers or groups of customers being served. And too much product-service independence can make it difficult—or impossible—for an enterprise to develop a truly unified approach to its customers. Convergys was composed of two sister units, the Customer Management Group (CMG) and the Information Management Group

(IMG), each with its own operations groups. The Information Management Group offers billing and other customer support systems for companies providing wireless, wireline, cable television, and Internet services. Its clients also include utility companies. The bill you get from your cable TV or cellular phone company might be generated by IMG. Or when you call your water company to find out why this month's bill is higher than last month's bill, the information the water company uses to answer your question might be generated by Convergys IMG.

Customer Management Group (CMG)	Information Management Group (IMG)
Lead generation and dealer referral programs	Real-time billing solutions
Customer acquisition and retention	Bill stream consolidation
Customer service	Switch management
Employee care services	Service order and traffic processing
Technical support	Receivables management
Business-to-business telesales and full account management	Credit assessment and collections
Market research and customer value management	Customer targeting and acquisition
Database marketing services	Interactive billing technology
Interactive customer services (IVR and Internet technology)	Service setup, provision and pricing
Customer relationship management services	Usage processing

IMG and CMG had been launched originally as subsidiaries of Cincinnati Bell. Both subsidiaries naturally developed their own unique methods and mannerisms to approach what appeared to be separate markets. And, as is often the case when two or more business units in a single corporation function independently, seemingly benign turf issues can slow or impede the flow of critical information between units, reducing the corporation's overall effectiveness. As each unit becomes more specialized, the chance of miscommunication, inefficiency, and wasteful conflict rises.

For example, two different Convergys units supported contact center services. Prior to being acquired by Convergys, these units had their own presidents, their own management teams, and their own processes. To avoid disruption, they were allowed to keep much of their original management structure intact. While this made sense from the perspective of managing internal processes and workflow, it made less sense from the perspective of managing clients.

Let's say a client needed a direct response campaign, complete with a television ad and an 800 number. The client's needs would be handled by the Convergys unit that specialized in providing teleservices. But if that same client came back a few months later and needed a retention program to keep the customers won over by the direct response campaign, another unit would step in. Often a whole new group of people would be involved, which had the effect of driving the relationship between the company and the client back to square one.

For the sales reps, these independent "silos" were a serious issue. So the sales reps tended to funnel accounts to units that were easy to work with and to avoid units that made their lives—and the lives of their clients—more difficult. As one manager diplomatically phrases it: "They took the path of least resistance. If they knew one unit wouldn't work with them the way they wanted, they might go to another unit and say, 'Help me!' "

This type of behavior, while completely understandable, served neither the company nor its clients. IMG, because of its product set, tended to focus more of its energies on technical issues and less on "softer" issues such as customer relationships. CMG, by virtue of its product set, was more attuned to customer issues. One of the challenges facing Convergys was figuring out how to capitalize on each group's strength while simultaneously fostering a sense of teamwork and interdependence. Somehow, the two groups had to become more tightly integrated. Convergys was counting on CMG to serve as its primary engine for growth, and CMG was counting on sales to its best existing clients to achieve its goals.

Before moving on with our story, it's important to discuss the nature of organizational change. While it's true that every functional area of a B2B organization is needed to support an enterprise-wide one-to-one customer relationship strategy, the sales force is likely to be at the epicenter of any transformational initiative. Far from being marginalized or trivialized by new technologies, the sales force will be augmented, enhanced, and empowered by these technologies. If success is to be built on client relationships, and relationships are defined principally by interaction, then the sales force itself is the engine of a B2B company's interaction with its customers. To the extent that new technologies are to have a positive effect on client relationships, in most cases—the vast majority of cases—the technologies must be employed to provide leverage for a company's sales force. So it's fair to say that the sales force will almost always be at ground zero of any B2B's enterprise-wide effort to reorganize.

Any organization trying to manage the transition from being product-driven to being customer-driven will discover quickly whether its sales force is an asset, an obstacle, or both. A sales force—any sales force—is by nature a work in progress. Its qualities are not static, but dynamic. It reacts to the world around it, adapting and evolving over time. The Convergys sales force is a good example of this evolutionary change.

Before implementing its one-to-one strategy, Convergys had one sales force for CMG and another sales force for IMG. Now there is just one sales force. The functional areas that support the sales force also were consolidated.

In addition to combining the sales force, Convergys unified the marketing departments. "So now we have one internal Convergys group responsible for identifying trends in the marketplace and positioning the whole company in the marketplace, as opposed to positioning just a piece of it," explains Lento.

The company's solution architects, who used to be scattered among four divisions, are now one group as well. "They can focus on understanding what the client wants and working out the best solution," says Lento.

None of these changes occurred overnight. They were steps in a process of change that took place over many months. But these changes began with a single idea—to grow the company by concentrating on account development instead of market penetration.

Self-evaluation

Lento and his team devised a straightforward plan, based on established one-to-one marketing principles, to reinvent Convergys CMG as a client-centric organization. CMG would set up a picket fence around the clients it identified as most valuable and most growable. These clients would be wooed, won over, and wedded to CMG's best salespeople. They would be actively managed, nurtured, and cultivated. These higher-value clients would also be protected from routine marketing efforts originating from other areas of the company. Less valuable clients would see no change in their level of service. For them, everything would remain business as usual.

Before the plan could become a reality, however, Lento's team needed better information about the existing customer base. They already knew that only a handful of clients accounted for an overwhelming portion of the group's current revenues. They also knew that very few of their clients—including the most obviously valuable ones—were buying multiple products or services from the group.

The team began by conducting an in-depth internal survey to evaluate precisely how the company collected customer information and how the information was put to use. From the data gathered in the survey, Lento's team would build a chart showing where Convergys excelled at customer-focused activities and where it fell short.

The evaluation process started with two days of detailed face-to-face interviews with the company's own top executives. Those interviews were followed up with telephone calls to gather additional information. About thirty Convergys executives were interviewed during the first round of the evaluation process. In addition to the questions revolving around key principles of one-to-one customer relationship strategy, the interviewees were asked to define the company's culture. Following this initial round of questions, another survey was prepared and sent out to a broader group of executives within the company.

The surveys provided Lento's team with enough information to begin the process of change. Among their findings, the surveys had confirmed the team's suspicions that ongoing turf issues between various subunits within the group would indeed retard the development of any client-centric initiatives.

After digesting this information, Convergys' management moved to consolidate some of the units and to hold their executives responsible for ensuring that customer relationships would be preserved. This was an important step in the company's evolution.

Calculating customer value

Since its inception, Convergys had calculated the value of its clients the old-fashioned way—by eyeballing last year's revenue and guessing at the "intangible" aspects of customer value. "Some of our guesses were better than others," Lento recalls. What Convergys needed now was a system of metrics, a reliable tool that could be applied scientifically to clients across the board. This would be absolutely critical to success.

Remember, Convergys operates in an environment that is complex even by business-to-business standards. Typically, the customer value skew is much higher in business-to-business scenarios than it is in business-to-consumer scenarios. For a gas station, a diner, a car dealer, or even Amazon.com, the range in customer value will be relatively narrow. In the business-to-business space, however, one strategic account can prove more valuable than a thousand nonstrategic accounts. The challenge is identifying which accounts have strategic value and which do not.

"That's why a wider array of metrics is needed in the business-to-business environment," explains Schultz. "If you are putting all your eggs into fifty accounts, you can't afford to know only three things about each account, you need to know ten things. You need more measures, and they need to be precise."

The first step was eliminating as much of the guesswork as possible. The next step was establishing a methodology for drilling down into the client data, since it was clear that for Convergys to succeed with its account development strategy it could not rely solely on past revenue to prioritize its clients. What was needed was a workable customer valuation model with some system for balancing weighted measures that would reveal the actual relative importance of each client.

Convergys created a system of metrics like this, and now calls its system its "Lifetime Value" model, or just its "LTV" model.

After hammering away at the problem for several weeks, Lento's team devised an LTV model based on six weighted indices, ranging from highly objective to highly subjective. Generally, more weight was given to the objective indices because the data behind them was considered more reliable and it

seemed sensible for the team to hedge its bets. But at the same
time the model was designed to be flexible, because the team
assumed that the relative weights would change as soon as it
was possible to measure the more subjective criteria, such as
Share of Client or Partnership, more objectively. The overarching goal of the first model was to break away from the traditional method of ranking clients purely in terms of tangible,
past years' revenue and create a system that would include less
tangible, nonrevenue measures. These would be metrics designed to capture a client's true potential to grow—its strategic
value to Convergys—as well as its actual, current value.

Index	Measures	Weight
Average Revenue Score	■ Current spending and projected spending	20 percent
Revenue Change Score	■ Year-to-year actual spending	25 percent
Current Relationship	■ Signed contract length ■ Total years as client	15 percent
Technology Entanglement	■ System integration ■ Reporting ■ Tele-Web ■ Email	20 percent
Share of Client	■ Outsource potential	10 percent
Partnership	■ Level of contact ■ Referenceable ■ Future value	10 percent

A brief glance at the index system reveals that annual revenue remains a critical basic measure of value, worth 45 percent when the Average Revenue Score and the Change Score are combined. No matter how finely you tune any value model, revenue is likely to play a dominant role. Yet each of the six indices plays its part in helping Convergys establish the value of its clients.

Average Revenue Score is determined by averaging a client's actual revenue this year and its projected revenue for next year. A large client with high projected revenue might rate a higher index than a large client with lower projected revenue. The large client with low projected revenue might even rate a lower index than a medium-size client with higher projected revenue.

Revenue Change Score is based on the difference between what the client spent with Convergys last year and what the client is spending with Convergys this year. This index gives the team a clear indication of how fast the account is growing or declining.

Current Relationship is a straightforward measure of the client's present level of commitment. "It tells us a lot about the state of the account," says Lento. "Do we have a signed contract? Is it a multiyear contract? How many years have they been a client?"

Technology Entanglement was seen as an especially important element in the company's customer development efforts. Let's take a moment to explore how technology entanglement works. Let's say the PC you purchased a few months ago for your home office crashes moments before you need to email an important report to a big client. You call the 800 number provided by the PC manufacturer. Because the manufacturer has outsourced its technical support service to Convergys, your call is answered by a Convergys customer support representative (CSR). Because the PC manufacturer and Convergys have integrated portions of their information systems, the Convergys CSR can access your customer data and guide you precisely through the appropriate restart procedure.

You don't know that your call was answered by a Convergys employee and you don't care. The entire process was seamless and invisible to you because the PC manufacturer had invested the time and the money necessary to integrate its systems with the systems of its technical support service outsourcer. Now if the PC manufacturer decides to change outsourcers, it must calculate the switching costs. That's what Convergys means by technology entanglement. It's a highly effective barrier against client defection. It's also a good leading indicator of strategic growth potential of a client.

"When we look at the Technology Entanglement index, we can tell if the client sees us as being more than just a supplier of butts in seats," says Lento. "A higher index means the client sees us as a strategic investment. Those are the kinds of clients we want." In general, clients with a higher index of technology entanglement are more loyal—and more growable—than clients with a lower index of technology entanglement.

Share of Client is based on the client's contact center budget and the percentage of that budget that is outsourced. The team acknowledged that its data in this area was sketchy, so it gave the index a relatively low rate.

Partnership produced a similar situation for the team. The numerical value of this variable is based on highly subjective criteria. Basically, the team had to rely on the judgments of the sales force to answer key questions such as "Does the client buy on price only?" "Are your contacts at a high level or a low level?" "Would the client serve as a good reference?" "Does the client regard Convergys as the supplier of a commodity?" "Does it regard Convergys as a future strategic partner?"

Lento's team knew it was imperative to include these non-revenue variables, but didn't give them much weight in the first iteration of its LTV model. As methods of collecting and analyzing client data improve, these indices will weigh more heavily in the reckoning of LTV.

In the meantime, the LTV model has become such an important part of the company's overall growth strategy that Convergys plans on using it to measure success internally. An employee who nudges a client up in the index ratings will be rewarded. "We're putting a little meat behind it," Lento says, "and making it part of everyone's compensation."

Hidden values revealed

With the LTV model in place, Convergys made some startling discoveries. Some of its clients rose in terms of their value, others fell.

Client F, a large technology firm, had been relegated to 94th place in the old ranking system, largely because of its relatively low average annual revenue. In the LTV model, Client F rose to 6th place because of its high Change Score and a high Partnership index.

Client I, a dot-com, climbed from 58th place to 9th place, based largely on its Technology Entanglement and Change

Top 20 clients	New rank by LTV	Original rank by revenue	Change in rank
Client A	1	1	0
Client B	2	2	0
Client C	3	62	+59
Client D	4	4	0
Client E	5	40	+35
Client F	6	94	+88
Client G	7	12	+5
Client H	8	20	+12
Client I	9	58	+49
Client J	10	3	-7
Client K	11	47	+36
Client L	12	78	+66
Client M	13	5	-8
Client N	14	72	+58
Client O	15	41	+26
Client P	16	23	+7
Client Q	17	9	-8
Client R	18	25	+7
Client S	19	52	+33
Client T	20	11	-9

Score indices. Client J, a telecom, fell from 3rd place to 10th place. Its prominent ranking had been based almost entirely on current annual revenue. Under the new LTV model, Client J's spending was offset by low levels of Technology Entanglement, Partnership, and Share of Client.

Seeing the results in black and white made it easier to begin reallocating resources around the company's best potential clients. In a little while, we'll show you how Convergys leveraged this strategy for impressive gains.

Covering all the bases

After setting up its LTV model, Convergys addressed the challenge of differentiating its clients by their needs. Lento's survey had revealed that most clients didn't have a static set of needs. Instead, most clients had needs that changed over time, corresponding to their particular stage of development. Convergys broke out these needs sets into four basic categories:

1. acquiring customers
2. billing customers
3. serving customers
4. growing customers

By defining the categories as stages in a natural life cycle, Convergys ensured that each client's needs would be served— or at least recognized—as that client grew and matured over the course of the relationship. This approach contrasts starkly with the typical methodology of defining product categories. In this case, the company's sales efforts are arranged around the client's own goals—not the sales team's.

Together with the LTV model, the needs-based categories provided Lento with a road map for deploying his resources more efficiently. It also created a guide that helped him assign accounts to the salespeople with the most appropriate skill sets and level of experience.

Deploying the sales force for maximum efficiency was essential to the overall success of the strategy. Based on his knowledge and understanding of the market, Lento believed he would achieve higher revenues if he assigned fewer accounts to his most experienced salespeople. His intuition was buttressed by the plain fact that 100 clients were generating 97.5 percent of the company's revenue. The remaining 500 clients accounted for just 2.5 percent of its revenue. Asking the sales force to provide equal coverage for all 600 clients was obviously not the most efficient way to proceed.

The year before Lento arrived at the company, each of its top ten sales reps was assigned fifteen accounts on average. In 1999, that average dropped to three. In 2000, it dropped to just two. By then, however, the company was routinely assigning more than one sales rep to its most valuable accounts.

Based on the new perspectives offered by the LTV model, with its weighing of nonrevenue variables, Lento had a pretty good idea which accounts should be assigned to the senior salespeople. But he still needed to figure out the best system for handling the remaining accounts.

The solution was to have two sales teams. The Direct Sales team was made up of veterans, proven winners with impressive track records of selling. The Sales and Marketing Account Coverage (SMAC) team was staffed with people who had less experience. SMAC functions as the inside sales force, dedicated to managing clients with the potential to become Most Valuable Customers (MVCs) or Most Growable Customers

(MGCs). The SMAC team also serves as a training ground for the Direct Sales team. Lento plans to promote at least two people from SMAC into the Direct Sales team this year. In addition, the SMAC team provides opportunities for people who prefer working closer to home and don't want to commit to the heavy travel schedules required of the Direct Sales team.

In general, resources and workloads were allocated according to customer value. Convergys grouped its clients, and potential clients, into four value tiers: Most Valuable, Most Growable, Migrators and Below Zeros.

Value tier	MVCs	MGCs	MIGRATORS	BZs
LTV rank	10th and above	11th to 50th	51st to 75th	75th and below
Customer management strategy	Served by Direct Sales force. 80 percent of effort spent retaining business. 20 percent spent growing business.	Served by Direct Sales force. 80 percent of effort spent growing business. 20 percent spent retaining business.	Handled by SMAC team. React to client needs as they are identified.	Handled by operations group. If operations group can't meet needs, request goes to SMAC team.
Manageable contacts per salesperson	Maximum of one. Most accounts have multiple reps.	Two to six clients per sales rep.	25 per sales rep.	NA
Frequency of contact	Every day or more.	Every day to a couple of times weekly.	As needed.	As needed.
Interaction costs	Relatively low, because the volume of business is already there.	Relatively high.	Low.	Low.

In the case of an MVC, the sales team's goal is to build, sustain, and grow the relationship. An appropriate level of dedicated, high-quality resources will be allocated to achieve that goal. One of the company's MVCs, for example, has been assigned ten Direct Sales reps.

In the case of an MGC, the sales team's goal is growing the account as aggressively as possible. High-quality resources will be allocated, but on a semi-dedicated basis. A Direct Sales rep may be assigned anywhere from two to six of these accounts, depending on their size and complexity. Note, however, that client growth will be measured relative to the LTV model itself. A client "grows" by achieving a higher and higher score on the LTV model. For instance, a moderately valuable client with a low partnership index can be made more valuable by improving the partnership index, because high-partnership clients can be expected to stay longer and do more types of business with Convergys.

Migrators are lower-value clients with the potential to become MGCs. They are managed by the SMAC team. Each SMAC rep may be assigned as many as twenty-five such accounts to watch over.

Below Zeros are clients on which Convergys loses money, just by serving them. Operations, rather than sales, is responsible for maintaining them. In some cases, their needs may be referred to the SMAC team. "We'll take a run at fixing the problem, but at some point we'll make a strategic decision to determine how they continue to fit into our client base," Lento says.

Upside, downside

The Customer Management Group at Convergys has proven the power of a carefully conceived, well-executed one-to-one customer relationship strategy. In 1999, the first full year the strategy was in effect, CMG revenues were up 28 percent from the previous year. Nearly all of that growth was generated by the group's top 100 clients, clearly validating CMG's client-centric vision. The measurable success of the strategy resulted in Convergys moving ahead to merge several functions that had been operating in separate silos. Lento, who had been brought in as head of the CMG sales and marketing team, was promoted and given oversight for all Convergys sales and sales operations. Although his workload has increased, he is in a better position to implement one-to-one marketing programs throughout the firm.

Lento acknowledges that reorganizing the sales force hasn't reduced the pressure on it. The pressure remains, but in a different form. For some, adjusting to this new kind of pressure wasn't easy. "The people who were transaction-oriented and always looking ahead to the next deal had to start thinking in terms of building long-term relationships with fewer clients," he says. "The old concept of 'safety in numbers' isn't relevant anymore. Nowadays you don't have nine or ten other accounts to fall back on if something goes wrong. Sure, that's a lot of pressure, but there is also the potential for lots of rewards."

All success, however, comes at a cost. Not all the sales reps liked the idea of working with fewer clients, says Lento. Some were clearly uncomfortable. "Everyone experiences a moment of panic when they realize what's happening," he says. "It's natural. You have to comfort them and explain the benefits. If that doesn't work, you tell them they don't have an option."

In the final analysis, many found they could not make the transition. "About a third could do it right off the bat," Lento says. "About another third were capable of doing it, but needed training. And about a third just weren't ever going to get there."

In the first half of 1999, the sales force experienced a 50 percent turnover. By the end of the year, however, turnover had dropped into the single digits, not only because all the ones who "weren't ever going to get there" had pretty much left by then, but also because of important changes in the hiring process. Sales reps are no longer recruited primarily on the basis of their ability to win new accounts. Today's sales rep is a team player, a person who inspires trust and can build relationships over time. "We're looking for people who know how to sell business-critical services," explains Lento. "We want salespeople who generate trust because they have a thorough understanding of the client's problems. We want salespeople who can get to know a client's business as well as the client knows it, so the client will trust them to deliver the right solution."

This returns us to the idea of the *trusted agent,* someone who can be relied on to act in the client's best interests. As the business environment grows both more competitive and more complex, trust is the best glue for holding a relationship together. In any complex selling situation, but especially when the vendor is handling the client's highly valuable and extremely confidential customer information, the salesperson's first task is to build a solid bond of trust between the buyer and the seller. This requires a new breed of salesperson, someone who can act as a consultant, a consensus builder, and a watchdog to make sure all the promised solutions are delivered.

"The new salesperson is solving business problems as opposed to just selling products and services. The new salesperson is expected to build relationships at the highest levels within the client's organization," says Lento. "It takes a different kind of person to do this job."

New kid on the block

Jay Halsted is an example of the new breed of salesperson. His official title is Senior Director of Business Development. He is currently assigned to the AT&T Broadband account, where he is a member of a team of ten sales and support people. His primary role on this team is developing new opportunities within AT&T Broadband.

Halsted has worked on a series of complex and challenging assignments. Most recently he was tasked with winning new business at TCI, a cable industry leader generally known for its reluctance to outsource customer care services. After TCI was purchased by AT&T, the company's name changed to AT&T Broadband.

Halsted saw the opportunity to establish a presence for Convergys and jumped. "The leadership at AT&T Broadband recognized there was value in outsourcing customer care functions, but because of the localized nature of their business, they really couldn't put a finger on it," he recalls. This was a new and very different environment from traditional TCI. For the next few months, Halsted did everything he could to find out about AT&T Broadband's needs.

One day he heard that AT&T@Home, a high-speed cable Internet service, had an interesting challenge: the high-speed cable Internet service was so popular that demand and usage had risen rapidly. As a result, the AT&T@Home call center was getting an increasing number of *incoming* calls from people who wanted the service. And the number and complexity of the technical support calls were also increasing. Halsted decided to make AT&T@Home's problem an opportunity. He spent time listening carefully to AT&T@Home's executive director explain the various challenges she faced.

"She was very knowledgeable about her business, and the problem she had to solve. She also knew that outsourcing was one alternative she could consider," said Halsted. The executive director eventually agreed to visit a Convergys call center.

Before the visit, Halsted knew he would have to see the world "through her eyes and build credibility for Convergys." He felt instinctively that she would not respond well to a traditional sales approach. "It was clear that many salespeople had come and gone, selling their wares and being rather assertive about it," says Halsted. "We made a conscious decision not to be assertive, but rather to be suggestive and to complement their management style rather than offset it." During the visit, Halsted took lots of notes, asked many questions, and listened carefully to everything she said. He wanted to make sure the prospect *knew* that he was doing all he could to genuinely understand her business. He was building trust.

A formal sales presentation was scheduled with the site visit. When the day came, the executive director arrived with one of her top managers and started firing questions at Halsted's team. Later, she told Halsted that her plan had been to attend the presentation, gather information, and go back to headquarters to make a decision. But as the day went on, Halsted recalls, the atmosphere changed from neutral to friendly. By about two-thirty in the afternoon, she turned to her colleague, shrugged her shoulders, and said, "I'm in." She contracted with Convergys to provide technical support, which is more complex than normal customer service. "Preparation met opportunity," says Halsted, "and we created a win-win."

Since then, the client has increased technical support operations with Convergys and is considering opening a dedicated contact center. Halsted attributes this success to support from his team and from his superiors, who encouraged him to spend the time necessary to cultivate a relationship with the client.

Halsted says the kind of patience and diligence it takes to develop a sincere relationship with a client feels natural to him. "I've had direct jobs where I'm supposed to sell to as many people as I can and then move on. But there is no comparison between that and what we're doing at Convergys," he says. "I like what I'm doing here. It gives me something to look forward to when I get up in the morning. I'm building relationships, adding value, and increasing the value proposition. It's exciting."

He said he recently received a compliment from a client that confirmed that view. "She said there were two things that were very appealing about Convergys. Number one, we take time to listen. She said that was very unusual. And, she said, number two, everything you have committed to, you have delivered. And that builds trust."

Some aspects of the sales process continue on as they have in the past, however. In addition to listening to his clients, interacting with them, and helping them develop custom solutions tailored to fit their individual needs, Halsted still occasionally takes them out for dinner. And, he says, he is careful to keep the conversation focused on the client's business needs. His primary role in these situations is to listen and to digest what the client is saying. "Seek to understand rather than be understood," he says. "And then try to add value."

Deeper is better

Mike Serpan is senior director of technology sales for Convergys. He used to be responsible for fifteen or more accounts. Now he has just two accounts, and the company has hired someone so that he will have another salesperson working with him on those two accounts. "This is a change I looked forward to," he says. "If you have only a few high-level accounts, you can penetrate deep into those accounts and put multiple efforts into that one client. You become more embedded in their ability to deliver their product. We want to become indispensable. The more things we have fingers in, the more we are indispensable."

Like Halsted, Serpan spends a good portion of his time interacting with potential clients to make sure he understands their needs. One of his biggest deals took six months to close. Most of that time was spent "understanding the client's challenges, understanding what was keeping them up at night, then trying to figure out what we could do to help them sleep better." Most salespeople working in traditional sales environments don't have the opportunity to spend much time getting to know their clients, he says.

"You have to have the confidence and the support to break away from the traditional way of doing things," he says. "You have to be able to get in there and pursue a strategy of going deep into the client. Once you get deep, the opportunities blossom like so many flowers. The greatest thing is that once you get the flow going, you won't have any problem getting work from that client."

Development strategies such as this are particularly appropriate when the product or service is complex. These kinds of strategies also require a different approach to compensation.

At many traditionally organized firms, the sales force compensation plan actually is a deterrent to forming long-term relationships. Unlike the salespeople at traditional companies, Serpan and his colleagues at Convergys don't have to choose between building client relationships and paying the mortgage.

"At most companies, you have a highly leveraged commission plan. Our bonus structure, however, allows us to pursue longer-term strategies. I am still motivated to make the sale, because I make a whole lot more money if I do. But I can still put food on the table if I don't," he explains. "If you have salespeople working in a fear mode, they'll sell whatever they have to sell as fast as they can. That's fine for the short term. But it is not nearly as effective for the long term."

Finding people who understand this philosophy, and can act on it, is a major challenge for any client-centric company.

"Most salespeople are used to meeting quarterly numbers or even monthly numbers," Serpan says. "That is short-term vision. That mentality doesn't play out here."

Even six months is now considered very fast when it comes to making a sale. "Another big deal I closed, it took me thirteen months to do that. That's more the norm, twelve to thirteen months to close a big deal."

And that, of course, is just the beginning of his job. "What we are really selling is our ability to perform. And so there is a constant delivery of product and services day in and day out. There is a saying in our industry: no good sale goes unpunished. And it's really true. Once you sell it, you have to do it. You have to open that facility, implement the right set of technologies, hire those five hundred people, train them, and get them going on the program."

Focusing on your more valuable clients also means you have to learn how to say "no" to clients who don't fit your long-term strategy. "You can't be afraid to tell people, 'You don't meet my profile. You might bring me $250,000 in revenue in the next two months, but then you'll go away.' That is one of the hardest things to do, to turn away business. But you have to be able to do that, to properly qualify clients based on the criteria you have set up."

This raises an interesting question: How do you balance the need for long-term growth with the need for immediate growth? The answer is by growing your top customers, because the revenue you gain from them will more than make up for any revenue you lose by not chasing after less valuable customers.

Rewarding teamwork, large deals

Compensation and incentives need to be completely aligned with business objectives if a salesperson is going to be expected to use one-to-one strategies. "If you tell me you want me to do this, then you need to walk the talk as well. Incent me properly and I'll go out and do it. For salespeople, it's really pretty simple. Incent them properly, train them properly, and they'll get the job done," says Serpan.

The compensation plan at Convergys is set up so that the salespeople have an incentive to improve not only their own lot but that of their teammates and company as well. "The idea is that we need the sales reps to focus on their individual contribution, but we also want them to be focused on their teammates and continually focused on the profitability of the revenue they bring in," Lento says. "Our compensation system must support all three initiatives."

The compensation package is a combination of base salary and several different bonus components. One is based on the company meeting its earnings goals for the year, paid out on an annual basis. Another component is tied to the individual sales rep's quota number. A third component is based on the sales performance of the team they have been assigned to. And then there is a special component called the large deal bonus. The large deal bonus is a single bonus for signing large contracts. It ranges from $5,000 to $50,000, depending on the size of the contract. It is calculated by taking the annual committed amount of the contract multiplied by the number of years of the contract.

Including time as a variable in the compensation equation

helped the sales force shift its focus from the present to the future. "What we are trying to drive, from a behavior standpoint, is a focus on negotiating long-term contracts," Lento says. "Before, the sales rep had no reason to care whether it was a one-year contract or a five-year contract. Now, if it's more than a one-year contract, there could be a significant difference in the large deal bonus. This helps us encourage our people to develop long-term relationships with the client."

If, for example, a sales rep at Convergys had a $100,000 total cash income target, $70,000 of that would be considered the base. Of the $30,000 that is the bonus opportunity, $7,000 would be based on the company's profitability, $7,000 would be based on the team's performance, and $16,000 would be based on the individual's revenue. The large deal bonus would be paid on top of that.

The large deal bonus was introduced in 1999. It has proven effective in driving the sales reps to more aggressively negotiate longer-term contracts, Lento says. That, along with some of the other facets of the compensation package, is a somewhat unusual feature when it comes to compensating salespeople. "Most of our competitors in the industry are on a commission transaction that says, 'All I'm really interested in is the next sale,' " Lento says. "We want to focus on our long-term relationships, so we need to make sure we protect the revenue we have and grow our new opportunities."

Lento says he is considering fine-tuning the plan to incorporate measures of technology entanglement and partnership potential. He is also considering moving to a gross profit model that puts less emphasis on pure revenue. "I like the basic model," he says. "The question is how do we put a stronger focus on profitability and on building technology entanglement."

The compensation plan and other facets of the new sales strategy have paid off. He notes that Convergys had always considered clients such as TCI to be prospects, even when those types of companies weren't interested in Convergys' service offerings. Then Halsted and his team were able to break through. "Now we are doing customer service with AT&T Broadband (TCI) and it's one of our fastest-growing accounts," Lento says. "And that is because of our dedicated focus on the account."

And there are clients like Citigroup. In 1998, the sales rep assigned to Citigroup had ten other accounts to manage. Negative growth was predicted for the following year. After refocusing its sales efforts, Lento's team was able to reverse the trend and grow the Citibank account by 20 percent.

Focusing the sales compensation plan on long-term profitability and relationship building also allows Convergys to do a better, more productive job at client acquisition. Under the new compensation plan, the most valuable accounts to win are the ones that are likely to be the most profitable over the long term—clients for whom Convergys can do the best overall job with its service offerings. The company's work with a well-known PC maker serves as one example of how patience is rewarded when the long term is taken into account. Serpan and his team needed almost a full year to land this company as a client. But Lento now projects that soon this personal computer manufacturer will emerge as one of Convergy's top twenty-five clients.

In addition to increased revenue, there are other benefits of working closely with clients. The increasingly collaborative relationships have led to several strategic partnerships. For example, one client came to Convergys with a problem: it was having trouble responding to emails from its customers. "We worked with them proactively and put some technology in place to do it in a more automated, consistent, and cost-effective manner. The proof of concept was about a year ago. Today, that technology is one of our major service offerings," Lento says.

The solution in this case was a joint marketing agreement and an equity investment in a company called Kana Communications. Kana provides customer communication software and services for businesses. "That has become a standard offering to all of our clients," Lento says.

"You can't have these kinds of conversations when you don't have reps that are focused on small numbers of clients," Lento says. "Our reps are now working with clients to figure out how to recognize issues and bring issues to the forefront, rather than waiting for an RFP to come through the fax machine."

This is a prime example of how a one-to-one enterprise finds products and services for customers, instead of finding customers for its products and services. After Convergys identified the client's need, it looked for a solution. The fact that the solution was provided by another firm didn't stop Convergys from acting in its client's best interest. In this instance, acting as a trusted agent for the client resulted in a strategic alliance that brought multiple benefits to all parties involved.

Saturday Night Fever or *Fosse*?

The integration of the CMG and IMG sales force began recently and should take almost a year to finalize, Lento says. When the process is complete, Lento plans to have eliminated the different titling schemes, compensation plans and ranges, and to have reconciled all the overlapping accounts. "This is what we have planned," he says. "Bring the teams together. Reconcile their differences. Put more feet on the street. And support the sales force through automation and training systems."

Lento and Schultz say they see attitudes changing significantly as the successes mount up. Convergys has developed an aggressive internal communication strategy to keep people informed about changes and the effects those changes are having on the work environment. As successful as that communications strategy is, Schultz says, "one pound of success tastes better than a hundred pounds of communication."

But old habits die hard and Lento concedes that he still encounters occasional pockets of resistance within the company. For example, Convergys recently held an executive forum called "CRM in 2000." Its purpose was to share the principles and practices of one-to-one customer relationship management with some of the company's best clients and prospects. Lento recalls that he had a difficult time selling the idea internally.

"The plan was to bring together fifteen high-level executives from existing clients or prospects and provide them with an event that would clearly differentiate us from our competitors," says Lento. He planned to use the event as an occasion to educate a few promising key clients about customer relationship management—how to interact with customers to build stronger and deeper relationships with them. Lento felt that such an event, if done correctly, could give Convergys a very effective sales message: (a) Customer interaction is important, and (b) we specialize in customer interaction.

"But when I proposed the idea," Lento added, "it was not broadly accepted or supported. Even some members of my team doubted our ability to pull it off. They said things like 'This idea has no value' and 'Nobody will show up.' "

But Lento forged ahead, booked rooms in the Millenium Hilton in New York City, and invited eighteen executives from sixteen companies. The night before the forum, Convergys executives dined with their guests in a private room at the "21" Club. The following day, all the executives convened for the forum. They listened to several presentations on CRM strategies. They debated the value of CRM and talked about the role CRM would play in fostering growth. They discussed global competition, margin erosion, customer loyalty, and the Internet. While they met, their spouses were treated to a private tour of the Metropolitan Museum of Art, followed by lunch and a shopping trip. At the end of the day, all the participants gathered for dinner at the hotel, where the theater critic from the New York *Daily News* regaled them with show business stories. Then the guests had a choice of attending that night's performance of *Saturday Night Fever* or *Fosse*. After the play, it was back to the hotel for refreshments and more conversation.

What emerged from all the dialogue was that while most of the executives had *heard* about CRM, few had any genuine depth of understanding of the business issues and processes involved. "They were very positive about moving in the direction of CRM, but none of them knew how to do it," recalls Lento. The event, by focusing on strategy rather than selling, whetted their appetites for more knowledge. Specifically, they wanted more knowledge about how Convergys could help them with their own customer-centric programs.

By the end of the event, the doubters had been transformed. Some of the same people who had told Lento the idea would flop said they were looking forward to the next forum. One of the company's largest clients offered the highest praise: "Nobody else is doing these kinds of things, and it really proves that you guys are different."

The event also provided a golden opportunity for Lento's sales team to make new contacts at existing accounts. Whole new departments within accounts suddenly emerged as solid prospects. Lento recalls dealing with a contact who had warned him not to talk with anyone else in the company. The contact's boss, however, attended the forum and was so impressed that he invited Lento to make a presentation to the company's global management group. "That alone pays for the entire event," says Lento.

The fact that Convergys leveraged the event to engage in some nicely executed market education, however, isn't what makes it remarkable or unusual. Many companies do this. What makes it worth mentioning is that Convergys set its sights on just a few high-level executives from just those clients most likely to increase their business with the firm, and that the company used the event to get them thinking about doing business differently.

Focus on clients

There is little question that the success of the company's one-to-one strategy was due in great part to the enormous time and energy it spent creating a logical methodology for differentiating clients. In this regard, Convergys is light-years ahead of most organizations. And yet its methodology was not the most important element of the strategy. What allowed Convergys to succeed where others have failed or are still struggling is that it made a commitment to support the managers and executives on the front lines of the battle for change. The single most critical factor in the firm's success was its willingness to embrace cultural change, move away from tradition, and try something new.

If the "moral" of the Convergys experience could be reduced to just four key points, they might be:

1. If you're going to adopt an account development strategy, you must know which accounts are really the most growable.
2. When compared with more traditional market penetration strategies, account development requires a far higher degree of collaboration, both internally and externally.
3. A sales force pursuing an account development strategy must be rewarded differently from a sales force pursuing a traditional strategy.
4. Cultural as well as organizational changes within the enterprise are necessary to ensure the success of an account development strategy.

As Ron Schultz notes, a string of early victories helped pave the way for Convergys. But in the end, the firm's own clients were the "secret ingredient" of its success. "If you pay attention to the folks you are already married to, you can grow your business quickly," he says. "Another thing we've noticed as we've become more introspective: We do some of our best work with the accounts where we have strategic relationships. The greater the interdependence, the better we can do. So it just makes sense to grow the big accounts bigger. We'll also grow the small accounts we think have the potential to become big accounts."

Tasks ahead for Convergys

Convergys is a large B2B company with a leading position in an evolving market. Moreover, as the result of a series of corporate acquisitions, the firm is made up of a patchwork of different organizations, with a variety of related and overlapping services. But the client acquisition sales strategy that had served the firm's various operating units so well for so long is no longer sufficient to sustain a competitive growth trajectory, so Convergys has decided to reorient itself to focus on share of customer rather than market share. It adopted an account development strategy, and to execute this strategy successfully it had to clear away all the underbrush of previous sales models, client views, and compensation schemes.

Convergys is clearly on an evolutionary path, and its story is only half complete. What we have with this case study is a snapshot of a completely new strategy in the initial stages of implementation, its true complexity still unfolding, and its long-term benefits not yet a firm reality.

But Convergys could probably accelerate the progress of its account development strategy by:

- Developing a more precise system for measuring its share of customer and estimating the strategic value of all its accounts in actual monetary terms. This would allow Convergys to focus its business development resources where the ROI is greatest. The monetary model of strategic value would have to be continuously validated and updated, as more information and results become available for analysis.
- Fully integrating the operations of its primary business units. This would allow a more seamless flow of customer data across all touch points (Web, call center, and billing).
- Managing customer data for its clients across all touch points. This could easily become the basis for much deeper levels of technology entanglement with clients, which should be one of Convergys' most important goals in the years ahead.
- Initiating a value-added service such as Premier Dell.com that would provide customers with better metrics about the status of their own operations and the outcomes of their customer-focused initiatives.
- Removing the remaining barriers between various divisions and business units. Then the entire organization can focus on customers.
- Further upgrading its sales force, with a hiring and continu-

ous training program designed to move the salespeople into an increasingly consultative role. The sales force should eventually be reorganized around the principal types of client needs already identified (customer acquisition, customer billing, customer service, customer growth)—the same needs that should be used to construct bundled solutions of Convergys services.

Novartis CP
Rediscovering the customer

Top line summary

When the biotechnology revolution threw the market for crop protection chemicals into a tailspin, Novartis CP found itself confronting a genuine crisis. A sudden and unexpected surge in foreign competition added to the company's woes. Instead of panicking, company management sized up the options and chose to develop a one-to-one customer relationship program to defend itself against lower-priced competitors. In the end, Novartis CP not only held its ground; it actually grew its overall business by focusing its efforts on its best customers.

While Novartis CP had been successful in its previous incarnation as a product-centric organization, it proved itself even more successful in its reincarnation as a customer-centric organization. But one thing is certain: If it had not responded by reinventing itself as a one-to-one enterprise, it would not have survived the crisis.

In a swiftly evolving economy, the ability to grasp the "big picture" and to respond by developing and executing the right business strategy is critical. At moments of change, quick reflexes can make the difference between falling behind or vaulting ahead of the competition. Companies that react too slowly, or too cautiously, are likely to find themselves waging an uphill battle against swifter foes.

Once a new strategy has been set, an across-the-board effort within the organization is required to achieve success. Teamwork and a shared sense of purpose are absolutely essential. Internal communications must be crafted with surgical precision to reinforce the message of change. If necessary, functional areas within the organization must be altered or reconstructed to support the new strategy. Once the ball gets rolling, the pace of change must be consistent. It must appear logical, reasonable, and inevitable. Progress must be monitored, measured, analyzed, reported, and rewarded throughout the organization. Management must strive for universal buy-in to ensure that every available human resource is working to achieve the same goal. "Godfathers," mentors, and sponsors with sufficient seniority and clout must step forward to help the strategy survive its infancy.

Transforming a traditional organization into a one-to-one enterprise is a group effort in every practical sense of the phrase. Nowhere is this illustrated more vividly than in the case of Novartis Protección de Cultivos. Six months after launching a one-to-one strategy, Novartis CP measured substantial increases in total revenue, share of customer, and share of market. The strategy worked—and continues to work—for three main reasons:

1. It was based on established one-to-one principles.
2. The unit's eighty employees understood the strategy and got behind it.
3. A broad portfolio of products made it possible to mass customize bundled solutions for individual customers.

Background

Novartis CP was a Latin American unit of Novartis AG, the Swiss life sciences firm. Based in Argentina, Novartis CP sold crop protection products such as herbicides, fungicides, seed treatments, and insecticides to dealers, who then resell them to farmers.

Over the years, the farmers had come to rely on a complex and costly array of crop protection products to safeguard their crops from various pests and predators. Although the Novartis sales force, which was headquartered in Buenos Aires, had some contact with the farmers, the dealers tended to "own" the customer relationships. This sense of ownership had evolved naturally over time. The rural dealers were physically closer to the farmers, and they tended to be more knowledgeable about the unique set of problems generated by each farm.

Appearances can be deceiving

Since the size of the agrochemicals market had been growing steadily for the past ten years, a casual observer could be excused for assuming that all was well. Traditional business logic dictated that as long as the market continued to expand, higher revenues and higher profits would surely follow.

Top management at Novartis, however, knew full well that by chasing market share, the unit would fall eventually into a classic trap of diminishing returns. They knew that selling to a *market* isn't the same as selling to a *customer*. A market has no loyalty; it simply responds to the harsh law of supply and demand. Selling to a market puts you at the mercy of your lowest-priced competitor. That means you're under constant pressure to drop your prices to remain competitive. If you're selling a commodity, the danger is even greater, because price is almost always the weapon of choice for the competitive predator. All too often, the end result of traditional sales and marketing strategies is climbing revenues and disappearing margins.

Still, it was hard to shake the idea of a linkage between a rising market and rising profits, especially when everything seemed to be going so well. But then everything changed.

The introduction of bioengineered crops that are resistant to many types of pests (and therefore require fewer pesticides or herbicides during their growing cycle) meant that farmers no longer had to spend huge sums of cash on chemical crop protection. Although these bioengineered crops had not been used broadly in Argentina, they had been widely embraced in neighboring Brazil. As the Brazilian market for crop protection products shriveled, the firms that had been selling these products in Brazil looked hungrily to Argentina as a viable market. Suddenly, Novartis CP found itself in a highly competitive arena.

Soon, more Argentine farmers were using some of the newer crops already used by their Brazilian counterparts. Within one short year, the total market for herbicides in Argentina dropped from $850 million to $750 million. In the case of soybeans, for example, the average farmer's spending for herbicides fell from $32 dollars per hectare to $12 per hectare! Similar declines in spending were forecast for other crops.

"It was like a bad dream," recalls Leopoldo Cid, marketing manager at Novartis CP. "Demand evaporated practically overnight. You can imagine the stress we felt." In the space of a heartbeat, $100 million in forecast sales dropped out of the Argentine crop protection market.

Carlos Weiss, Novartis CP's chief executive, knew that the previous year's sales gains would be short-lived if he and his team didn't act quickly to change their strategy.

Anyone who has ever stood at the edge of a diving board and looked down can sympathize with Weiss. There is a world of difference between knowing you must do something and actually taking the leap. For Weiss, fate intervened in the form of an invitation to attend a Harvard Business School Executive Forum. At Cambridge, Weiss met the legendary John P. Kotter, a Harvard professor and an ardent advocate of change management. "He was the trigger that motivated us to get going with the transformational changes we needed to make in our strategy," recalls Weiss. "He also inspired us to move forward with the structural changes we needed to implement in our organization. These structural changes, in turn, would make it possible to carry out the new strategy."

Energized by his conversations with Kotter, Weiss returned to Argentina to draft a new strategic plan for the unit. After weeks of meetings and memos, his team achieved an epiphany.

Weiss recalls the moment when the unit's view of the world

changed. "After many hours of discussion and brainstorming among all levels of our organization, one very simple, very clear truth emerged—the farmer is our customer."

Weiss outlined a basic three-point strategy:

1. Build farmer loyalty
2. Build reciprocal agreements with dealers
3. Build customer share and market share

To achieve these goals, the unit would have to reorganize, beef up its staff, and invest in new information technology. The company would be guided by one-to-one principles as it fleshed out its skeletal plans.

Backed by the upper management at regional headquarters in São Paulo, Brazil, they moved swiftly. So swiftly, in fact, that the plan began yielding positive results after a mere three months. Those results gave them the confidence to press further and faster. After six months of steady gains, share of customer among the unit's top tier of customers had increased from 20 percent to 70 percent. Market share rose by 20 percent. Revenue was up 4 percent.

How was all this accomplished in so little time? The answer is suggested by the name they coined for the unit's one-to-one strategy. They called it Primero el Productor, which means "the farmer first." The name sent a clear signal to the sales force. The unit would recover by building relationships with its end users, the farmers. But there had to be a well-defined plan, a road map to guide the sales force as it took up the task of reinventing itself.

One of the primary reasons we chose to write about Primero el Productor is that it offers a textbook example of how to plan and execute a one-to-one program quickly. It mirrors the logical progression of steps we envisioned as we were developing the theoretical framework for one-to-one strategy. Indeed, Primero el Productor embraces our four basic implementation steps: Identify, Differentiate, Interact, and Customize.

Sense of urgency

Physicists like to say that the dimension of time was created to keep everything from happening all at once. The management team at Novartis CP would likely agree with this observation. From their perspective, everything *was* happening all at once. They believed, probably correctly, that any delay would be fatal. So they began moving ahead as quickly as they could. One of their first steps was to survey their customer base to get an accurate sense of where things stood. For the survey to be meaningful, they would have to gather the names of as many customers as possible—no small feat, considering there were more than 100,000 farmers in Argentina and almost all of them were purchasing their crop protection products through a dealer.

They began populating a rudimentary database with names of farmers culled from lists maintained by the Ministry of Agriculture and from a set of names collected at random during a major agricultural exposition. It was not an auspicious beginning, but it was a beginning. Knowing the names of the farm-

ers, as well as the size of their farms, would enable Novartis CP
to begin pushing ahead to the next step, differentiating them
by value to the sales force.

Novartis CP also appealed to the dealers, offering them incentives to share customer information. In this instance, the
timing was perfect. In addition to experiencing the same
shrinking market for crop protection products, the dealers
were reeling from a worldwide drop in farm prices that made it
extremely difficult for them to collect money owed to them by
the farmers. To a cash-strapped dealer, the chance to partner
with Novartis CP in a well-conceived one-to-one initiative
seemed like manna from heaven.

This early attempt to involve the dealers ultimately would
serve two purposes. It would not only speed the harvest of
names for Novartis CP, but it would also erect a roadblock
against the company's competitors who, facing the same dire
circumstances, attempted to bypass the existing distribution
chain entirely. These attempts proved unsuccessful, largely because of stiff resistance from the dealers, who were able to
leverage their long-standing relationships with the farmers to
fend off efforts by the manufacturers to "disintermediate" them.
"Some of these dealers got really angry," recalls Cid. "Our competitors really messed up by trying to go around the dealers instead of trying to work with them. The dealers are very
important in this business because they have very strong relationships with the farmers."

Realizing the danger that could result from mismanaging its
distribution channel, Weiss made sure that each of the approximately eighty dealers who resold Novartis crop protection
products in Argentina got a personal visit from a Novartis CP

manager. "It was very hard work," recalls Cid. "The dealers thought they owned the farmers and that Novartis should sell only to them. But we had to make them see that we were partners in a common cause—meeting the needs of the farmers. And we were willing to make commitments to the dealers. We took steps to improve their profitability, to ensure them a measure of exclusivity within their territory and even to incent their sales reps."

By working with the dealers from the very beginning, Novartis CP established the groundwork for channel relationships based on trust and mutual need rather than suspicion and pure self-interest. This lesson is an important one to learn, because channel conflicts are guaranteed to surface when companies that traditionally sell their goods or services through distributors or dealers try to build bridges to the end users.

Tiers of value, clusters of need

After accumulating the names of 400 farmers, Novartis CP launched a survey to understand more about how the farmers viewed their own needs. The heart of the survey was a lengthy questionnaire prepared by ASK NV, a Belgian market research firm best known for its work in the agrochemicals industry. The questionnaire was designed to find out what the farmers actually wanted, what they valued, what factors they considered before making a purchase, and how they viewed themselves. Jan Martin Suter, a Novartis marketing executive who was familiar with ASK's approach, was confident that the farmers would sort themselves into easily definable clusters. These clusters would enable the unit to start building one-to-one relationships by treating different farmers differently.

After the questionnaires were completed and collected, they were shipped to Belgium for analysis. As they waited impatiently for the results, Suter and Cid realized they had to drastically pare down the questionnaire. It was simply too long and too complicated. "So we trimmed it down, from a hundred questions to about twenty," recalls Cid. "We needed to find the absolute fastest way of surveying the farmers and analyzing the data." By now they had collected the names of another two hundred farmers. They quickly dispatched teams armed with the newer, slimmed-down questionnaire to these farmers and once again relayed the results to Belgium.

Meanwhile, the team worked on ranking the farmers by value. Their analysis began with the classic 80–20 pyramid. In a marketplace of 100,000 farmers, roughly 20 percent of the farmers accounted for 80 percent of the unit's revenues. The good news was that, for the moment, there were 80,000 farmers that wouldn't require active customer management. It also meant that 20,000 farmers would have to be managed aggressively and intelligently if the program were to succeed.

This topmost slice of the pyramid was divided again, this time into four tiers of descending value. The formula they used to assign customer value was:

Yield per hectare × spending in dollars per hectare × total hectares under cultivation

A brief examination of the formula reveals a few of Novartis' assumptions about the relative importance of different farmers.

While the formula takes into consideration the size of the farm, it also considers the willingness of the farmer to spend money and the magnitude of his or her success. Moreover, in a strictly mathematical sense, the formula reduces to:

$$\text{Yield per hectare} \times \text{total spending in dollars}$$

If you think about this, what it means is that a farmer's total spending is important, but if two farmers spend the same amount of dollars on chemicals for their acreage, then the farmer with the richest yield per hectare will be given priority as a more valuable customer.

Because farms are fixed, long-term businesses, the variables in this equation—spending on chemicals and agricultural yield—do not vary significantly from year to year. Therefore, as the "proxy variables" in a customer valuation plan, they should be considered fairly reliable "circumstantial evidence" of a customer's real potential with Novartis. In the absence of more detailed data, this formula was a good beginning, and it was enough for Novartis. "With everything happening so quickly, we couldn't afford to waste time," says Weiss.

Even before the data had been fully analyzed, Weiss moved to begin identifying the most valuable farmers, the top 100 or so of the 100,000 total farm operators in the country, and to place them under the active management of a sales rep. Each sales rep was assigned just a few PEP farmers to manage (PEP being the acronym for Primero el Productor). These PEPs clearly represented the unit's Most Valuable Customers.

At the same time, the unit continued collecting data from company sales records, cooperating dealers, and a variety of government sources. The marketing team studied county maps showing the size of the farms, the number of hectares under cultivation, and the type of crops grown.

From this data the unit identified three more value tiers. There were 2,600 Top farmers, followed by 6,500 Important farmers and 10,800 Productores del Comercio, who would be managed indirectly. In this lowermost tier, local dealers would be responsible for handling face-to-face relationships, while the Novartis call center in Buenos Aires would be responsible for fielding technical and service-related questions, as well as reaching out with telemarketing campaigns.

A customer management strategy was outlined for each of the four tiers. The most hands-on approach was reserved for the PEPs, who were most likely to generate the most profitable relationships with the sales force. As an indication of just how personal they wanted the relationship to become, they nicknamed the PEP management strategy "belly-to-belly." Although the nickname is amusing, the decision to adopt a highly personal approach to the farmers was not made lightly. Sending a sales rep into the Pampas to visit a farmer, sit down with him, talk with him, get to know him, and develop a grasp of his problems would be both expensive and time-consuming. But Novartis believed the possible gains could justify the costs, provided that the sales calls were allocated to the right farmers. And they believed that developing intimate business relationships with their best customers would give them a strategic advantage, an edge that would be more difficult for their competitors to match with each passing day.

Weiss was acutely aware that the additional money spent on these "belly-to-belly" visits would have to be offset by savings gained from spending less on customers with less potential. And while he drew significant comfort from knowing there were 80,000 customers he didn't have to worry about at all, he also knew the sales force—as well as the functional departments supporting it—would need to be expanded and enhanced to cope with the task of actually managing 20,000 customers.

Value tier	PEP	Top farmers	Important farmers	Productores del Comercio
Number of customers in tier	104	2,600	6,500	10,800
Customer management strategy	"Belly-to-belly"; completely customized offer	Face-to-face; mass customized offer	Group meetings; mass customized offer	Indirect; through dealers and call center
Manageable customers per sales rep	4	100	250	0
Frequency of contact	10+ times annually	4 times annually	1, then hand off to call center	0
Interaction costs	High	Medium	Low	Minimal

Under the plan, each sales rep was responsible for setting up a schedule of regular contacts with the PEP farmers assigned to him. The next tier, the Top farmers, could expect face-to-face visits from their sales reps, but on a less frequent basis. More important, however, would be the difference in how the sales proposal or offer would be generated. In the case of the PEPs, Weiss expected the sales rep to conceive a unique, totally customized offer for each customer. Top and Important farmers would be offered mass customized solutions developed by Cid's marketing team. An early draft of the unit's customer relationship management plan provided a rough blueprint of the PEP strategy.

The unit's managers now felt confident that they had developed a workable methodology for differentiating customers by value. The "picket fence" was in place.

The next piece of the puzzle would be trying to figure out how to differentiate the farmers on the basis of their needs. For the top 10,000 or so farmers, those that were to receive some type of interaction with or contact by the sales reps, true relationship building would require Novartis to understand something about each farmer's needs. Keep in mind that Novartis sold more than thirty chemicals for hundreds of different crop configurations.

The first step in the process would be categorizing farmers into different clusters, based on some aspect of how they approached their business, or their worldview, or the type of technical issues they faced in operating their farms. Novartis offered thirty chemical products for sale for a variety of sometimes overlapping uses, so one aspect of treating different farmers differently was simply understanding each farmer's own particular crop situation. This would require the sales reps to develop a relatively high level of technical expertise. But keep in mind that chemicals are chemicals. They are commodity products, and simply understanding which chemicals to suggest to a farmer, even in a complex operating environment, might not be sufficient to win that farmer's allegiance.

Novartis also knew, however, that farmers approach their lives and their businesses in different ways. They are individual human beings, and they have different psychologies, different desires, and different preferences. So if Novartis sales reps could start with an understanding of each farmer's "hot buttons," based on that individual farmer's own psychology and worldview, they not only would be able to tailor the farmer's recommended crop protection solution but also would be able to pitch their case to the farmer in a way that would strike a more resonant chord. They could match not only their product combination but also their method of selling to the individual needs of the farmer they were selling to.

This would mean breaking the customers into understandable clusters of farmers with similar psychological needs. After months of work—what seemed an eternity to Suter and Cid—ASK finished its analysis of the farmer questionnaire data and it proposed a method for categorizing farmers in just this way. The data showed a clear pattern of needs differences, which could be broken into six basic categories. ASK developed an algorithm for assigning a farmer to one of these categories based on the farmer's questionnaire answers. Each category of farmer, or cluster, was characterized by a unique set of key personal needs and attitudes. To make it easier for the team to distinguish one cluster from another, they were color-coded.

Cluster	Key personal needs
Yellow	Craves leadership role, must be a winner. Needs to see ROI.
Turquoise	Needs a feeling of success, strives to win recognition from peers.
Green	Wants latest technology, wants to learn more, improve abilities. Concerned about the environment.
Purple	Demands high-quality service, puts a premium on satisfaction, but enjoys a challenge.
Gray	Needs to feel secure, wants to belong and to be sociable.
Blue	Wants technical help and support, but is very loyal to current dealer.

The plan called for each sales rep to be equipped with a lap-top loaded with the questionnaire and the algorithm. When a sales rep visited a farmer, the first order of business would be completing the questionnaire. The algorithm would place the farmer into one of the six clusters and the color corresponding to that cluster would pop up on the sale rep's screen.

With this insight, the sales rep could propose an agrochem-ical solution for the farmer that had been developed in concert with Novartis' R&D department, and the rep could "pitch" that solution in a manner designed to match the farmer's own individual needs, based on the cluster he belonged to. The so-lutions themselves were mass customized by creating standard-ized combinations of the unit's thirty available products. Delivery options, financial incentives, and ancillary products such as crop insurance could also be included in the offer, but these additional options could be configured in such a way as to appeal to the particular type of farmer being sold to.

Having the questionnaire and the algorithm loaded on the laptop of each sales rep was considered critical to the plan's on-going success. Using these tools would enable the sales rep to plant the seed of a one-to-one relationship into every selling situation.

The clusters, with their mass customizable solutions, would enable the sales rep to respond meaningfully to what the farmer had told him, closing the loop on the first stage of the Learning Relationship between the company and the customer.

What is key here is that Novartis CP was developing an ability to automate its sales and marketing efforts, making it possible to deliver products and services in a more individualized fashion than ever before.

A stronger sales force

No sooner was the plan off the drawing board than one truth became glaringly apparent: The existing sales force was not prepared to perform its new mission. The list of problems was daunting:

- A twelve-person sales force simply was too small to cover the countryside effectively. New hires would be needed. To cover the regular contacts with top customers planned in the table on page 205, the sales force would have to be roughly twice its current size.

- The sales staff didn't have the technical training necessary to interact with the farmers on a level high enough to establish trust and inspire confidence. The existing sales training programs were limited in scope and not designed to provide the reps with the specific technical knowledge they would require.
- There was no formal system in place to manage the information required to develop Learning Relationships with the farmers.
- The existing compensation plan had been designed for a traditional sales environment, not a one-to-one environment. There were no specific incentives or rewards for customer-focused behavior.

Clearly the sales force didn't have the breadth or depth to fulfill the new responsibilities envisioned by Weiss and his management team. The first order of business was increasing the size of the sales force. "When we counted up how many farmers we needed, we realized we could never make the program work with only twelve sales reps," says Weiss. "So we began by doubling the size of the sales force. We felt that was the only way we could get the right amount of coverage."

Juan Nava, the unit's sales manager, and Cecilia Rodriguez, the unit's human resources manager, were concerned with ensuring not only the right *amount* of coverage but also the right *kind* of coverage. They decided to forgo the traditional method of hiring people on the basis of their previous sales experience, choosing instead to focus on people with a mix of technical and social skills likely to be appreciated by their customers. In the past, the sales reps had been culled from the ranks of Argentina's educated city dwellers. Under the traditional sales system, this type of hiring had made sense—after all, the reps worked mostly in Buenos Aires and rarely had face-to-face dealings with the farmers. They weren't expected to possess superior agricultural knowledge. They were, however, expected to possess the negotiating skills necessary to establish solid working relationships with the dealers. As long as the dealers controlled the relationships with the end users, the best a sales rep could hope for was to negotiate the best possible contract with the dealer. This fact of life was something the management at Novartis CP wanted to change as quickly as possible.

So the sales force would need to undergo not only a change in size but a change in culture as well. The new sales reps would need a new set of attitudes, behaviors, and skills to accomplish the goals set by management. The sales team would have to abandon its present role and adopt a more aggressive, proactive approach. Above all, a sense of urgency was needed.

Under the new system, the reps would spend most of their time on the road, traveling through various rural areas to forge relationships with the farmers. Their goal would not be to circumvent the dealer, but simply to figure out the best way to turn the farmers into more profitable customers. If the reps did their job properly, Primero el Productor would reap benefits for both the manufacturer and its channel partners.

The new sales reps were called Delegados Técnicos Comerciales, or DTCs. The idea for changing the job title was inspired by Sergio Lazen, who had worked with Weiss in Chile. Lazen believed it was important for the farmers to know that the DTC was neither purely a salesperson nor purely a technician, but an amalgam of both. Lazen was careful, however, to make sure that the adjective "técnico" preceded the adjective "comercial" when the title was formalized. "It's a small distinction, but an important one," Weiss notes. "Going forward, a key driver in the relationship will be the sales rep's technical skill. That will make it possible to sell the kind of multicrop, multiproduct programs we'll need in order to increase the amount of business we do with each of our selected farmers."

Unlike the previous generations of sales reps, the DTCs would more likely be culled from local agricultural colleges rather than from big-city universities. They would be people who felt comfortable riding long miles through the countryside to meet with the farmers and, perhaps even more important, people the farmers would learn to respect and trust. Because the DTCs would function more or less autonomously in the field, they would need a much higher level of technical fluency than their predecessors.

"This is a tremendously complicated selling situation," explains Cid. "We offer thirty different agrochemical products. Each farmer grows three or four different crops. Each crop requires four or five different products. The average single farmer buys twelve to fifteen different products from us. That's a lot to keep track of. At a minimum, the DTC has to know as much about crops and chemicals as the farmer. To really succeed, the DTC has to know *more* than the farmer."

To achieve and maintain this critical level of technical fluency, the unit worked feverishly to develop a training program. "This is where we really made a huge effort," says Cid. "We wanted the farmer to consider the DTC as a valuable resource, a trusted expert who can deliver reliable information on a timely basis. Without continual training, the DTC can't keep up to date on all the new technology. So we train, train, train. It's like a mantra."

Planned and organized by Rodríguez, training primarily takes place during a series of three-day sessions held eight times annually in Buenos Aires. Outside experts are brought in to discuss the latest developments in biotechnology. Leading specialists brief the DTCs on the current state of each major crop. "We invite the gurus, the best brains in agriculture and technology, to speak about specific problems facing particular crops," says Nava.

The training sessions also include structured internal dialogues to keep everyone on the team abreast of everyone else's progress. Members of the R&D team discuss the advantages and disadvantages of products sold by various competitors. The marketing team presents an overview of its current strategy, along with progress reports and projections for upcoming periods. All seventy members of the unit participate in discussions designed to familiarize them with the ongoing one-to-one initiatives. Current methodology is reviewed and discussed, along with ideas for improving the Primero el Productor program or streamlining the processes required to keep it going. The unit's management team also holds smaller meetings every Monday to share feedback, discuss problems, and monitor progress. "The major difference between the old sales force and the new one is this fierce concentration on formal training," says Nava.

Cid agrees. "As we evolve toward knowledge-based selling, we need to develop a sales force that can partner with customers to solve their problems. And you can't solve someone's problems unless you know them, understand their needs, and fully comprehend the technology required to address their needs."

Load a sales rep's mind with sufficient technical knowledge and he can begin functioning like a technical advisor, says Nava. "The idea is for the farmer to see his sales rep as an encyclopedia of knowledge, someone ready to answer his most difficult questions and solve his most intractable problems.

Show me the money

Devising a compensation plan that provides clear, consistent rewards for customer-focused behavior is one of the most difficult challenges facing any organization that wants to become a one-to-one enterprise. Each functional area of the enterprise will present its own unique obstacles to change. Few employees will welcome any change that puts their present pay package at risk, despite the prospect of future gain. And any CFO worth his or her salt will want to know *precisely* how each and every proposed change in compensation will be funded before signing off on a new plan. Where will the money come from?

Anticipating these hurdles, Weiss went ahead with a hybrid pay plan that recognized the primacy of revenue while simultaneously providing incentives for reps who achieved the goals of Primero el Productor. "It's quite complex," Cid concedes. Roughly 80 percent of a DTC's annual compensation is fixed salary. The remaining 20 percent is paid in the form of a performance bonus. This bonus depends not only on the DTC's total sales revenue but also on his ability to sell new products and higher-margin products. Additionally, the DTC must personally meet with the PEP, Top, and Important farmers assigned to him. Last but not least, the DTC must make certain that the goods and services delivered are actually paid for. All of these factors, plus a regional goal devised to create a spirit of competition among the unit's five sales regions, play a role in the DTC's bonus equation.

So far, the bonus program seems to be having its intended effect, says Nava. "The DTCs are very conscious of their bonus potential and pay close attention to how well they're performing relative to their goals. It's a big deal for them to get the bonus and they're very careful about following the guidelines."

Cid would like to be able to reward the DTCs for growing share of customer, but knows that aspect of the comp plan will have to wait until more data has been compiled. "The problem is, we have no records from the past. So we don't really know which customers we are retaining or growing. Next year, we'll have enough data to know and to make comparisons."

Cid's comments underscore a critical point: A long-term customer relationship strategy requires huge amounts of patience and stamina. Planning, implementing, and managing a one-to-one strategy isn't something you do overnight. It's a gradual process, with ups and downs, good days and bad.

Weiss and his team harbor no illusions about the pay plan. At best, it's a work in progress. They are considering modifications to the plan that would allow them to reward non-sales employees for contributing to the success of Primero el Productor. For example, if someone working in R&D suggests a solution to a sales rep that results in a markedly larger or more profitable sale, that technical person should be compensated for his or her contribution. The problem is devising a comp plan that doesn't rob Peter to pay Paul. Unquestionably, Primero el Productor has demonstrated how difficult it is to create a plan that is logical, fair, and relatively uncomplicated. What seems evident is that the pace of change can't move much faster than the pace of revenue growth or you'll simply run out of cash.

Managing information

Under enormous pressure to show results quickly, the management team decided to delay the purchase of an automated data management system for the sales force. This decision had an upside and a downside. The upside was that it gave them more time to research the available choices and arrive at a prudent, well-reasoned decision that would satisfy regional management in São Paulo. The downside was that the current system involved collecting customer data and storing it in a cumbersome, inadequate database that effectively stripped most of the value from the data.

The upside won, mostly because the management team shared a gut feeling that hunting around for the perfect data management tool, installing it, and training everyone to use it properly would simply prove too much of a distraction during the initial—and most difficult—months of their one-to-one project.

Eventually, they chose Pivotal eRelationship Intrahub, a relatively new product designed for midsize operations without the resources or the need to purchase an end-to-end CRM system. Pivotal was also deemed a good, defensible choice since other Novartis units around the world already were using Pivotal products and were satisfied with them. Additionally, the system could be configured to allow selected dealers and customers to use their Web browsers to view information stored in the database. While this feature was not a primary factor in the team's choice of vendors, gaining the potential to build relationships over the Internet was considered a significant advantage.

For the time being, however, the team was more than happy to use the Pivotal system simply to begin creating a more effective web of communications within the unit. The job of making sure that everyone was properly trained to use the Pivotal system fell to Juan Cassagne, who led the unit's newly formed Area de Relacionamiento con el Cliente, or ARC. The name means "client relationship center" and it was intended to be exactly that—a sort of virtual focal point for all the unit's efforts to integrate the various functions of its several departments around the farmers.

As chief of ARC, Cassagne was officially responsible for managing the unit's database, call center, and marketing com-

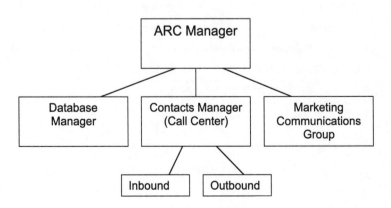

munications group. Partly because of his previous experience as a direct marketer and partly because ARC had quickly evolved into the unit's information nexus, Cassagne also was tapped for the unofficial role of cultural change agent.

"It's a hard job. For example, I'm not in charge of implementing the database. But I *am* in charge of making sure the sales reps understand how to use the system and understand why it's valuable to them, why it's essential to our one-to-one effort here," explains Cassagne. "So I have to change the culture of the sales force. I have to meet with each of them, stay with them for a while, and teach them to use the system so they can see its benefits. Sometimes I even go on sales calls with them. Ultimately, the idea is to get the reps to champion the system. Then they will be able to teach others and expand the experience."

So part of Cassagne's role is to function as an internal salesman for the idea of relationship-based selling. From his perch in the organization, he clearly understands the need for consistency of effort across the unit. "When one of our reps goes out to visit a farmer, he's trying to understand the totality of that farmer's business and all the problems that farmer will face in the coming year. Then the rep can offer a comprehensive solution that's tailored to answer the farmer's needs. And the pricing for this solution will be based on yield—after all, that's what the farmer is concerned about."

Creating a knowledge bridge

Basing the price on the success of next year's crop raises an interesting question: Isn't it risky to tie the cost of a customized solution to an expected outcome, in this case the farmer's yield? Unquestionably the answer is yes. On the other hand, the Novartis team saw a unique opportunity to create something deeper than a buyer-seller relationship with the farmers by sharing some of their risk. The team also knew that managing this type of relationship—and profiting from it—would depend on the unit's ability to marshal as much knowledge and skill as possible to assure that the customized solutions offered to the farmers would produce results in the field.

To achieve this, Novartis CP created yet another department, one that would serve as a sort of "knowledge bridge" between R&D, marketing, and sales. The department became responsible for:

- Reaching out to the scientific community to establish relationships with agrochemical experts.
- Acting as a liaison between R&D and marketing to develop individually customized and mass customized solutions for customers. These solutions would include not only agrochemical products but technical support as well.
- Serving as the in-house technical support team for the sales and marketing staffs.

The overarching goal of the new department, however, would be to ensure the ongoing credibility of the sales force. Without credibility, it would be impossible for the sales reps to build trusting relationships with the farmers. "Each area of the country has its own distinct ecology," says Cassagne. "You go a hundred miles to the north, the farmers face a very different set of problems than the farmers a hundred miles to the south. And agricultural products that work one way in the northern climates don't necessarily work the same way in the southern climates. There are no 'by the book' answers. If the sales rep is going to help the farmer, he's got to be very knowledgeable."

Nava, the sales manager, offered this perspective on the power of knowledge: "It puts us in a stronger position when we talk to the dealers. First, the DTC now has scientific knowledge at his fingertips. Second, the DTC has a relationship with the farmer, so he's getting his information straight from the source, not secondhand. He doesn't need the dealer to explain the farmer's problems because the farmer has already told him."

Seen from these various angles, the decision to formalize the role of a "knowledge bridge" seemed reasonable and necessary. "What we're really doing is knowledge-based selling," says Cid. "You have to know what you're talking about. In the future, selling knowledge will be more important than selling products. So we've got to *get* smarter and *stay* smarter."

This raises another interesting question: Is a company that sells knowledge *smarter* than a company that sells containers of crop protection products? Theoretically, it shouldn't make any difference. But on an intuitive level, we know that it does. Organizations that value knowledge and understand its intrinsic worth in the marketplace tend to evolve very differently from organizations that focus solely on tangible products. A knowledge-based organization is likely to develop an internal culture that shares information, encourages new ideas, and rewards innovation. In today's super-fast competitive environment, these characteristics are absolutely essential. On the other hand, organizations that dismiss the notion of intellectual capital or discourage the evolution of a culture based on knowledge are likely to find themselves at a severe disadvantage.

Cultural differences aside, an organization that adds knowledge to its product line will find that it is much, much easier to mass customize information than it is to mass customize tangible products. We almost always advise companies looking to mass customize some aspect of their goods or services to begin by mass customizing something intangible, such as a Web-based billing service or an email newsletter.

Bumps along the road

None of Novartis' managers expected the program to unfold without a hitch. Almost as soon as the clusters were unveiled, it became apparent that two of them should be eliminated, because farmers who fell into those clusters were unlikely to respond positively to any form of active customer management by the company. There was little to be gained by pursuing farmers who had indicated strong feelings of loyalty toward their local dealers, for instance. In those cases, the original relationships would continue undisturbed, except for occasional outbound telemarketing or direct mail campaigns.

Another challenge that required attention was the lack of "critical mass" in the customer database. Although the Sisyphean task of populating the database had been anticipated, it remained daunting—and time-consuming. "We are working hard and it's getting better every day," Cassagne says wearily. "Right now, we can identify lots of customers, but we can't differentiate all of them. So when a prospect calls us, we can't immediately tell if it's worth sending a rep out to talk to him. Knowing if he's a hot prospect or a cold prospect is extremely important to us because it's very expensive to make a sales visit. So we need to be very sure before we commit a rep to a sales call. And we're not there yet. In four to six months, we'll have the best database in the country, but we're still working on it."

In the meantime, Cassagne is making the best of his direct mail campaigns and passing most of the leads along to the dealers for follow-up visits. It's a transitional strategy, which is entirely appropriate for such a transitional time in the unit's history. In a similar vein, Novartis CP launched a card-based loyalty program called Agrolider, which enables the farmers to accumulate points when they purchase Novartis products from the dealers. The points can be exchanged later for rewards. It's a tried-and-true approach, a good starting point for enriching the database. If it also builds loyalty in the short term, so much the better.

Of all the obstacles facing the unit, the greatest was one that remained out of anyone's direct control. Because of unexpectedly low prices for agricultural produce, many of the farmers simply did not have the cash to pay the dealers what they owed. So the first order of business was collecting as much of this debt as possible. This, unfortunately, meant the DTC had to perform double duty as a bill collector, a role that was not likely to endear him to his future customers. Aware that this unwelcome duty imposes a severe burden on the sales force, Cassagne says the unit is hiring additional people to provide administrative support for the DTCs. The problem of debt collection remains a front-burner issue, however, because the dealers need a steady flow of cash to stay afloat. If they go under, the unit loses its distribution system. "Many of these products can't be delivered by mail," explains Cid. "One role of the dealer is to help us deliver our products to the farmer."

Impressive gains

Happily, the results of Primero el Productor were better than any of the managers at Novartis CP could have imagined. Three months into its one-to-one program, the unit had registered impressive gains despite a rapidly shrinking market. The unit's best customers had been identified, surveyed, ranked by value, sorted by needs, and assigned varying degrees of hands-on account management. Customers of lesser potential value had been delegated to existing distribution channels. Customers of little value weren't cut off—they just weren't allocated any direct resources, which allowed the unit's sales force to concentrate on the most valuable and most growable customers.

In the program's first six months, average share of customer increased from 20 percent to 70 percent among the PEPs. The combination of declining market and higher revenues hoisted the unit's market share by 20 percent. As this is being written, the crop protection market in Argentina continues to shrink, while this Novartis unit's revenues continue to grow.

One last note before leaving Argentina: A few weeks after launching Primero el Productor, the unit's human resources group decided that something unique and memorable was needed to symbolize the ongoing effort. So they set up a bell in the hallway. The idea was that someone would ring the bell every time a DTC contacted one of the PEP farmers on his list. When days went by without a sound, the team began to wonder if the bell had been such a good idea after all. Then someone rang the bell. A few hours later, another ring. Now hardly a day passes without the bell ringing. As of this writing, the DTCs have already surpassed their initial goal of signing up 104 PEP farmers. Cid now estimates the DTCs will sign up 130 PEPs before the program is fully one year old. "Let me tell you, it's a good feeling to hear that bell ringing. It's music to my ears."

Tasks ahead for Novartis CP

Faced with the sudden decline of its market, Novartis CP realized that its best chance for survival lay in unlocking the hidden value of its end-user customers, the farmers who used its agrochemicals. Embarking on a crash campaign to identify and focus on the highest-value farmers, Novartis CP had to change its internal culture and redirect its energies from selling products to managing relationships. The fact that Novartis CP was able to succeed on both fronts, external and internal, is a testament not only to the flexibility and resourcefulness of its people but also to the utility and value of a well-executed one-to-one relationship strategy.

However, the crop protection unit (now part of Syngenta) should consolidate the gains it has made during the initial phases of its Primero el Productor program. The firm needs to emphasize (a) getting better leverage from the information it now has on the top producers and (b) streamlining its customer-facing operations so as to make it possible to expand the breadth and depth of the entire relationship-building process.

Perhaps the greatest asset the crop protection brings to the table is its potential to help the farmers manage their own businesses more effectively and more profitably, and this is a very valuable asset. In the months ahead, the unit should develop this potential. Imagine if the unit could provide a tool that would make it easier for individual farmers to manage their inventories of crop protection chemicals, fertilizers, soil treatments, seeds, bags, twine—anything and everything required to manage a farm. The unit could develop a Web-based system such as Premier Dell.com, or it could do something far simpler, such as providing each farmer with a special notebook to record the use of materials and then offering to review the notebook at regular intervals. The team could also offer a program of automatic replenishment to guarantee that a farmer never runs short of vital supplies. Some things the unit should do:

- Develop a more robust customer information system, with a richer and more useful needs-based segmentation of customers.
- Refine the customer valuation criteria in order to prioritize the total financial resources to be allocated to different customer tiers.
- Introduce a greater degree of automation at as many touch points as possible, to ensure that customer data is being captured and stored systematically.

- Move as many of its customer interactions to the Web as possible. As the telecom network in Argentina becomes stronger and more dependable, strategies for Web-based interactivity will become more practical. In the meantime, Novartis might consider providing PCs, low-cost PDAs, or perhaps Internet access for its PEP farmers.

- Create and implement a strategy designed to treat different distributors differently, in the same way the PEP program treats different farmers differently.

- Develop a formal system for rewarding sales force behaviors that lead to customer growth and retention, not just new sales.

- Consider a system of customer portfolio management, as opposed to territory management. Novartis should have a customer relationship manager for each of the psychological clusters it plans to address in its sales and marketing effort, and these customer relationship managers should be setting individual objectives and strategies for "their" customers, to guide the field sales people.

- Implement a system to identify inbound callers in real time, then develop the right set of interactions to differentiate customers when they call in.

- Introduce value-added programs and services for farmers, such as risk management, inventory management, or automatic replenishment of chemicals and other supplies.

- Pursue alliances with trade and industry associations to generate "expert advice," perhaps in the form of a monthly newsletter that could be sent to customers either electronically (for free) or via traditional mail (for a nominal charge).

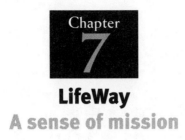

LifeWay
A sense of mission

Top line summary

Every revolution begins with a vision. Turning that vision into reality is the hard part. Compare the American Revolution and the French Revolution. Both began with visions of an egalitarian society based on natural laws. The American Revolution was followed by an unprecedented era of growth and prosperity. The French Revolution was followed by the Reign of Terror and Napoleon Bonaparte.

Turning a product-focused company into a customer-focused enterprise is indeed akin to staging a revolution. The "vision thing" is important, yes, but the real test is implementation.

When top executives at LifeWay Christian Resources decided on "customer intimacy" as a strategic goal for their firm, they left it to the division managers to sort out the details. Anyone who has ever been tasked with putting together a customer-centric initiative can testify to the difference between "talking the talk" and "walking the walk."

How would LifeWay's managers leap this chasm between vision and reality? The goal was set, but for more than a year limited progress was made toward it. Then some LifeWay managers and employees began reading our books and quickly realized that they could construct a workable CRM implementation program for LifeWay simply by applying the I.D.I.C. methodology— Identify, Differentiate, Interact, and Customize.

What follows is the story of a company that consciously sought to adopt a customer-focused strategy, learned a practical implementation methodology simply by reading about it in our previous books, and made remarkable strides before they even contacted our consulting firm. We were, of course, delighted to get their call, and the fact that their managers had all read the material and were comfortable with our terms, methodology, and general business objectives made everyone's job much easier.

At the end of the day, however, the credit for transforming LifeWay goes to LifeWay. No organization, no matter how well-equipped or well-intentioned, can refocus its business operations without a huge expenditure of time and energy. Blood, sweat, and tears are the basic ingredients of any revolution, and LifeWay's was no different in that respect from the others described in this book.

The first four case studies in this book describe B2B organizations that have made significant strides toward becoming a one-to-one enterprise. This next case study profiles a one-to-one initiative that is still very much a work in progress. We thought it would be useful to examine an organization that is taking the primary steps of a long and possibly difficult journey.

Everything about LifeWay Christian Resources qualifies it as the "business unusual" case study in this book. What can Fortune 1000 companies as well as dot-com start-ups learn about B2B from a hundred-year-old Christian organization in Nashville that sells Sunday School materials and other religious products to churches? Before you say, "Not much," read this chapter. You will be intrigued, as we were, when we looked into LifeWay's transformation.

In many respects, the challenges facing LifeWay Christian Resources are similar to the challenges that Bentley Systems and Convergys met and eventually overcame. In the case of Bentley, high market penetration and good earnings made it difficult to mount a successful argument internally for change. In the case of Convergys, the absence of objective data supporting a customer-centric approach to sales and marketing was a major obstacle to change.

What sets LifeWay apart from the previous case studies is a very high level of genuine support for customer-centric strategies at the senior management level, the use of employee teams to accelerate learning, and the speed at which changes are being made.

New vision, ancient principles

In 1991, a new management team led by LifeWay's corporate president, Jimmy Draper, was brought in to refocus a business that had become inefficient and resistant to change. When the new team stepped in, LifeWay had a total revenue of $202 million and a net income of $1.9 million. Over the next few years, the new team succeeded in enhancing the company's products, repositioning its chain of more than 90 retail stores, upgrading its internal systems, and streamlining its business processes. By the end of fiscal 1999–2000, total revenue exceeded $372 million and net income exceeded $12 million.

Yet in 1998, as the decade neared its close and the new millennium loomed, top management at LifeWay began questioning whether improvements like these would be enough. Rather than resting on their accomplishments, they began crafting a new vision statement that would require LifeWay to judge its success by more than improved financials; it would focus on how well it was helping its customers meet their needs and succeed in their ministries. The new vision statement, drafted in spiritual language, affirmed the new outward focus:

As God works through us, we will help people and churches know Jesus Christ and seek His Kingdom by providing biblical solutions that spiritually transform individuals and cultures.

Granted, it's not the kind of vision statement many of us are used to reading. But everyone at LifeWay knew what it meant, and that's what counted. In addition to the new vision statement, the Executive Management Group articulated five core values and corresponding operating principles that would guide the organization for the future. LifeWay's *Vision, Values, and Operating Principles* were printed in a booklet, dubbed "the white book," and given to all employees. It became the "constitution for behavior" for LifeWay in the future.

Core Value 3 in "the white book" focused on LifeWay's customers and laid the foundation for the one-to-one initiative that would emerge a year later. The Customer Core Value stated:

Our customers are our reason for existence. Knowing our customers, not just knowing about them, and meeting their expressed, unexpressed, and unknown needs is essential to achieving our vision.

So in everything, do unto others what you would have them do unto you . . . (Matthew 7:12)

The booklet then listed the Operating Principles that would support the Customer Core Value:

- We will treat our customers with sensitivity and kindness.
- We will maintain a personal involvement with our customers to gain insight into their needs and expectations.
- We will share customer information throughout the organization.
- We will make it easy for customers to do business with us by aligning our business processes to meet our customers' needs.
- We recognize that our customers ultimately determine the value of our products and services.
- We will seek to solve customer problems on every occasion.

During this period of strategic thinking about the future, chief operating officer Ted Warren led LifeWay's management group to consider three corporate value disciplines—product excellence, operational efficiency, and customer intimacy. He then challenged the organization to choose one discipline to which LifeWay would commit itself. After careful consideration and discussion, the Executive Management Group fixed its sights on customer intimacy.

Ted Warren explained the importance of this decision. "We knew that producing excellent products would always be important to us as an organization and we were committed to continually improving our products. We also believed that operating efficiently by understanding our business processes was essential. Yet none of this would matter," Warren said, "unless we focused on meeting the needs of our customers and helped them succeed in their mission."

The management team assumed that in the years to come every good company would have superior products, and every good company would operate efficiently. "But ultimately, the focus on customers," Warren said, "would separate the great companies from the good ones. We didn't just want to be a good company."

As a result of the work of the Executive Management Group, the mission, the vision, the values, and the operating principles were in place and created the conceptual wellspring from which the one-to-one initiatives that are now reshaping the company's future would flow. Yet the new focus on customers was, in many ways, a return to the company's historical roots.

Created for its customers

Headquartered in Nashville, LifeWay was launched in 1891 as
the Sunday School Board of the Southern Baptist Convention.
Initially, the board's chief objective was making sure that Baptist churches in the South had a reliable supply of books and
learning materials for their Sunday School programs. Prior to
the creation of the Sunday School Board, Southern churches
relied on literature published and distributed by the American
Baptist Publication Society of Philadelphia. While the differences between Southern Baptists and their Northern cousins
might not seem very great to a casual outside observer, those
differences were very real when viewed from within. So it was
no small thing that the churches of the Southern Baptist Convention had to buy their books from an organization based in
Pennsylvania. In spite of the needs of the churches, some leaders in the early convention were cautious about establishing a
new organization. After much deliberation, the convention
granted approval for the organization's formation, with an important stipulation—the new enterprise would not receive donations from the churches or from the Southern Baptist
Convention. Instead, the Baptist Sunday School Board would
generate its operating funds through the sale of products to the
churches. With that directive, the first Executive Secretary,
J. M. Frost, borrowed $5,000 from his wife's family estate and
began the new work, laying a solid foundation for a robust
ministry funded by a strong business.

The Sunday School Board, which became LifeWay Christian Resources in 1998, has grown steadily. Now with over
$400 million in revenues, it sells thousands of religious items

ranging from CD-ROMs to church steeples. LifeWay's customer base includes more than 38,000 Southern Baptist congregations and over 18,000 churches of other denominations.

The historical fact that LifeWay was created at the end of the nineteenth century as a direct response to the unmet needs of a specific group of customers—the churches of the Southern Baptist Convention—foreshadowed LifeWay's decision at the end of the twentieth century to implement a customer-centric ministry and business strategy.

Acting on the vision for the churches

While all of LifeWay's divisions implemented initiatives in response to the corporate commitment to focus on customers, one division, LifeWay Church Resources, led the way in incorporating the principles of one-to-one strategy.

Despite LifeWay Church Resources' success in the marketplace, there was a growing feeling among division management that the organization was neither achieving its full spiritual missions nor attaining its commercial potential. Division president Gene Mims grew impatient with the pace of change and the inertia of "business as usual." Over a period of months, he began pushing the division management team to move beyond the rhetoric of "customer intimacy" and instead change the company. Through what his management team jokingly referred to as "big thoughts from a gentle leader," Mims began wielding his forceful leadership style to focus on the future.

Initially, he articulated his views in the executive summary of the division's 1998 strategic plan. "We are fast approaching the day," Mims wrote, "when product excellence alone will no longer be enough to meet the needs of our customers." The statement was a lightning bolt aimed at the heart of the organization. The division prided itself on the success of products such as *Experiencing God,* a book by Henry T. Blackaby which has sold over 3.5 million copies and been translated into more than fifty languages. The division also produces a small group Bible study curriculum that is used by millions of people throughout the United States and in more than twenty foreign countries. And the division won plaudits for other initiatives such as *True Love Waits,* by Mark Devries, an abstinence program for teenagers which has been used worldwide. Later Mims explained, "I knew we needed to communicate to the organization that things were about to change. The ship was leaving the dock and dragging the dock behind us. We were not going back." For the future, Mims declared that LifeWay Church Resources would henceforth devote itself to meeting the needs of its customers—the churches.

At the same time, Mims began articulating a new value proposition aligned with a customer-centric strategy. "Our success as an organization is linked to the fortunes of the churches. If we help the churches do better in their ministry, they will take care of us," he told his management team. The irony of the statement was that during the 1990s LifeWay Church Resources had actually been doing better than its customers. While the division's revenues had grown steadily to over $160 million, the ministry impact of the churches in the aggregate had lagged. This imbalance, according to Mims, was inappropriate and was unacceptable for the future.

The things Mims was saying rang true with his management

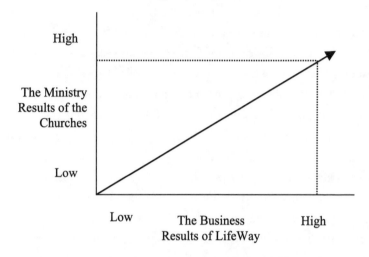

Linking LifeWay to the Churches

team, many of whom were former pastors and all of whom were actively involved in churches in the Nashville area. "Although LifeWay faces the same pressures as any other business, ultimately we exist not to make the most money possible, but to help the churches who are our customers achieve their goals," says John Kramp, director of operations for LifeWay Church Resources. "So we began asking ourselves, 'Are the churches who buy our products reaching more people? Are they having a greater spiritual influence on the people in their communities? Do the families who attend the churches stay together longer? Are the children of these families doing well in school; are they staying off drugs?' Are people's lives being transformed to the point where they are having a positive impact on their communities? We had to answer 'no' or at least 'not enough.' So we knew something had to change."

The division managers knew it would be difficult to create a

practical strategy that took into account hard business goals
and less tangible ministry goals. The tension between business
and ministry had always existed at LifeWay. In recent years, division leaders had measured the success of their spiritual mission by the level of product sales to the churches. That simple
equation was no longer adequate, which meant Kramp and his
colleagues would have to devise a new one. Despite a reasonable degree of trepidation, the management team was confident that it could design a strategy and implement a plan that
would make it possible for the entire organization to shift from
a product focus to a customer focus. "Since many of us now in
business roles at LifeWay have been pastors and church leaders
in the past, we know about living in the shoes of our customers," says Kramp. "We can easily remember being LifeWay
customers ourselves and understand many of the needs of our
customers."

While the management team affirmed the need for a change,
the tone of Gene Mims's interaction with his division management team became increasingly forceful. One day, he walked
into the conference room where the team was seated. In his
hand was a silver metal lunchbox with the name MIMS written
in bold black marker on the front. The lunchbox had belonged
to his father, who had worked for years in the field on gas
pipelines. "Every morning, my dad picked up this lunchbox,"
Mims said as he banged it down hard on the wooden conference table. "That was the signal from my dad that it was time
to get to work. And that's what we're going to do—get to
work." So the metal lunchbox became a regular fixture at the
meetings. The time for "happy talk" about customers and customer intimacy was over. It was time to get to work. The divi-

sion managers didn't know all that Mims had in mind—and what would unfold over the next months.

Transforming the organization

Bridging the gap between good intentions and measurable results would require a series of organizational changes. Barriers between operating and publishing groups within the division would have to fall, or at least be rendered more permeable to the flow of information. Interdepartmental communication would have to be encouraged and facilitated, so knowledge and learning could be shared rapidly. The best way to achieve these goals was to establish weekly sessions at which top managers from various departments could gather to hammer away at the issues. These daylong "Monday Meetings," as they were called, would become the heart of the strategy development process that Mims led.

Division managers and employees were assigned to teams to speed the process along. Kramp led the Customer Team, whose job was to learn more about LifeWay's customers and their needs. Mike Miller led the Message and Models Team, whose job was to develop a ministry framework and process for helping churches solve problems. The Organizational Options Team was led by David Francis. The team's role was to develop a new organizational structure to support LifeWay's customer-focused strategy. Gary Rhoades would lead the Implementation Team, which would guide the organization's transition to the new organizational structure. Gary Hauk was tapped to lead the Communications Team, whose task was generating and managing internal communications throughout the LifeWay organization to ensure that all employees understood the new customer-centric strategy.

Each week, the teams worked separately on their various assignments while continuing the ongoing responsibilities of their "day jobs." Then on Mondays, each team would present their findings. "The hardest thing about the Monday Meetings was that we were always presenting 120 percent of what we knew," Kramp says with a smile. "So most presentations began with a retraction of at least part of what we had presented the previous Monday." Transforming the LifeWay organization became a consuming task for the managers and employees involved in the teams and the presentations. Together, they generated and shared an immense amount of learning, about their customers, their organization, and themselves. Many commented that they had never learned so much and yet felt so stupid at the same time. The platform for learning was set and the pace of focusing on the customer accelerated.

When in doubt, start with your customers

The Customer Team, led by John Kramp, Steve Blount, Tom Carringer, Earl Nobles, and Judy Kizer, jump-started the accelerated learning process by assessing information about Life-Way's church customers. What they learned was invaluable in defining reality for the present and future.

In our chapter on Convergys, we demonstrated how in some business situations it is not only possible but also practical and desirable to move forward aggressively with a strategic initiative even when there isn't enough objective data to justify such a move. If you've read this far, you know that we're not talking about acting on "gut feelings" or "raw instinct." We're talking about constructing a formal methodology for using the subjective data you already possess to rank your customers according to their long-term worth and to prioritize the allocation of your resources so that different customers can be treated differently.

One of the underlying lessons of the Convergys case study is the importance of getting comfortable with a high level of ambiguity, uncertainty, and subjectivity. When properly organized, "soft" data can provide powerful insight for a one-to-one B2B. The critical factor, however, is organization. Without a formal system for collecting, analyzing, and utilizing the data, there will be no sure way to distinguish between reality and fantasy. So while it may sound strange, in order to make rational progress you must devise a system to objectively assess and evaluate the subjective variables you already have.

The Customer Team at LifeWay began by taking inventory of the information it already had on hand. Fortunately, LifeWay had over fifty years of data that offered the team a window of insight into its customers. Each year, the majority of churches in the Southern Baptist denomination file a voluntary disclosure statement called the Annual Church Profile. The statements include highly detailed information on attendance, donations, expenses, Sunday School enrollment, conversions, baptisms, and other metrics used by the churches to measure how well they are doing.

In addition to the annual statements, Kramp and his colleagues accessed exhaustive sales and other transactional data for the division, as well as from other business units at LifeWay, such as LifeWay's chain of more than 90 retail stores and its extensive B2C and B2B online stores. All that information, combined with third-party demographic data, became building blocks for what the Customer Team was learning. For three months in early 2000, the team pored over the data. Their analysis was presented in LifeWay's Customer Project Phase One Report, a 100-page document that would become a rough blueprint for its long-term one-to-one initiative. The presentation to the division managers in a marathon Monday Meeting enabled the leaders to take a quantum leap forward in their collective understanding of the challenges facing the churches and the need for LifeWay to radically change its strategy.

Ironically, the document begins with a well-reasoned and very candid argument for maintaining the status quo. The debate is framed by the question: "What are the benefits of treating all customers the same?" A series of answers follows. The first two are especially revealing:

- Without any doubt it is easier to treat all customers in the same way than to go through the demanding rigor of developing and implementing an operating environment in which we treat different customers differently.
- Our history as an organization supports the notion that it is good, even right, to treat all customers the same.

It's fair to say that almost any B2B organization contemplating a one-to-one initiative would find common ground with these opening statements. Other reasons cited by LifeWay for treating all customers the same way, all of them mentioned in the opening paragraphs of the Phase One Report, included:

- It costs the organization less to require customers to conform their behavior to the organization's standards than for the organization to conform its behavior to the customer's standards.
- Serving a mass market with products and services requires less work by the organization. Business can be conducted at a slower, more leisurely pace.
- Information system requirements are less demanding if only transactional data is captured and stored.
- The organization can continue directing most of its energies toward product excellence and operational efficiency.
- What happens if the organization can't meet the needs of its customers? What happens if treating different customers differently becomes a slippery slope of ever-escalating demands?

It seems as though the Customer Team had developed a pretty strong case against building one-to-one relationships. Then they ask: "Why treat different customers differently?" Here are their answers:

- *LifeWay's stated commitment to customer intimacy is not consistent with a mass-marketing philosophy.* "We can assume that some, possibly all, of our customers would like to be treated differently from the way that we have chosen to treat them today. It is inconsistent to herald a commitment to 'customer intimacy' while simultaneously dictating the terms of the relationship."

- *LifeWay's sense of spiritual stewardship requires it to treat different customers differently.* "Currently, we treat the majority of our customers in basically the same way. . . . We can assume that we are doing more than some customers require . . . and doing less than what other customers require."

- *A sense of fairness.* "It is not appropriate for us to extract more money than necessary from some customers to provide services to customers who have not asked for, and do not pay for, that level of service."

- *In a digital economy, product excellence alone will not assure survival.* "Successful companies will differentiate themselves on the basis of their relationships with their customers. In the emerging marketplace, there will be no alternative. Many companies can provide good product. A one-to-one enterprise will become intimate with its customers and use what it knows about each customer to provide treatment not available elsewhere."

Of course, we all know which side of the debate won the day. But we thought it would be instructive to reprise for you how LifeWay anticipated the arguments, both pro and con, that its one-to-one initiative would engender and how LifeWay took the trouble to articulate and consider all sides of the discussion, not just the one favored by top management.

The Customer Team also recommended using Identify, Differentiate, Interact, and Customize—the four basic implementation steps of one-to-one strategy—as a general guide that would make it easier to manage the initiative after it got rolling. "We already had a language for publishing and a language for finance that helped us discuss these parts of our business," said Kramp. "What we lacked was a language that helped us talk about what we wanted to do for customers. I.D.I.C. gave us that common language."

In Phase One of the initative, LifeWay Church Resources would tackle only the first two steps, Identify and Differentiate. LifeWay, unlike Novartis CP, was not facing external pressure to move quickly. Its pressure came from within. That didn't make the pressure any less real, however. The division's president, Gene Mims, had sent a clear message that change was necessary, but the managers knew he wasn't expecting miracles. On the other hand, they knew that Mims had put the initiative on a fast track and was expecting to see results soon.

Describing a universe of customers

After laying the groundwork for its one-to-one initiative, Life-Way tackled the first implementation step: *Identify your customers.* For LifeWay, this meant much more than collecting names and addresses. It meant establishing a formal system for describing customers by specific attributes, such as size, growth rate, total sales, and other concrete measures. LifeWay believed firmly that it would be impossible to begin the next implementation step, differentiation, without first devising an objective method for classifying constituents within the customer base. LifeWay's refusal to "leap" from one implementation step to the next without first constructing a logical bridge is admirable.

Descriptive measure	Defining question
Size	What is the average annual Sunday School attendance?
Growth groupings	Is church attendance growing or declining?
County population change	Is the church located in a growing community?
Total LifeWay sales	What is the church's level of spending with LifeWay compared with other churches of comparable size?
Sales change	Has the church's level of spending increased or decreased over time?
Gross profitability	Does LifeWay make money or lose money selling to this church?
Baptisms	How many baptisms annually?
Sunday School attendance	Is Sunday School attendance growing?
Undesignated receipts (nonspecific donations)	What is the current level of nonspecific donations received by the church?
Per capita measures (sales, baptisms, donations) compared to Sunday School attendance	What are current ratios of per capita sales, baptisms, and nonspecific donations to Sunday School attendance?
Ethnicity	What is the dominant ethnic makeup of the church?
Generational	What is the ratio of senior adults to all adults?
Pastoral transitions	How long has the current pastor been at the church?
Lifestyle segmentation	What types of people attend the church? What types of people are in the surrounding community?
Denomination	What is the church denomination?

Kramp knew the job of properly identifying customers wouldn't be easy. "No matter how long we spend preparing data and analyzing it, we will never have *enough* information and predictive insight," says Kramp. "Instead, we tried to identify a limited set of descriptive measures that would allow us to develop a relative ranking of our customers so we could prioritize our work with them."

After several days of meetings and discussions, LifeWay compiled a set of fifteen measures that would describe the basic architecture of its customer universe. Each descriptive measure was accompanied by a defining question. (See preceding page.)

The team examined Sunday School attendance figures from 32,835 churches and divided the churches into four size categories:

Size category	Sunday School attendance	Percent of sample
Small churches	Less than 100	69.7%
Medium churches	100–499	27.5%
Large churches	500–999	2.0%
Mega-churches	More than 1,000	0.68%

LifeWay next examined the growth patterns. "We developed a scale ranging from -4 to +4 that grouped churches based on their annual change rate for Sunday School attendance between 1994 and 1998," Kramp explains. "In this scale, a +4 church grew by 30 percent or more during these years. A -4 church declined by 30 percent or more."

The change rate analysis showed that about 17 percent of

the churches had experienced very high rates of growth, about 18 percent had experienced very high rates of decline, and about 29 percent had plateaued. About 16 percent were growing at a slower pace than the +4 group and about 20 percent were declining at a slower pace than the -4 group.

Growth category	Definition	Percent of sample
-4	More than 30 percent decline	18%
-3	21 to 30 percent decline	8.0%
-2	10 to 20 percent decline	11.7%
-1	Plateaued—less than 10 percent decline	13%
+1	Plateaued—less than 10 percent growth	15.7%
+2	10 to 20 percent growth	9.8%
+3	21 to 30 percent growth	6.6%
+4	More than 30 percent growth	17%

LifeWay understood intuitively that for its church customers average annual Sunday School attendance could provide a more accurate proxy measure of a church's potential value as a customer than Sunday service attendance or total membership numbers.

Gradually, LifeWay worked its way through all fifteen descriptive measures. At the end of this wearying process, the managers recognized that their effort was still a work in progress and would probably remain so. Some of the descriptive measures compiled so diligently by the team would not be immediately useful. And key specific questions about the needs of individual churches remained unanswered and would require direct interactive discussions with the churches themselves. To keep moving forward, LifeWay needed to know:

1. What goals is the church pursuing?
2. What strategies is the church utilizing to pursue its goals?
3. What operating programs or ministries is the church implementing to support its strategies?
4. Which operating programs or ministries used by the church do its leaders consider to be successful, adequate, struggling, or failing?
5. Who influences the pastor, staff, and church leaders as they set goals and decide on strategies and then implement operational programs or ministries? Will the church listen to advice from LifeWay?
6. What special challenges is the church facing at this time?

"The answers to questions such as these can be discovered only as a result of interaction with the church," says Kramp. "This kind of knowledge can be drawn from a limited number of customers with whom we seek to establish an ongoing Learning Relationship." But which customers would be included in this limited set? To answer that question, LifeWay began the second implementation step of building one-to-one relationships: Differentiate your customers.

The IPO model

"Because of our mission, we felt it was inappropriate to focus only on sales or profitability in our customer valuation process," says Kramp. "Instead, we developed a model that lets us consider valuation in three important dimensions—impact, profitability, and opportunity."

The initials of these three dimensions conveniently spell IPO, which is what Kramp's team chose to name its differentiation process. "For *impact*, we focus on two descriptive measures: growth in Sunday School attendance and growth in baptisms. With these two criteria, we can determine if the church is growing and what kind of growth it is experiencing. For *profitability*, we focus on two financial measures: LifeWay sales and costs of service. By evaluating this data, we can determine the most appropriate level of service to provide. For *opportunity*, we focus on pastoral transitions, generational changes in the congregation, changes in lifestyle segmentation, and changes in the surrounding community. The goal here is to see if LifeWay can help the church solve a problem, achieve a goal, or capitalize on an opportunity."

When the team ranked 38,606 Southern Baptist churches in its database from the perspective of the IPO model, 2,000 accounts jumped out of the crowd. All the tedious hours, days, and weeks of painstaking number crunching now paid off. Kramp's team identified "top customers" in all four categories of church size (Small, Medium, Large, and Mega) and across all eight growth groups (ranging from -4 to +4). These 2,000 churches also accounted for more than 30 percent of LifeWay's total sales revenue, a fact that raised the team's comfort level. Confident that they had succeeded in identifying the company's best and potentially most growable customers, Kramp's team prepared for the more challenging aspects of the project which were still to come.

IPO dimension	Descriptive measures used to differentiate customers
Impact	■ Sunday School attendance ■ Baptisms
Profitability	■ Sales ■ Costs of Service
Opportunity	■ Pastoral transitions ■ Generational ■ Lifestyle segmentation ■ County population change

Tying business results to customer needs

Based on the exhaustive presentation by the Customer Team, the management group faced its work with a new, more realistic and practical perspective on the LifeWay customer base. In this context, Gene Mims began asserting his assumption that what was good for the churches would be good for LifeWay. Mims challenged the team leaders to view customers' needs on three levels. These three levels of needs, he explained, could only be discovered within the context of an ongoing relationship.

Mims sensed that by focusing on customer needs, LifeWay could free itself from the trap of traditional build-to-forecast approaches that rely heavily on market research, educated guesswork, and extensive testing. While the traditional ap-

Levels of needs	How a customer would describe these levels	Actions required by LifeWay
1. Expressed needs	The needs I know about and can tell you about.	Record expressed needs of the customer in database
2. Unexpressed needs	The needs I know about but have not told you about.	Ask questions to determine unexpressed needs of the customer; record answers in database.
3. Unknown needs	The needs I have but cannot yet express.	Develop Learning Relationship with customer to discover needs that are presently unknown or inexpressible.

proaches focus exclusively on developing *markets*, the nontraditional, one-to-one strategies focus on developing *customers*. The traditional approach was a one-way street. The organization didn't know what an individual customer really wanted, and even if it knew, it wouldn't have had the capability to respond to that knowledge. In contrast, the one-to-one approach is a two-way thoroughfare. The organization must develop the capacity to know what the customer wants and then provide precisely what the customer wants, when the customer wants it.

At this point in the process, the work of the Customer Team and the Message and Models Team began to dovetail. Together, they devised a methodology for collecting, analyzing, and storing customer information at all three levels. The first level (expressed needs) would be the easiest to manage, at least initially, because the customer had already specified his needs to LifeWay. In this situation, LifeWay would simply record the information so it could be accessed later.

The second level (unexpressed needs) would be harder to manage (again, initially) because it would require LifeWay to develop procedures to ascertain and record the customer's needs in a standardized way that would make one church easily comparable with, and distinct from, other churches across the customer base.

The third level (unknown needs) would, of course, be the hardest to manage, both initially and over time, because it would require LifeWay to establish an ongoing Learning Relationship with the customer. A Learning Relationship would enable LifeWay to uncover needs that were hidden, inexpressible, or presently unknown. It would be at this level of need that the strongest bond between LifeWay and a customer could develop. LifeWay realized that if it could rely on its experience with some customers to deduce what other, similar customers might want (but didn't know about or hadn't realized), then it could begin to visualize its business in terms of leading its customers, one at a time, to better and more successful outcomes.

Yet all of this—the focus on the needs of customers—was contingent on LifeWay implementing a strategy that could build its relationship with its customers as illustrated in the chart on the opposite page.

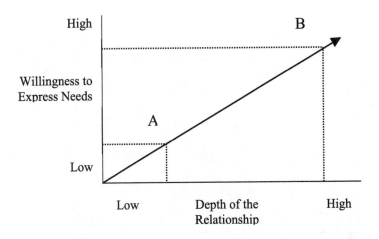

In this graph, point A illustrates that if the depth of the relationship is low, the willingness to express needs is correspondingly low. On the other hand, point B illustrates that if the depth of the relationship is high, the willingness to express needs will be correspondingly higher. LifeWay's one-to-one approach affirms the strategic significance of focusing on customers' needs and recognizes that LifeWay cannot be successful in helping churches without moving from level 1 to level 3 needs. Therefore, at least partly, LifeWay earns the opportunity to help churches be successful by deepening its relationship with its customers.

As part of this relationship-building strategy, the Message and Models Team, led by Mike Miller, Louis Hanks, Barry Sneed, Jay Johnston, and David Fields, presented their report—what they called "The MAP." This was the "method and process" LifeWay would use as a dialogic tool in the future to interact with churches, build relationships, understand needs, and help churches solve problems. The MAP would become a foundational part of LifeWay's emerging strategy and commitment to help the churches.

A Church MAP (Method and Process)

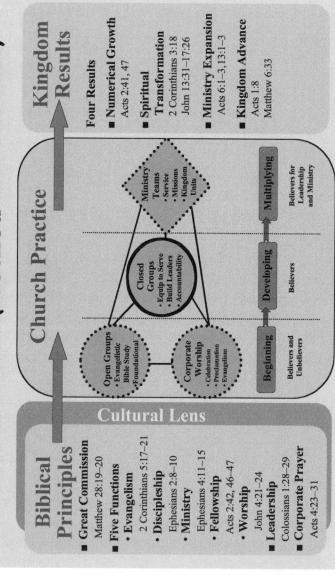

Biblical Principles

- **Great Commission**
  Matthew 28:19–20
- **Five Functions**
  - **Evangelism**
    2 Corinthians 5:17–21
  - **Discipleship**
    Ephesians 2:8–10
  - **Ministry**
    Ephesians 4:11–15
  - **Fellowship**
    Acts 2:42, 46–47
  - **Worship**
    John 4:21–24
- **Leadership**
  Colossians 1:28–29
- **Corporate Prayer**
  Acts 4:23–31

Cultural Lens

Church Practice

Ministry Teams
- Service
- Missions
- Kingdom Units

Closed Groups
- Equip to Serve
- Build Leaders
- Accountability

Open Groups
- Evangelistic
- Bible Study
- Foundational

Corporate Worship
- Celebration
- Proclamation
- Evangelism

Beginning — Believers and Unbelievers

Developing — Believers

Multiplying — Believers for Leadership and Ministry

Kingdom Results

Four Results
- **Numerical Growth**
  Acts 2:41, 47
- **Spiritual Transformation**
  2 Corinthians 3:18
  John 13:31–17:26
- **Ministry Expansion**
  Acts 6:1–3, 13:1–3
- **Kingdom Advance**
  Acts 1:8
  Matthew 6:33

Matching solution sets to customer needs

As we saw in the Bentley case study, it is essential to match so-lutions with needs. Bentley had 85 products and several thou-sand customers, so matching customers individually to products, or suites of products, would have been complex and more difficult than the company could manage. Instead, Bent-ley created just 11 account scenarios describing the needs of certain types of accounts and then listed the product and ser-vice bundles most likely to serve their needs. This made it far easier for Bentley to match solutions with customers on a more routine and reliable basis. Mapping customers into account scenarios initially, of course, meant Bentley could then develop ever more customized configurations of products and applica-tions for individual customers.

At LifeWay, Gene Mims knew that the organization's huge array of products, programs, and services was indeed a mixed blessing. In one way it was a competitive advantage, because it meant that LifeWay could potentially offer more to its cus-tomers than anyone else could. In another way, though, the dazzling assortment of possible solutions made it more difficult for LifeWay to focus its energies on the needs of particular cus-tomers, or types of customers, most of whom didn't need the full range of solutions to achieve their individual and immedi-ate goals.

Ideally, the process would result in a logical balance between needs and solutions. In other words, as more needs are discov-ered, more solutions are developed. This is a significant depar-ture from traditional strategies of product development, sales, and marketing. In a traditional organization, the product would be developed first, based on a mathematical, but still largely theoretical concept of what the market "wanted." Then the marketing team would be tasked with creating demand for the new product. The sales force would then go out and push the product until the market was saturated. LifeWay was planning to do the exact opposite. Mims reasoned that with this approach Life-Way's extensive set of "customer solutions" could become an immediate asset and a bridge that would help its financial performance while it worked to help churches improve their long-term ministry performance.

The Needs and Solutions Matrix

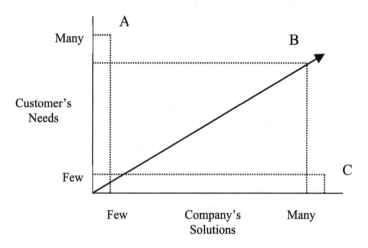

Point A illustrates a company that has a relationship with a customer expressing many needs. But unfortunately the company has few solutions to meet those needs. Point C illustrates a company that has a relationship with a customer expressing few needs. The company has many solutions here, but they are solutions for problems and needs that the customer simply doesn't have. Point B illustrates the optimum situation. The company with many solutions is relating to a customer expressing many needs.

One-to-one methodology at LifeWay

Although Mims and his management team had been using terms such as "customer intimacy" and "customer-focused" to describe the new strategic direction for LifeWay Church Resources, they lacked a common, practical language for expressing its goals or measuring its progress as a customer-centric enterprise. In keeping with its overarching mission of ministering to the spiritual needs of its customers, LifeWay devised what it calls *One-to-One Ministry*.

LifeWay's methodology offers two valuable lessons:

First, no process of change, no matter how compelling, can be imposed from without. It should be integrated into the organization as seamlessly as possible. Modifying, tailoring, reworking,

Help the Churches

We face daily the pressure of our concern for all the churches. 2 Corinthians 11:28

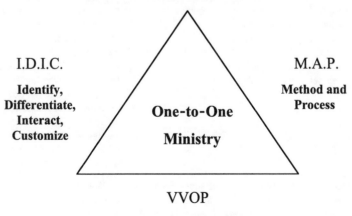

I.D.I.C.

Identify, Differentiate, Interact, Customize

One-to-One Ministry

M.A.P.

Method and Process

VVOP

Vision, Values, and Operating Principles

and translating the change process—whether it's one-to-one relationship building or some other strategy—to make it feel comfortable and natural is absolutely essential for any organization that's serious about reengineering its business philosophy.

Second, it demonstrates clearly that customer needs are the heart and soul of any customer relationship management initiative. Everything circles back to the needs of the customer—the implementation steps describe the surest path for not getting lost in the thicket of competing interests.

As LifeWay Church Resources continued its change initiative and prepared to implement a new organization to support its strategy, the division leaders developed the following matrix, which envisions the implementation steps they will face as they launch their One-to-One Ministry strategy with their customers, the churches.

	Identify	Differentiate	Interact	Customize
Need Level 1 expressed or articulated The goal: listen and remember	Secondary information and transactional data that is "remembered" and available in the "brain"	Needs—hypothesis-based Value—weighted equation-driven	LifeWay to churches: catalogues, planning guides, etc. Churches to LifeWay: process and respond to requests and feedback	Do consistently what we tell customers we will do Tell customers what we can and will do in response to what they ask us to do—even if we say "no"
Need Level 2 unexpressed or unarticulated	Information that is secured through strategic use of "golden questions" used	Needs—deep insight into cluster-level needs (ex. "growing churches")	LifeWay to churches: interaction online or with	Begin to offer customers a set of options that can be "customized"

	Identify	Differentiate	Interact	Customize
Need Level 2 The goal: ask, listen, and remember	to secure information that cannot be known easily through secondary or transactional data	Value—increasing emphasis on "opportunities" based on information (ex. pastoral transitions)	customers in group settings using feedback mechanisms (conferences with feedback forms)	based on the choices made; ensure that LifeWay can deliver what is promised based on each combination of options
			Churches to LifeWay: process all information church leaders disclose and use as a basis for action	
Need Level 3 unknown or unarticulated	Deep insight into cluster-level needs (ex. "growing churches")	Needs—deep insight into the root issues facing specific churches	LifeWay to churches: cluster-level interaction with	Multiple forms of interaction that focus on root causes to the problems
The goals: ask, listen, discern, and remember	Deep insight into specific churches as a result of a robust, long-term Learning Relationship that draws on all points of interaction	Value—emphasis on the willingness of the church and its leaders to seek help from LifeWay and to collaborate to find solutions	churches that focuses on root issues; individual church consultation as required and justified by value to organization	of churches ranging from conferences, products, Internet, and various forms of personal consultation
			Churches to LifeWay: process all requests for help based on predetermined "ministry rules"	

Organizational change

After months of Monday Meetings, the management group realized they would need an action plan to begin testing their assumptions. They would need to design a formal bridge connecting the spiritual and business sides of the LifeWay organization.

"We knew it was the right time to widen our net and include more of our employees in the process," recalls Mike Miller, leader of the Message and Models Team. "So we invited fifty of our best people from all over the LifeWay organization to attend an eight-day session of training, brainstorming, and strategizing."

Prior to this intensive session, however, several shorter meetings were held to resolve the issue of differentiating the churches by need. By the last of these meetings, LifeWay narrowed the spectrum of needs down to four clusters—Small, Growing, Stable, and Declining. Basically, where a church was in its life cycle would determine its cluster.

The longer session began with three days of training, feedback, and discussion. Then the fifty participants, dubbed the "Discovery Group," were divided into teams. Each team was assigned a particular cluster and given the task of developing a unique strategy for that cluster. "It was one-to-one marketing at the grassroots level," says Miller. "Each cluster had different needs, and so each cluster required a different strategy."

The teams were given five days to formulate strategies and prepare a presentation. The presentations were essentially summaries of each team's "best of breed" ideas for treating the different clusters differently. The teams also developed "enhanced needs sets" for each cluster. These sets, which essentially identified and described *potential* needs, would provide LifeWay with a road map for growing its relationships with individual churches within the clusters. In a sense, developing the enhanced needs sets required LifeWay to ask itself essential questions such as: "What *else* should we be doing to meet this customer's needs?" "What's the next step?" "How can we provide even *more* help to this particular customer?"

One of the most important aspects of the entire exercise was that it forced the Discovery Group to define the roles and responsibilities of a new class of leaders and employees. For the moment, figuring out precisely *how* these leaders would be organized was less important than describing accurately what they would actually *do* in a one-to-one organization. The recommendations the teams developed were given to David Francis and the Organizational Options Team to use as they formulated new organizational design options.

In addition to generating ideas and concepts that could be narrowed and refined in the next round of planning, the intensive session also created an atmosphere of excitement and expectation. When participants were asked to describe the eight-day experience, they used words such as "passion," "commitment," "thrilling," and "miraculous." One person compared the process to the Lewis and Clark expedition. Not surprisingly, several expressed their feelings by quoting Scripture or invoking biblical imagery. Even Mike Miller, one of the leaders of the Discovery Group process expressed his surprise at the impact of the experience. "We expected our folks to learn a lot during the eight days," he said. "We were not prepared for the level of enthusiasm and commitment people showed. It was remarkable."

Developing champions for change

In our second book, *Enterprise One to One*, we wrote that no one-to-one initiative undertaken by a single department within a larger organization would survive for very long without support from the organization's other functional areas. Our premise was that you can't have a "one-to-one marketing department" or a "one-to-one customer service department." Any organization that is serious about treating different customers differently will need to become a one-to-one *enterprise*. And a one-to-one enterprise can't be an archipelago of loosely connected departments. A genuine one-to-one customer development strategy requires a very high level of integration among the various departments and functional areas that make up the enterprise—it just won't work any other way.

Any management team attempting to implement a one-to-one strategy is going to encounter varying degrees of resistance as it reaches further and deeper into the organization for support. It is often difficult to predict who will help and who will hinder. Because of the Discovery Group process, LifeWay empowered about fifty people in its organization to be champions for the new focus on customers. Many of the original fifty volunteered for the next iteration of development, which would formalize strategies for each of the clusters and create a prototype one-to-one initiative. From this group of volunteers,

LifeWay selected seven to work full-time on the prototype initiative and others to assist in part-time capacities.

For practical reasons, LifeWay decided Nashville would be the epicenter of the prototype. "It is basically the easiest place to start," Kramp explains. "It's an area of growth, activity, and vitality. And many of our employees attend the local churches, so we'll have a ready supply of 'soft data' available as the prototype moves forward." The prototype included 520 churches, a sample large enough to provide good data, but small enough to be manageable. It was the place to start, to learn, and to prepare for a new organization, a new strategy, and a new one-to-one focus.

Getting down to work for customers

The silver lunchbox that Gene Mims had slammed on the conference-room table months before illustrates the dividing line between companies that pursue CRM strategies as a "fad of the month" and those who commit themselves to focus their organizations on their customers. Becoming a customer-focused company demands that people quit talking about it and "get to work," as he puts it. If the vision is compelling, if the values are clear, and if the operating principles are strong, an organization can reinvent itself. "Focusing on customers and helping them succeed is the heart of LifeWay. It's just who we are," says Ted Warren. "And given who we are, it would have been impossible for us not to change."

Tasks ahead for LifeWay

LifeWay is a company with a dual mandate—to make a profit and to serve a greater spiritual purpose as well. With thousands of products to offer thousands of customers, LifeWay had to choose between two quite different paths. One path was to continue offering the same products and services to everyone, regardless of need, letting customers sort through the firm's many alternatives on their own. This path had the advantage of being easy to implement, causing little organizational disruption and requiring no significant IT systems upgrades. The other path was to recognize that each customer had different needs and to begin treating different customers differently.

LifeWay chose the second path and began developing a one-to-one initiative that would transform it from a product-centric organization into a customer-centric organization. To accomplish this goal, LifeWay realized that it would have to develop and manage ongoing Learning Relationships with its customers. Without such relationships, how would LifeWay ever know what its customers really needed? Moreover, without such relationships, why would its customers even care about LifeWay?

The company also realized that it needed to develop a formal system for ranking its customers by value. Fortunately, much of the data LifeWay needed for this step was already on hand in the form of annual surveys completed by the individual churches. After culling through the survey data for months, LifeWay was able to determine which metrics offered the best clues to a customer's value.

With a valuation model in the works, LifeWay could move on with confidence to the next step of the process, differentiating its customers by their needs. Once again, LifeWay relied on information it already had to achieve its immediate purpose. Many of LifeWay's current managers were former LifeWay customers. So they were able to provide a wealth of insight and knowledge about customer needs. LifeWay made sure the managers got the opportunity not only to make valuable contributions but also to assume leading roles in the development of the one-to-one program.

LifeWay is on the road to reinventing itself as a one-to-one enterprise. Several challenges remain, however. To stay on course, LifeWay should:

- Continue identifying decision makers and influencers at each church. In this market, the primary influencer is likely to be the pastor. But pastors don't remain with a congregation indefinitely, so LifeWay must develop a practical system for tracking them throughout their careers.
- Provide each LifeWay employee with a clear perspective not only on the concept of a one-to-one strategy but also on how the shift to a customer-centric business model is likely to change that employee's duties and measures of success. The metrics of LifeWay's IPO customer valuation model should be discussed, explained, and used throughout the organization.
- Develop a formal set of business rules for collecting and analyzing customer information. This will be especially important in the ongoing development of LifeWay's larger church customers.

- Confirm that all IT systems are integrated and continue integrating other parts of the organization—product development, production, delivery, call center, Web site, billing, customer service, sales, and marketing—into a seamless one-to-one enterprise.

- Teach the organization how to anticipate and recommend products for each customer, rather than filling orders. This will likely require a big investment in the development of business rules, and a process for automating personalization, especially for the smallest church customers.

- Avoid missteps by piloting each new one-to-one initiative. LifeWay made a wise decision in launching its pilot program close to home. Now it will have to figure out the best way to scale its one-to-one model to fit the rest of the organization.

Virtual B2B

Describing the current wave of technology-driven business activity sweeping across the economic landscape as a "sea change" seems an understatement. What we have here is a global transformation, a kind of "systemic" change that can truly be understood only in terms of analogy or metaphor. Imagine, for instance, that you lived in a city made of steel and woke up one morning to discover the entire city had been turned to glass. Everything that had been opaque would be transparent, everything sturdy would be fragile. One false move, even the slightest slip, and—boom!—everything around you could shatter.

Nowhere is this transformative energy hitting with more sheer force than in the realm of business-to-business commerce, where the Internet is recasting and remodeling nearly every existing relationship.

We would be lying if we said we could accurately predict where all this is heading. So we won't even try. We can, however, offer some warnings and suggestions, based on what we've seen so far. We will help you ask some of the right questions, even if nobody knows all the answers yet. One truth appears self-evident: Any B2B organization that isn't developing a robust online presence had better team up quickly with an organization that is—for the simple reason that having a fully transactional Web site today is just as essential as having a telephone. You simply won't be able to remain in business without one.

But what exactly do we mean when we say that a Web site is "fully transactional"? We mean exactly this: That it accurately reflects the complexity, richness, and flexibility of a face-to-face, business-to-business relationship. It remembers who you are, it remembers your complete history of transactions, it remembers your negotiated pricing schedule, it remembers your specific needs, and it delivers value-added content and offerings based on your unique requirements as a business customer. Another term for this might be a "one-to-one Web site" and, yes, they do exist. Dell's Premier Pages Service represents one very good example.

And there are other examples of B2B Web sites that are becoming truly "one-to-one" in their functionality, with varying degrees of sophistication. We often point to Cisco as another near-perfect example of a Web-based CRM success. The Cisco Connection Online Web site now handles roughly half of Cisco's total sales, delivering online customer service, tracking orders, and facilitating software downloads. More than half a million times a month, Cisco's customers hit the site to report technical problems, check orders, and download software.

Many customer-service inquiries are actually handled by other customers!

Still, Premier Dell.com, Cisco Connection, and other services like them represent a small fraction of the Web's real potential as a virtual marketplace. What's more exciting—and more threatening to any B2B organization—is the rise of B2B exchanges.

Indeed, no book on B2B business in the Internet age would be complete without examining the dynamics of online B2B exchanges, marketplaces, and portals. There are a number of business models, pricing structures, revenue-generating schemes, and organizational constructs that operate within the realm of the "B2B exchange" today. But certainly, as a business phenomenon, the rise of B2B exchanges represents one of the most dramatic and transforming results of the Internet.

Rather than scrolling through an address file and making phone calls to identify the possible suppliers or buyers for some industrial product, many businesses today can simply call up a Web site that lists dozens, or maybe tens of thousands, of suppliers of the product. And usually these suppliers are immediately available, just a mouse click away. They can be organized or prioritized not just by price but by geography, product specifications, shipping criteria, and other important buying factors, including credit terms, quality representations, and so forth.

Moreover, because of the self-service, collaborative nature of Web interactions, the suppliers and buyers at a B2B exchange list themselves on their own initiative. Not only do they require little administrative overhead or maintenance, but getting them signed up often involves little if any sales or promotional effort. They are attracted to an exchange because other suppliers and buyers are already there. They come because not to come is to shut off an important potential source of revenue or product sourcing. B2B exchanges have the potential to improve the economics not only of buying but also of selling.

Most of the major research firms predict that B2B e-commerce will literally explode over the next few years, completely dwarfing the B2C Internet revolution that helped fuel the world economic boom of the late 1990s. Jupiter Communications predicted in October 2000 that by the year 2005 the total amount of online B2B commerce will have grown from an estimated $336 billion (year 2000's level) to approximately $6.3 *trillion*. In a major study of procurement and e-commerce activities across twelve major industries, Jupiter found that in five of these sectors more than half of all procurement would be taking place online by the year 2004, driven in large part by the rise of B2B exchanges. The heaviest and most immediate users of B2B e-commerce are likely to be telecommunications and computers, followed closely by aerospace and defense, chemicals, electronics, and automotive vehicles and parts.

Other firms predict similar explosive growth. AMR Research predicts a $6 trillion B2B e-commerce level by 2004, and adds that industry leaders will probably do 60 to 100 percent of their transactions online over just the next two years. Boston Consulting Group predicts $4.8 trillion by 2004, and Forrester predicts $2.7 trillion by 2004. No matter how you slice it, no matter what you call it or how you analyze it, we're talking about something that is simply and truly breathtaking in its implications. The annual benefits in terms of increased efficiency and productivity alone—the benefits that come from streamlining such a vast quantity of commercial activity—are enough to boggle the mind. The Internet is just Viagra for our maturing Western economic system.

We said at the beginning of this book that the rise of B2B exchanges is both good news and bad news for most B2B companies. While it's certainly good news in terms of cost reduction and procurement efficiency, it's bad news for any seller whose margins are now protected by the veil of imperfect information—and that includes a large number of sellers, probably the majority of sellers throughout the world. Thus, for a B2B firm whose industry is about to have an exchange introduced, it is now more important than ever to focus on creating and managing individual customer relationships, so as to avoid being whipsawed by the cost-transparent pricing likely to be found on the exchange.

But what about the B2B exchanges themselves? Do one-to-one strategies and customer relationship management have any lessons for an exchange that can make it more likely to succeed? Forrester predicts 3,000 B2B exchanges will be launched by 2001 alone, but only 5 percent of these will survive. Goldman Sachs predicts 10,000 such exchanges by 2003, although many will fail. So, while there does appear to be real gold in them thar Internet hills, the actual likelihood of succeeding with a B2B exchange, given the intense competition for this real estate, appears small indeed. But are there some strategies that an exchange can employ to increase its long-term probability of success? The answer to that is "yes," and these strategies derive almost entirely from applying the basic principles of

CRM and building one-to-one relationships with the B2B exchange itself. That's what we're going to explore in this chapter of our book.

The growing season

Ask the owner of any garden center how long his year lasts and he'll tell you sixteen weeks. That's how long his selling season lasts. For the rest of the year, he either breaks even or loses money. Compressing an entire year's work into those critical sixteen weeks is the mathematical equivalent of working 78-hour days for four months.

Any business that offers to shave hours or even minutes off the garden center owner's daily task time is going to get his attention fast. But once you've captured his attention, how do you make him your customer, keep him loyal, and grow his business into a more and more profitable relationship?

John Cochran, a former aerospace marketer and amateur horticulturalist, has an answer. He is the CEO and co-founder of e-Greenbiz.com, an online exchange for buyers and sellers of "green industry" products. Born and raised in Alabama, trained as an aerospace engineer, Cochran is a poster child for the "next generation" of B2B entrepreneurs. To Cochran, the Internet isn't much different from the missile guidance systems he sold back in the 1980s—a means to an end. The last thing he would ever call the Internet is "sexy"—not because he doesn't think it's interesting, but because he knows his customers don't care how it works as long as it helps them manage their businesses.

"Many of the people I deal with are afraid of the Internet," says Cochran. "And it's not just the people in the green industry. It's the same in the construction business and the chemicals industry. Some people don't understand the World Wide Web or they have misconceptions of it. They think that if they push the wrong button on their computer, a truckload of supplies is suddenly going to show up at their door."

Cochran says he still spends a fair amount of time educating potential customers. "I ask them to think of our Web site as a replacement for their fax machine. That's something they can relate to, because practically everyone who owns a garden center already has a fax machine. I tell them the Web site is like a better, faster, more powerful fax machine with a color display. And then I tell them that, unlike their fax machine, the Web site will remember who they are, what they need, and when they need it."

Like other B2B exchanges, e-Greenbiz.com matches buyers and sellers electronically. For both sides of the deal, this means transactions occur in seconds, instead of days. And while each side of the deal has its own set of unique needs and issues, there is a common need for speed. "If there's one thing that's consistent between buyers and sellers, it's the desire to save time," says Cochran. "If you're on the buy side—whether you're a garden center owner, a landscape contractor, or the director of purchasing for the city of Salt Lake—you are going to be spending a lot of your time searching for goods and then trying to purchase them. Because the supply base is very fragmented, just finding the right information about a product can be a very time-consuming and cumbersome process."

For a small or medium-sized business with just a few employees, there just isn't enough time in the day to complete a list of jobs and source all the necessary products. "Until now, your level of success depended largely on your ability to manage your time," says Cochran.

E-Greenbiz.com users, though, can log on anytime, day or night, to find and purchase the goods they need to complete their jobs. "With this system, they do a lot of their sourcing at night and on weekends. It reduces their phone and fax time dramatically. What used to take hours now takes three clicks of a mouse," says Cochran. "The reduction of time is an extremely high-value proposition."

In its first nine months of operation, e-Greenbiz.com has signed up nearly 2,300 businesses, most of whom log on to the site to make purchases as well as sales.

B2B exchanges such as e-Greenbiz.com also help their customers serve *their* customers better by putting more timely and higher-quality information at their fingertips. "If a customer comes into a garden center looking for a rare hydrangea or a unique type of birdhouse, the chance of finding the right catalogue and then finding exactly what the customer wants— while the customer is standing there—is highly remote. But if you're using the Web site, you can search for the item, price it, and even order it—all while the customer is still right in front of you."

The system's ability to remember purchase histories allows buyers and sellers to interact more efficiently and more speedily. "All the transactional information is maintained on the system," explains Cochran. "So a buyer can log on with a user name and a password, pull up previous purchase orders, and basically regenerate new orders based on the stored data easily and quickly."

On the sell side, the system's ability to provide greater efficiency translates into better inventory control, improved supply chain management, and smoother cash flow. Cochran says most of e-Greenbiz.com's 2,300 users register as both sellers *and* buyers. The green industry isn't the only industry in which everyone seems to be selling and buying from everyone else at the same time. Remember the "Great Chain of B2B-ing" diagrams we presented back in Chapter 1? When there are multiple links between producers of raw materials and end users of finished goods, there are likely to be several "mini-chains" within the larger chain of supply. This becomes apparent when you track a typical day of transactions on e-Greenbiz.com.

"The nurserymen use the system to sell their goods to the garden centers. But they also use the system to purchase plastic pots, growing medium, fertilizer, heaters, lights—sometimes even entire greenhouses. It takes the whole supply chain to produce a single plant."

Managing information

"One of the problems with the green industry is that a lot of the businesses keep their information in spiral-bound notebooks," says Cochran. "If you ask the guy running a garden center grossing $15 million a year to tell you which of his products earn him the most money, he won't be able to give you an answer. He'll tell you which products have the highest margins and which products are the best sellers. And he may have a hunch as to which product is actually earning the most money, but he won't have the data to back up his hunch." And what if you ask which *customers* earn him the most money? Here again, he might have a hunch, but he won't have a system for identifying his best and worst customers.

With a Web-based data management system at his disposal, the garden center owner can easily discover which of his products are selling profitably and which aren't. Armed with that information, he can manage his inventory in a way that minimizes his risk and maximizes his profits. He'll also have access to data that could help him differentiate his customers by value, so he could begin treating different customers differently.

Suppliers can use the system to plan marketing campaigns, test new products, create surveys, and gather feedback much more quickly and efficiently than in the past. "Let's say you're a fertilizer company and you're launching a new product. We could pull down information based on customer profiles in the database and generate a list of high-value prospects for you. We could provide all the marketing services you would need to create awareness and generate sales." Theoretically, a seller could introduce a new product, test it, improve it, and test it again—without ever leaving the exchange.

Cochran envisions the day when online exchanges such as e-Greenbiz.com serve not only as marketplaces but also as IT departments for their customers. "Once we've gathered enough information, we can be your back office as well as your front office. And that, by the way, is the key to customer loyalty. If you let us e-warehouse your information for you, someone would have to approach you with an incredible value proposition to pull you away from us. Your switching costs would be prohibitive."

Coming from anyone else, those words might sound cold or calculating. But when Cochran utters them in the plain-speaking language of an engineer, they seem nothing more than a straightforward statement of fact. Let's look at the reality of the situation: Most small and medium-sized businesses don't have the capital to invest in a fully transactional, one-to-one Web site. What e-Greenbiz.com is proposing is to become an outsourcer of one-to-one technology. If this sounds like the business model of an ASP (Application Service Provider), don't be too surprised. As computing moves out onto the Internet, information-based services are sure to follow. E-Greenbiz.com is not alone in anticipating this trend. What makes e-Greenbiz.com so interesting is that it has seen how this migration can be leveraged as part of a customer development strategy.

One of e-Greenbiz.com's messages to potential customers is a straightforward appeal to their sense of survival. By offering a range of Web-based, information-rich services, it is basically saying to customers, "We can help you compete with Wal-Mart and Home Depot by giving you access to the same kinds of information technology they use."

From begonias to high steel

Another excellent example of one-to-one at work in an exchange environment is e-Steel. Auctions may work for generic products, but in the steel industry, where any batch may carry many dozens of attributes, pricing is not as important as the need to obtain or deliver precise specifications. Accordingly, cost-focused auctions represent only 5 percent of e-Steel's transactions. The real value proposition, says Sherry Sigler, an e-Steel spokesperson, "is the creation of a marketplace for primary products where brands, relationships, service, delivery, and the actual attributes of the steel are all part of the deal."

E-Steel's fundamental strategy has been to deliver an e-commerce solution that addresses the most critical needs of the industry, be it negotiation, branding, credit, or supply chain initiatives. According to strategic services director Gene Moses: "From day one, this has required an acutely one-to-one focus." For example, a primary concern in the steel industry is the need to screen bid or offer pricing and inventory information from competitors. The e-Steel site therefore gives sellers and buyers precise control of their broadcasts. As Moses explains, "you can post any information you like and at the same time specifically exclude who has access to it." E-Steel's Broad-Vision-powered "Steel Direct" functionality is patent-pending.

Users of the site are carefully screened, explains Sigler, to ensure they are creditworthy, reputable market participants. Once a visitor is recognized by the exchange, the site is highly personalized for that visitor and that visit. For example, the site gives users the ability to save searches or postings, making repeat business easier to execute. Ironically, as advanced as it is, the site does not use matching engines or other technology to "morph" its look and feel. As Moses explains, this is as much a conscious choice as it is a matter of priorities. "We've devoted our time to personalizing the exchange itself and the shopping experience, not the waiting room." Moreover, "our very strong sense from the market is that privacy is a critical concern, and users would feel more comfortable directing the site's look and feel themselves." In any case, in the effort to become an ever more value-added site for the steel industry, user-directed "waiting rooms" will be rolling out "very soon," says Moses.

Another one-to-one strategy is to run as deeply into users' operations as possible. Systems integration is a huge technological challenge, and e-Steel's approach is to attack this objective incrementally. For example, e-Steel has just delivered Data Jet, an XML-based application enabling sellers to load inventory information into the system with only a few clicks. As Moses explains, this has two benefits. First, simply providing a seller with the capability for displaying large amounts of inventory information is useful. A seller might have an Excel spreadsheet with sixty specifications relating to his product. While entering this much data for each batch of steel would be labor-intensive, it is still in a seller's interest to do so, since any additional attribute might represent additional value for a buyer. Second, since e-Steel automatically updates a seller's inventory information, over time it is much less work for the seller to execute transactions via the site as opposed to offline. The continual expansion of such capabilities, says Moses, improves the value proposition for both buyers and sellers. In addition, of course, it tends to make each party more loyal to the exchange.

E-Steel now has some 3,500 companies participating on the site, representing ninety-eight countries at last count. Participants include steel mills, service centers, fabricators, distributors, and major original equipment manufacturers (OEMs). E-Steel's success and continued growth, explains Sigler, is very much one-to-one-driven. "We are listening to our customers and we are improving the range and customization of services. This is very much a learning-oriented, one-to-one enterprise."

Lions and tigers and portals—Oh my!

Whether it is buyer-centric, seller-centric, or neutral, an online B2B exchange is simply a cyber "place" where firms who want to buy or sell can find and arrange deals with firms who want to sell or buy. It is a cyberspace meeting place for buyers and sellers, an online mechanism to "clear the market," ensuring that supply meets demand. But there are a large number of additional services and features that could accompany such a pure demand-supply mechanism, and the variety of business models among B2B exchanges is breathtaking.

Vertical exchanges exist in particular industries; the more obscure and narrowly focused the industry is, the more usefulness can often be obtained from a vertical exchange. Plastics.net is a B2B exchange where buyers and sellers who deal in plastics can meet, online, to negotiate prices, secure contracts, and agree to sales transactions. Buyers get competitive bids, and sellers save the costs involved in generating sales.

Horizontal exchanges link buyers and sellers within a certain discipline, rather than within an industry. Logistics.com allows shippers and their customers to find each other, and in so doing each party is likely to find a more immediate and cost-efficient partner. In this purest form, a B2B exchange is simply a mechanism for ensuring that the supply of a commodity-like product or service meets demand for that product in an efficient and timely manner.

A firm can do business at a B2B exchange without suffering any of the "friction" of thumbing through old contact meeting notes, business card files, or Rolodexes, making phone calls and pursuing dead ends. Moreover, the pricing model employed by an exchange can be altered to fit the type of commodity or product being sold. Not just auctions, but English auctions, Dutch auctions, reverse auctions, private auctions. And not just haggling over individual prices, but sealed bids, call markets, and multiple-attribute auctions.

Going beyond the pure mechanism of matching supply with demand, however, a B2B exchange can also offer a number of additional services in conjunction with the sales being explored or consummated at the site. A B2B exchange with additional services might describe itself as a "marketplace," although a more apt term might be "shopping mall." At such an exchange, not only do sellers display their wares in more detail, offering technical data specifications, pictures, diagrams, or maps, but the site might also feature related products and services, order histories, financing options, and so forth.

Probably at the top of the food chain of B2B exchanges is the vertical Web portal, sometimes called an "affinity portal," "vertiport," or "vortal." This is a site not only for consummating e-commerce transactions but also for acquiring information, education, and other services associated with a particular business issue, process, or problem. Vertical Web portals feature things like discussion groups, advice columns, and even online consulting, all related to the basic problem being solved.

The genealogy of portals

In the beginning (circa 1996), "portal" was a Web buzzword. AOL and Yahoo! were ancient Internet mariners that provided gateways to the Internet with business models based on advertising, subscriptions, or both. They were the first in the portal space and continue to rule the high seas of the general portal market. Now users rely on portals, such as Yahoo! and Excite, for everything from email and calendars to bulletin boards, chat rooms, and even full-service tool kits to organize communities of their own, complete with messages and photo albums.

Soon a new breed of portals began springing up, such as RealHome.com, which serves homebuyers and homeowners, and Smalloffice.com, a B2B portal that provides content, commerce opportunities, and business tools to small companies. Vertical portals like RealHome and Smalloffice are aimed at specific interest groups and focus on providing customers with a gateway to unbiased information from other sources. Instead of generating revenue primarily through advertising and subscriptions (à la Yahoo! or AOL), the vertical portal's business model is more skewed toward e-commerce.

Lucent launched myLucent for its service provider customers to help them get information about Lucent products and services. Solution Finder helps customers narrow their areas of interest based on their business needs. MyLucent also allows customers to place and track orders. "Our customers want to get information about us by the means that's most effective for them," says Mary Whelan, Lucent's e-business vice president of service provider networks. "For us, it's an opportunity to target specific segments with special offers."

Portals have also evolved to meet the needs of the corporate market, offering a central entry point to information from numerous sources. Pure corporate portals—a huge area these days—provide a single, easy-to-access starting point for a company's own internal constituents to locate information, participate in a business process, or collaborate with other users. They can be valuable resources for employees, suppliers, partners, or stockholders, serving a variety of roles, from supply chain extranet to employee-focused intranet. One type of corporate portal is the enterprise information portal (EIP), a gateway into a company's corporate news and information (typically an intranet for employees and partners). Merrill Lynch predicts this category will reach $14.8 billion by 2002. It also claims EIPs will exceed the investment opportunities of the massive enterprise resource planning (ERP) market.

OK, end of the terminology discussion—what's the real, one-to-one moral of this story? We think that as Web users become more savvy, relying more on sophisticated B2B exchanges and specialty portals, the most successful exchanges will be the ones that are customer-oriented, rather than simply product-oriented. A good exchange, and one that will be more likely to succeed in a storm of heavy competition, should *solve problems for its visitors.* A corporate customer should be able to use a B2B exchange as an access point for increasing its profit or revenue, reducing its costs, improving its sales or production cycle, or bettering its own customer relationships.

Some manufacturers, such as Raytheon, a product and service provider to the aerospace and defense industry, create exchanges where buyers may purchase competitors' products as well as their own. (How better to communicate trust than to feature competitors on your own exchange?) At Everything Aircraft.com, Raytheon features not only its own aircraft parts but also those of other manufacturers. "Working with a wide variety of suppliers is critical," says John Carroll, general manager of EverythingAircraft. "A potential buyer will hit your site once, maybe twice, looking for a particular part before they go somewhere else—if you don't have the parts buyers need, you lose in this business." (As an added bonus, of course, when you sell your competitors' products on your own site you can more easily estimate your share-of-customer with each customer.)

No matter what the scenario, to survive over the long term an exchange must be designed not just to connect buyers and sellers but also to solve problems for its customers—to develop relationships with them. But what are an exchange's opportunities for a longer-term relationship with the end customer (whether a buyer or seller)?

Basically, you need a compelling, value-based argument for customers to keep coming back to you. One of our clients, an air conditioner manufacturer and wholesaler, had virtually no contact with its end customers, in this case homeowners. From the end customer's perspective, the distributor or installer was the supplier. So there was no compelling reason for a homeowner to have a relationship with the air conditioner manufacturer. On the surface, that makes sense—if you buy a central air conditioning unit, you're probably familiar with the service company that installed it. You may also be familiar with the brand, but it probably wouldn't occur to you that you have a relationship with the manufacturer. And this is, in fact, the real issue. Will your customers *want* to have an ongoing relationship with your brand? Can you build a sense of *community* around your branded site? If the answer to both these questions is "yes," then building your own exchange can make sense.

Some of the early vertical Web portals emerged from bricks-and-mortar businesses that decided to build virtual communities online, such as Commerx PlasticsNet.com, an e-marketplace for the plastics industry, and Chemdex, an e-marketplace for the life sciences industry. In each of these cases, the exchange epitomizes a "community," facilitating communication among the customers of the exchange.

Creating your own vertical portal could cost upward of $150 million. Before it catches on, your end customers must think of your company as the solution to a significant set of their needs. The air conditioner manufacturer we worked with satisfied only a small subset of homeowners' needs. Their full set of needs—everything from buying a new deck to painting a house to fixing a garage door—is typically handled by a service contractor. Therefore, we recommended that our client form a partnership with a homeowners' portal, such as RealHome.com, rather than create one from scratch.

Show me the value-added services

The Holy Grail of business goals for any B2B exchange is to grow large enough to become virtually the only exchange of any significance in its primary market. As with many other areas of activity during the Internet gold rush, important benefits derive from the "network effects" of establishing an early lead in the number of buyers and sellers trafficking at a B2B exchange. Whoever gets there first, in terms of having the most buyers and sellers gathering at a particular cyber-location, has the best chance of maintaining its number-one position permanently. In essence, a B2B exchange truly succeeds if it can establish its dominance and become a "benevolent monopoly," overseeing all the e-commerce transactions within its particular domain.

However, one important and often overlooked criterion of success, if market dominance is the final goal, is the degree to which an exchange can block competitors by generating genuine loyalty on the part of the buyers and sellers who use the exchange. There are many ways in which a B2B exchange can make money, and we're going to review these business models now. Note that some of the more sophisticated revenue-generating activities, such as providing ancillary information services and value-added services, are also excellent vehicles for generating long-term customer relationships.

The simplest and most common business model for any B2B exchange is to take a share of the sales transaction. By taking a small piece out of the middle of each transaction, something usually ranging from 0.5 to 5 percent, the exchange's value is immediately linked to the overall value of the consummated deal. No deal, no cost to either party. This is by far the most lucrative business model. Large, established markets, like the stock exchanges, make money primarily in this way. It is also one of the most easily and immediately scalable business models, because buyers and sellers can "sign up" to participate in the exchange at no cost whatsoever to themselves—only having to pay when and if a deal is struck.

An exchange organized on the World Wide Web has many additional ways to make money, however. It could charge for the listing itself, becoming in essence a "media" firm—like the Yellow Pages. No matter whether a sale takes place, an exchange could charge a seller for displaying his goods, or it could charge a buyer for the privilege of looking. It could charge sellers higher prices for listings that are more preferentially displayed, while showing other sellers at little or no charge in order to fill out the Web site with enough listings to make it attractive for buyers to come.

The dominant airline reservations systems in the United States, SABRE (owned by American) and Apollo (owned by United), got into antitrust difficulties in the 1980s when the preferential listing of flights by American and United, respectively, was deemed to give these carriers an unfair competitive advantage over other airlines. But unlike the Web, the airline reservations networks were closed systems, requiring travel agents to buy their own dedicated terminals in order to take advantage of the convenience of automated bookings. This meant that once an agent had committed to one system or the other, it was nearly impossible for another reservations system to gain a foothold, so those carriers who did not already own reservations systems were, in effect, being permanently shut out of the distribution system.

It remains to be seen whether a similar antitrust issue will be raised with respect to large Web-based B2B exchanges that are owned or operated by one of the vendors themselves. However, the fear that an exchange owned by one or more participants with an economic and competitive interest in the transactions will be biased against non-owners will certainly play a role in determining the non-owner participants' willingness to transact there as well as the government's level of interest.

In addition to transaction fees and listing fees, an exchange can also make money simply by selling advertising access. In almost any horizontal or vertical application, there are all sorts of specialized merchants who might not directly participate in the industry but who nevertheless have a sincere interest in selling things to the industry's participants. Even though in most instances advertising revenues by themselves will not be sufficient to pay the entire cost of operating an exchange, such revenues can be an important supplemental revenue stream.

An exchange could make money by selling information directly, even when this information is *not* linked to particular sellers or buyers. Information regarding the proper water filtration techniques for different types of impurities and climates is valuable to civil engineers dealing in this arena. It makes little difference whether an exchange actually sells this type of information outright, in the form of research reports or studies, or offers it as an enticement to attract buyers and sellers to its Web site. Either way, providing reliable and up-to-date technical information is an activity calculated to add value to an exchange's business model. But in addition, when a user requests information like this, the exchange is learning something important about the user, and it could leverage what it now knows to make it easier for that user to find relevant information in the future.

Over and above these forms of revenue generation, an exchange could earn a profit by playing a role in authoritatively "certifying" individual sellers or buyers as qualified in some way. An exchange could certify that a seller meets certain objective, unbiased standards of quality, and then stand behind this certification with an implicit or even explicit satisfaction guarantee to the buyer. This tactic received a lot of press attention in the B2C space, when Amazon began certifying its auction sellers, in contrast to eBay, which takes a more "caveat emptor" approach. In the B2B space, very few exchanges now offer this service, even though it could prove to be an important point of leverage in establishing an exchange as a true, benevolent monopoly. In an effort to achieve dominance, an exchange should be trying to add those services that tend to define and enforce the "standards" governing commercial transactions. The rise of the Web offers a remarkable standards-setting opportunity in almost every domain of e-commerce.

Finally, a B2B exchange should set its long-term sights on generating revenue and customer loyalty by offering a variety of value-added services. Even for exchanges purely concerned with connecting the buyers and sellers of commodity products, the total cost of ownership, or the total cost of acquisition, of those products, is usually more than the actual material cost of the products themselves, and sometimes much more. Just a few of these value-added services might include:

- Transaction history maintenance
- Order status reports
- Installation assistance
- Operation consulting
- Standardization advice
- "Smart" invoicing
- Auto-replenishment
- Data storage
- Back end/front end integration (technology entanglement)
- Data mining/pattern analysis
- Load or throughput optimization
- Collaborative supply chain management

While some of these features may seem "bleeding edge" now, we guarantee they'll be standard for every one-to-one B2B exchange in the near future—some of them perhaps by the time you hold this book in your hand.

What to do?

Regardless of the business model, the industry, or the complexity of the products and services involved, certain strategies are indeed key to enhancing the competitive strength of a B2B exchange. Many of these strategies are directly applicable to any one-to-one enterprise.

In the short term, one of the most important things to do is to try to become a destination. The achievement of "destination status," says VerticalNet chief technology officer Dave Ritter, "leads to greater transaction volume in our business communities." And how. Whether we're dealing with a technology firm's Web site such as Cisco Connection, or a building materials site such as Owens Corning's, or a pure B2B industry exchange such as meatandpoultry.com (one of the 50+ "communities" in the VerticalNet family), the most important goal is to become a true value-added "destination" for customers.

Cisco.com is an example of a site that has become such a true destination for technology managers. Although a verified purchase order or service agreement is required to experience the site's full functionality, the depth and breadth of information is astonishing. As senior manager of corporate communications Michael Hakkert explains, from this one Web site customers can choose from several dozen job- and industry-specific newsletters. In addition, Cisco publishes its own controlled-circulation print and online magazine, *Packet*. Certainly not overlooked by the firm, a third-party organization recently cited *Packet* as one of the top three most influential forms of customer communication from Cisco, just behind the sales force and Cisco.com itself.

An information-intensive yet readily searchable B2B site is a powerful strategic weapon. With the rise of business exchanges like Chemdex, specialty chemical maker Sigma-Aldrich became concerned by the potential insertion of an intermediary between it and its customers. But Sigma-Aldrich is not losing any volume to the exchanges. In fact, its Web site was chosen as the best in the chemicals industry by *Chemical & Engineering News* as well as by *Network World*, beating out Chemdex, SciQuest, and even competitors such as Fisher Scientific. "We know our customers' needs better than any business exchange," explains vice president and chief information officer Larry

Blazevich. "We have over 1,900 Ph.D.s on staff. We have the world's largest online library of chemical information. The aggregators may have 185 editors, but how many Ph.D.s? How much of a knowledge database? They can compete, sometimes, on price, but they can't match our end-to-end capabilities."

The same can be said of GE Plastics. Their Polymerland site is an example of a company with a wide-coverage catalogue, with listings driven by customer needs. The site is now attempting to go "deep" in terms of content, offerings, and end-to-end integration for specific solutions.

Providing more complete, front-to-back electronic processing of a product purchase and installation is another winning strategy. The more integrated your solution to a participant's problem, the more opportunity you will have to engage that participant in a longer-term relationship. One way B2B buyers are achieving this is via e-commerce platforms such as Commerce One, Ariba, and Intellisys. Battling these exchanges, leading B2B companies themselves also try to provide end-to-end processing.

Sigma-Aldrich, for example, consolidates the wares of five ERP-integrated divisions representing over 130,000 products sold to over 1.3 million research chemist or corporate procurement customers. Though approached via a combination of EDI (still a staple of the chemicals and pharmaceuticals industries), call centers, extranets, and its Web site, www.sia.com, the company still fulfills 95 percent of its orders on a same-day or next-day basis. "Our customers want it right, and right now," says Blazevich. To that end, "we now have full end-to-end e-commerce integration. You can find what you need, see it in the inventory, and order it—all at the same time. Then you know it will arrive tomorrow, and the payment will be processed automatically." Though it has taken over four years to complete the company's internal SAP implementation, the company was able to rapidly add full e-commerce capability utilizing software from Haht Systems. As Blazevich explains: "Installing the Haht architecture took less time than it took simply to read some vendors' responses to our RFP." Says Blazevich, "Our customers and our organization are now benefiting from the effort."

In the final analysis, it will be important to organize everything at your B2B exchange around individual customer needs. Different customers will need different things, even at an exchange that deals in commodity products. By organizing the entire site around customer needs, rather than around product varieties, or service selection, an exchange can position itself to create relationships with its users, whether they are buyers *or* sellers. If you're dealing in commodity products, then emphasize value-added services such as the ones already mentioned— things like throughput optimization, order status checking, or inventory maintenance. Even though they may buy the same commodity products, different users are still likely to have different inventory issues, different payment processes, different ordering parameters, and perhaps different manufacturing or delivery processes.

Increasingly, one-to-one exchanges offer collaborative supply chain management features such as product design, forecasting, and scheduling. These types of features allow buyers and sellers to interact in real time, customizing products and services on the fly. Basically, this means a buyer gets what he needs when he needs it. It also means that a supplier doesn't have to manufacture or stock goods until they're actually needed by a buyer. This is a significant step beyond "just in time" manufacturing. This is more like "instantaneous fulfillment," or something very near to it. Certainly, the availability of such value-added services would dramatically speed the process of mass customizing products, compressing weeks or even months of work into mere days.

Whatever you call it, it's safe to predict that value-added features such as collaborative supply chain management will likely prove essential to the long-term viability of any exchange aiming to be more than an auction site.

The one-to-one future for B2B exchanges

In the long run, the only dependably competitive business model for a B2B exchange will be to establish relationships with its customers. Even "benevolent monopoly" B2B exchanges will not be immune from having their business undermined by technology unless they, too, can find ways to build, cultivate, and strengthen individual relationships with their participants, over time.

The primary culprit in this march toward relationship building is, again, technology. Consider, for instance, how increasingly advanced information and interactive technologies are likely to shape the evolution of B2B exchanges. As the capability of this technology improves, exchanges will find themselves in more and more of an "open architecture" environment. Over the long term, as the best B2B exchanges seek to provide ever more encompassing and turnkey services for their participants, these exchanges will need connections between themselves and various other sites or exchanges dealing in related products and services.

If the most successful exchanges will be the ones able to attract the most buyers and sellers, effectively blocking out the competition, then it is important now to align your own B2B exchange with other exchanges or corporate Web sites. The idea, of course, is to create a friction-free channel for incoming and outgoing traffic. Just as software programs are more useful when they are compatible with other software, exchanges will be more useful to participants when they are compatible in all respects with other exchanges.

As the Web infiltrates every industry and takes over every commercial interaction, one can easily see a future of modular, interconnected exchanges, with small groups of exchanges together providing a multifaceted but seamless *set* of transactions for their participants. B2B exchanges will join together both vertically and horizontally, forming networks that offer increasingly automated, turnkey solutions for clients. Not just selling batches of rolled steel, but scheduling the mill's throughput, procuring the iron ore and coke for the batches, finding and reserving the rail cars required, and filing the environmental impact forms. Not just procuring aircraft engines, but delivering, installing, maintaining, and servicing the engines, doing the safety reporting, and ensuring regulatory compliance.

It is inevitable that B2B exchanges and portals in similar industries will glom together over time, forming larger and larger constellations of sites—"ecosystems" of exchanges and service-rendering sites, providing ever more integrated suites of solutions for the participants. As this happens, the World Wide

Web's own relentless efficiency dynamic will be constantly sucking the friction out of individual B2B exchanges themselves, generating a new and even more lethal form of cost transparency.

This means *any* business model that depends for its success on imposing a toll on isolated, independent transactions, as they occur within a B2B exchange, is doomed to long-term failure. As inevitably as capital seeking a higher return, transaction tolls will be hammered down, down, down, toward their natural level in a completely frictionless economic system—zero.

Nor will even the most benevolent of B2B exchange monopolies be able to maintain its monopoly for long. The "ecosystem" will simply grow around monopolies. Like a boulder blocking a tree root, the tollgate erected by a B2B exchange to tax the transactions going through it will simply be broken, eroded, or evaded into irrelevance, as modular exchanges in other areas adapt themselves to compete. Other constellations of exchanges will inevitably be driving to provide broader and more comprehensive solutions to their own participants, converging into the offending monopoly's space in the process.

As a result, probably the single most important rule for long-term competitive success, in designing and operating a B2B exchange, is to construct the business model in such a way as to be adaptable to a completely open, nonproprietary, frictionless ecosystem of interconnected exchanges. The business model must generate a profit even when transaction tolls spin down to zero.

What business model can possibly do this? Only a business model based on managing customer relationships, one customer at a time.

Chapter 9

Return to the future

Generals often make the mistake of assuming the next war will be similar to the past one. The truth is, almost all of us expect the future to be a repeat of the past, and this same mistake often afflicts even the smartest, most accomplished business leaders.

But the world we live in now has changed so radically in the past few years that fighting yesterday's competitive battle today is almost guaranteed to fail. Cheap and powerful computing technologies, combined with the near-zero cost of engaging individual customers in complex communications over the Internet, have dramatically transformed the landscape of business competition.

The companies hit hardest by the changes brought on by these technologies are the largest ones, companies that had waged successful campaigns in the past. Like the armies of Napoleon and Robert E. Lee, they often had the smartest and most capable leaders. Some of these successful, profitable firms are now faced with the prospect of near-certain ruin. Their only hope in some cases is to renounce many of the very organizational structures and business practices that made them so successful in the first place.

The competitive business battles of the last century were fought among the hedgerows and fences of sales and customer acquisition. But as the business-to-business landscape flattens out and becomes a featureless plain, imperfect information no longer provides the cover it once did. Each combatant's weapons and weaknesses are becoming visible to all. The rules of engagement have changed.

If there is a single overriding lesson that emerges from the five case studies in this book it is this: In the frictionless one-to-one future, B2B organizations must do a lot more than just sell. They must climb ever upward within each individual customer organization, involving themselves more and more intimately in the customer's business, helping each client to manage its own business ever more efficiently and effectively, one customer at a time. Only in this way can a B2B organization improve relationships with its customers enough to provide traction for its own profits. The companies that build relationships most successfully do it by concentrating on just a few important but often difficult tasks:

Account development
One of the surest ways to strengthen any B2B customer relationship, account development is a difficult and complex tactic to execute well. Growing an account into a larger and more profitable asset involves more than simply winning the next contract. A business must use the latest computer tools to track

individual actors within the account and map their relationships with one another. Treating different individuals differently within a corporate account is an intuitively powerful idea, but one that is for most firms extremely difficult if not completely impractical. Today, however, Web technology does in fact enable companies to approach this ideal. Those that do it successfully are far more likely to survive in the new, frictionless battlefield of B2B exchanges and e-business.

Knowledge-based selling

In turn, one of the most important keys to successful account development is *knowledge-based selling*. But a sales force created to deal competently with the customer acquisition struggles of the last century is often not going to be prepared for knowledge-based selling. Sales skills, tenacity, and the ability to hit a quota are still valuable, but in the current century consultative thinking will be more important than any of these other attributes. It should be no surprise that the expertise required to help a customer solve a problem is quite different from, and often more expensive than, the talent required to persuade a buyer to sign a contract. More than one of the companies we examined had to completely reinvent its sales strategy, and even its sales force structure, retraining the salespeople or hiring new ones and then equipping them with different, more technologically sophisticated tools. As we learned from our cases, to be successful a company must measure the results of its sales effort differently and redraw its compensation plans to better match its success metrics.

Embracing information technology

Of all the various leverage points that might allow a firm to sell its knowledge to clients and develop deeper customer relationships, probably none is as powerful as technology itself. To be successful, a B2B organization must not only be familiar with the latest technology for managing customer information and interactions; it must embrace this technology head-on and deploy it with vision and purpose. It is the meteoric development of these revolutionary information technologies that has brought us to this situation to begin with, and probably the single biggest point of leverage any B2B company could hope for today is simply to be technologically competent and innovative. When Dell uses the Web to reach deep into its corporate customers' organizations and strike up one-to-one relationships with the individual users of its equipment, it is leveraging technology to the maximum. Information technology is what permitted Convergys and Novartis CP to prioritize their customers in the most rational way. And information technology is how Bentley is converting the purchasers of its software seat licenses into longer-term subscribers to a series of business-managing services.

Total cost of ownership

One way to zero in more effectively on the problem a client faces, from the client's own perspective, is for a B2B organization to focus on the total cost of ownership of its product or service as it must be employed to solve the client's problem. A traditional sales-and-marketing approach almost always focuses primarily on transactions individually. But in building customer relationships, the key is to reorient the business, away from the immediate need to generate sales transactions and toward the long-term need to solve the customer's broader problem, over time. So what are the *informational requirements* that accompany the product or service you are selling? What extra *services* do your customers often have to provide for themselves in order to employ your product or service? What *obstacles* lie between your customer's decision to purchase and install your product and his successful use of it to solve his own problem? Dell's Premier Pages Service helps a company reduce the total cost of owning Dell products by providing a convenient, Web-based system for managing procurement and ordering. Bentley's SELECT program allows clients to (1) ensure that their architects and engineers always have the latest software version and (2) manage their own "seats" in a more flexible way, reducing their cost of ownership in the process. The real payoff comes in the collaboration with the customer: The process of reducing total cost of ownership requires participation and investment on the part of the customer, and reinvesting that effort would be added to the cost of switching to your competitor.

Channel management

One of the biggest problems often faced by B2B organizations trying to initiate individual customer relationships is that all these activities and interactions must take place within an outdated and often hostile channel structure. Novartis plotted a strategy to ensure that their dealers are not cut out of the farmer relationships. Bentley organized resellers to participate in joint sales calls on large accounts. It's clear from the successes we've documented that for client relationships to succeed when a third-party sales channel is involved requires a company to co-opt the channel members themselves. They must do this in order to structure some type of win-win situation—unless, as is the case with Dell, the business grows up in the direct-to-customer world to begin with.

Cultural change

And finally, regardless of how well a firm deals with all the issues of account development, knowledge-based selling, and the like, one final, extremely important lesson learned from our B2B case studies is that managing individual customer relationships almost certainly will require not just organizational but *cultural* changes within the B2B organization itself. *Attitudes* have to change, not just processes. Even organizations that have well-developed, client-focused traditions, such as Convergys, with their handful of large corporate customers, are likely to find that reorienting themselves to develop accounts and manage longer-term relationships involves a good deal more than just a new set of business processes or a revamped sales force. The magnitude of the "attitude change" needed at a firm might even necessitate installing a "cultural change officer," as Novartis did. And LifeWay, having bought into the whole premise of relationship management as a means for furthering its corporate strategy of customer intimacy, nevertheless dedicated an immense amount of organizational effort toward the education of its managers and their participation in the change process.

All five B2B organizations profiled in this book are striving to become "best of breed" in the customer relationship arena. All five believe that attaining a consistent level of excellence in things like account development and knowledge-based selling will assure them continued growth and profitability. No, actually it's more than that—most of our subjects believe that without such excellence, if their effort to build sustainable customer relationships fails, then their long-term prospects are bleak.

Managing customer relationships is so intuitive an idea that it sounds simple. Conceptually, it is simple. The problem is implementation and execution. Implementing a program to develop and manage hundreds, thousands, or even millions of individual customer relationships is possible, but it is certainly not easy, and our five case studies amply demonstrate this.

So why bother? Why even put up with all this corporate angst? Because in today's Real Economy, the technology-powered, increasingly frictionless landscape of transparent costs and one-click customer defection, absolutely the only dependable strategy for protecting and enhancing your bottom line is to cultivate healthy, profitable, long-term customer relationships, one customer at a time. For B2B firms especially, customer relationships will spell the difference between success and failure.

Endnotes

Chapter 1. The Once and Future Business Strategy

Page 6: For our discussion of the effects of market-making Web sites on B2B suppliers, we relied heavily on our own business experience. We also found useful information in several timely articles, including: Ross Banham, "The B2B Bazaar: Market Leader VerticalNet Expands the Universe of Online Trading Communities," *Executive Edge*, April–May 2000, pp. 33–37; Mick Brady, "No Overnight Success for B2B," *E-Commerce Times*, July 21, 2000; and Bob Tedeschi, "E-Commerce Report: A Mad Dash to Create Electronic Marketplaces for Business-to-Business Transactions," *The New York Times on the Web*, January 24, 2000.

Pages 17–18: A "supply chain" is a value chain for a company looking up, toward vendors and suppliers. A "demand chain" is the value chain looking down, toward customers. We realize that these descriptions are oversimplifications. For detailed discussions of supply chain issues, see the following: Fred A. Kuglin, *Customer-Centered Supply Chain Management: A Link-by-Link Guide* (New York: American Management Association, 1998); "Dell Outlines B2B Commerce

Strategy: Meeting Supplier Demand," *Business 2.0 on the Web*, March 2000; Sean Donahue, "Supply Traffic Control: How i2 Keeps Sun's Global in Its Backyard," *Business 2.0 on the Web*, February 2000; Lisa R. Goldbaum, "I2 Plays with the Big Boys in B2B," *Forbes Magazine on the Web*, December 22, 1999; William J. Lewis, "Forging the Value Chain," *Intelligent Enterprise Magazine on the Web*, January 20, 2000.

Chapter 2. The *Real* Economy

Page 21: For an in-depth discussion of Keynesian cycles, we recommend visiting the Biz/ed/Institute for Fiscal Studies (IFS) Virtual Economy Web site at http://www.bizednet.bris.ac.uk/virtual/economy/library/economists/ keynes.htm.

Page 24: Kathleen McGuckin-VanGelder's pen-and-ink illustration of the F-117A Nighthawk was based on photographs posted on *Air Force Link on the Web* at http://www.af.mil/news/factsheets/F_117A_Nighthawk.html.

Page 27: The discussion of Internet-based B2B purchasing trends was based on reporting by Joshua Hallford, "B-to-B Buying Picks Up Speed," *The Industry Standard on the Web*, September 25–29, 2000.

Pages 27–28: The figures we refer to in our discussion of lower B2B supply costs were contained in a research report by Rakesh Sood et al., "B2B or Not 2B (version 1.1)," Goldman Sachs Internet Research Labs, November 12, 1999.

Page 28: Our discussion of how online B2B is likely to reduce procurement costs dramatically was based on our own business experiences and observations, as well as information contained in several articles, including: Associated Press, "General Electric Launches Personal Finance Site," February 8, 2000; Bloomberg News, "General Electric Forms E-Commerce Division," March 6, 2000; Claudia H. Deutsch, "G.E.'s Management Methods Are Put to Work on the Web," *The New York Times on the Web*, June 12, 2000; Laura Cohn, Diane Brady, and David Welch, "B2B: The Hottest Net Bet Yet? Business-to-Business Web Outfits May Wind Up Having Even More Impact than E-tailers," *Business Week on the Web*, January 17, 2000; Nick Earle, "The Future of B-to-B Is C-to-C," *The Industry Standard on the Web*, April 24, 2000; Douglas Frantz, "To Put G.E. Online Meant Putting a Dozen Industries Online," *The New York Times on the Web*, March 29, 2000; Bill Gurley, "Above the Crowd," *Unity Mail Express*, March 20, 2000; Julie Landry, "Big Three Automakers Face Big B2B Challenges," *Red Herring on the Web*, February 9, 2000; Jennifer L. Schenker and Tony Glover, "The Trillion-Dollar Secret Beneath the Hype: The Internet Is Fostering a Silent Revolution Through Online Exchanges That Allow Fast and Efficient Trading Among Corporate IT Systems," *Time Digital*, February 28, 2000, p. 10; David Smith, "The B2B Revolution," *The Times* (London), March 5, 2000, News International section; and David M. Walker, "B2B Systems Must Offer More," *The Age* (Australia), February 29, 2000.

Page 29: Our discussion of how General Mills leverages its B2B e-commerce strategy to gain competitive advantages over larger rivals was based on a telephone conversation, September 14, 2000, with Thomas Forsythe, director of corporate communications at General Mills.

Page 29: The intertwining of the "old" economy and the "new" economy to produce something very different is a concept we discuss frequently at the Peppers and Rogers Group. The idea of the "real" economy was introduced to us in an article by Jacob Schlesinger, "Puzzled Investors Seek the Real Economy As the Idea of Old vs. New Loses Potency," *The Wall Street Journal on the Web*, March 22, 2000. For a good overview of the "new" economy, we recommend reading Kevin Kelly, *New Rules for the New Economy: 10 Radical Strategies for a Connected World* (New York: Viking/Penguin, 1998).

Page 30: Our discussion of brand building in an online environment was based on our own business experiences, and on a report by the Aberdeen Group, "Customer-Centric E-Business: The Next Evolution of CRM," June 2000.

Page 30: The impact of cost transparency on modern commerce is discussed and analyzed in a useful article by Indrajit Sinha, "Cost Transparency: The Net's Real Threat to Prices and Brands," *Harvard Business Review*, March–April 2000, pp. 43–50.

Page 31: The quote from Andy Zimmerman about the critical role of online relationships in online commerce was contained in a press release, "PricewaterhouseCoopers and Vignette Form Strategic Global E-Business and Customer Relationship Management Alliance to Help Clients Build Dynamic Online Business," *Vignette.com*, November 1, 1999.

Page 31: Our comments on the nature of the Efficient Market were based on Adam Smith, *The Wealth of Nations* (1776; reprint, Prometheus Books, 1991).

Page 43: Dr. Johnson's pithy observations about decision making under highly stressful circumstances can be found in James Boswell, *The Life of Samuel Johnson* (1791; reprint, Viking Press, 1979).

Page 47: For an excellent discussion of the concept of addressability, we recommend Robert C. Blattberg and John Deighton, "Interactive Marketing: Exploiting the Age of Addressability," *Sloan Management Review* (Fall 1991), pp. 5–14.

Page 48: Our interview with Cyndi W. Greenglass originally appeared in a staff Q&A, "It's All About People," in our monthly magazine, *1to1: Using Technology to Manage Customer Relationships*, September 2000, p. 44.

Page 51: A marketing purist might talk about wants and needs as if they were two different things. When we use the term "needs," however, we are using it as a catchall term for a customer's total, comprehensive set of motivations.

Pages 55–56: Jean Calembert of ASK, a Belgian market research firm, emailed us a generic version of the color-coded, needs-based customer differentiation matrix. Calembert developed the original chart, which has been used in a variety of formats by several of his clients.

Chapter 3. Dell: The Automated Relationship

Page 67: Our case study of Dell is based on extensive telephone and email interviews that we conducted from July through October 1999. We interviewed Chris Halligan, director of Dell's Relationship Online group; Kristena Bins-Turner, business development manager, Premier Dell.com; Robert Langer, then director, Dell.com, and currently vice president of business development at all.com; Cliff Mountain, vice president and general manager of Dell's Large Corporate Accounts Division; and Andy North, a Dell media representative. Patrick Vogt, who succeeded Chris Halligan as director of the Relationship Online group, also contributed information about the Premier Dell.com service. Sarah Lavender of Dell's communications team confirmed the factual accuracy of our text in September 2000.

Dell is not a client of the Peppers and Rogers Group.

Page 84: For our description of Eastman Chemical's online initiative, we spoke in April 1999 with Fred Buehler, director of electronic business at Eastman Chemical Co. We also gleaned useful information from several magazine and newspaper articles: Daniel Lyons, "Michael Dell's Second Act," *Forbes Magazine*, April 17, 2000, p. 208; "Eastman Pilot Links IT Infrastructure with Supplier and Customer; Based on WebMethods B2B," *WebMethods Home Page*, February 23, 2000; Joe Bousquin, "Eastman Chemical Scrapes Rust (Belt) and Takes B2B Plunge," *Street.com*, March 9, 2000; Eric Chabrow, "Buying a Piece of E-Business: Eastman Invests in Partners," *Information Week*, March 6, 2000; Daniel Roth, "Dell's Big New Act," *Fortune on the Web*, December 6, 1999.

Page 89: We based our discussion of the value chain largely on our own practical experience as consultants. We also found useful information in Michael E. Porter, *Competitive Advantage: Creating and Sustaining Superior Performance* (New York: The Free Press, 1985); John H. Dobbs, "Competition's New Battleground: The Integrated Value Chain," white paper, Cambridge Technology Partners, 1998; Gary McWilliams, "Dell Shifts Strategy to Make Servers Its No. 1 Priority," *The Wall Street Journal*, April 6, 2000, Technology Journal, p. B6; McWilliams, "Dell Computer Posts 21% Rise in Earnings, Topping Estimates," *The Wall Street Journal on the Web*, May 12, 2000.

Page 99: We found a useful discussion of the Internet's impact on competition, collaboration, and margin erosion in an article by Adam Dell, "Claiming Space on the Value Chain," *Business 2.0 on the Web*, July 1999.

Chapter 4. Bentley Systems: Preaching to the Choir

Page 107: Our case study of Bentley was based on extensive telephone, email, and in-person interviews that we conducted from June 1999 through January 2000. We interviewed Warren Winterbottom, senior vice president of sales; Greg Bentley, chief executive officer; Paul DeStephano, regional channel director; Yoav Etiel, former senior vice president, marketing; Charles Ferrucci, vice president, marketing; Andy Smith, project manager; Brad Workman, vice president, building engineering products; Pat Elnicki, proposal manager; Randall Newton, editor, *MicroStation Manager*; Frank Conforti of Project Bank, and Huw Roberts, MicroStation TriForma product manager. Greg Bentley confirmed the factual accuracy of our text in September 2000.

Bentley Systems has been a consulting client of the Peppers and Rogers Group.

Page 115: Our description of the relationship between Bentley and one of its channel partners, ModernTech, was based on a July 22,

1999, telephone interview we conducted with Joe Kirby, Modern-Tech's chief executive officer. He provided valuable information and insight about Bentley's strategy for building stronger bonds between the company and its various resellers.

Page 139: Our description of the role and responsibilities of a project manager at Bentley was based on an August 24, 1999, telephone interview we conducted with Kyle Talbott, an NBBJ architect. Talbott's highly detailed description of his firm's ongoing relationship with Bentley helped us develop a deeper understanding of how Bentley's project managers help maintain and develop one-to-one relationships with existing customers.

Chapter 5. Convergys: Racing for the Best Clients

Page 149: Our case study of Convergys was based on extensive telephone and email interviews that we conducted from October through November 1999. We interviewed with Bob Lento, senior vice president of sales and marketing at CMG; Ronald Schultz, then chief operating officer at CMG and now president of the CMG business unit; David Dougherty, then president at CMG and now chief development officer at Convergys; Jay Halsted, senior director of business development; and Mike Serpan, senior director of technology sales. Renea Morris, public relations manager at Convergys, confirmed the factual accuracy of our text in September 2000.

Convergys has been a consulting client of the Peppers and Rogers Group.

Page 152: We provide a very detailed discussion of the difference between actual value and strategic value in our second book, *Enterprise One to One: Tools for Competing in the Interactive Age* (New York: Currency/Doubleday, 1997), pp. 32–42 and 99–105.

Page 154: There is little question that the traditional call center outsourcing business model is transforming itself rapidly into something that is both new and substantially more customer-focused. In fact, many companies now refer to their call centers as customer contact centers. For a more thorough examination of the evolving call center outsourcing market, see Mary Wardley and David A. Shiang, "Customer Relationship Management Market Forecast and Analysis, 2000–2004," report, International Data Corporation, 2000.

Chapter 6. Novartis: Rediscovering the Customer

Page 193: Our case study of Novartis CP is based on extensive telephone and email interviews that we conducted from February to November 1999 with Novartis managers and executives. We interviewed Leopoldo Cid, marketing manager, Crop Protection; Carlos Weiss, chief executive officer, Crop Protection; Jan Martin Suter, marketing chief, Novartis SA; Juan Nava, sales manager, Crop Protection; Cecilia Rodríguez, human resources manager, Crop Protection; and Juan Cassagne, chief of finance, Crop Protection. We also spoke with Daniel Altomonte of Pivotal Corp. to get a better understanding of the unit's new customer contact system. Carlos Weiss and Jan Martin Suter confirmed the factual accuracy of our initial text in December 1999.

In December 1999, Novartis AG and AstraZeneca PLC announced plans to spin off their agribusiness units and merge them to form a new company. Pending regulatory approval of the plans, Novartis CP entered a "quiet period" and officials in Argentina declined to review a final draft of the chapter or to provide additional information. The substance and accuracy of our report was confirmed again, however, by Newton Washington and Jan Martin Suter in a telephone call on February 23, 2000.

In October 2000, Novartis AG shareholders approved the proposed spin-off and merger to create a new corporate entity, Syngenta. In a press release posted on the company's Web site, Novartis chairman Dr. Daniel Vasella said the transaction would allow Novartis to strengthen its focus on core healthcare activities and prepare for "the anticipated launch of a substantial number of new pharmaceutical products over the next three years."

Novartis CP is not a client of the Peppers and Rogers Group.

Page 195: We based our description of the problems facing the agrochemicals industry on our interviews with Novartis officials and several highly useful articles, including: Andrea Knox, "A Revolution Moves to the Field," *Philadelphia Inquirer,* October 5, 1999; David J. Morrow, "Market Place: Three Drug Companies Are Moving to Dump Their Agricultural Units as Worldwide Sales Decline," *The New York Times on the Web,* January 29, 1999; Morrow, "Rise and Fall of 'Life Sciences': Drugmakers Scramble to Unload Agricultural Units," *The New York Times on the Web,* January 20, 2000; and Morrow and Andrew Ross Sorkin, "2 Drug Companies to Combine Troubled Agricultural Units," *The New York Times on the Web,* December 2, 1999.

Page 201: We conducted a comprehensive telephone interview on January 19, 2000, with Jean Calembert, managing director of ASK Business Marketing Intelligence NV, to gain an understanding of the needs-based cluster strategy used by Novartis CP in its PEP program.

Page 206: Under a "picket fence" transition strategy, a firm's topmost customers are fenced off and individually managed, while the bulk of customers continue to be treated to the same basic marketing solicitations and offers as they always had been. See *Enterprise One to One: Tools for Competing in the Interactive Age* (New York: Currency/Doubleday, 1997), p. 88.

Chapter 7. LifeWay: A Sense of Mission

Page 227: Our case study of LifeWay is based on telephone and email interviews between July and October 2000 with John Kramp, director of operations at LifeWay Church Resources. We also drew extensively on our own consulting experience and knowledge of customer differentiation strategies to paint a complete picture of LifeWay's steady evolution from product-centricity to customer-centricity. The factual accuracy of our text was confirmed in October 2000 by Kramp; Ted Warren, chief operating officer; and Gene Mims, president.

LifeWay has been a consulting client of the Peppers and Rogers Group.

Page 227: For an extended discussion of the concept and practical aspects of customer intimacy strategies, see Michael Treacy and Fred Wiersema, *The Discipline of Market Leaders: Choose Your Customers, Narrow Your Focus, Dominate Your Market* (New York: Perseus Publishing, 1997); and Wiersema, *Customer Intimacy: Pick Your Partners, Shape Your Culture, Win Together* (Santa Monica: Knowledge Exchange, 1996).

Page 235: LifeWay considers *Experiencing God*, which emphasizes the idea of revelation through personal relationship with God, to be one of its most successful products, in terms of both commerce and ministry. Henry T. Blackaby and Claude V. King, *Experiencing God: Knowing and Doing His Will* (Nashville: Broadman & Holman Publishers, LifeWay Christian Resources, 1990).

Chapter 8. Virtual B2B

Page 267: Our discussion of Cisco Connection Online is based on material that appeared originally in a magazine article by one of our senior staff writers, Bill Millar, "To Be B-to-B Virtually: The Challenges of Business-to-Business CRM Online," *1to1: Using Technology to Manage Customer Relationships*, November 2000, p. 27.

Pages 268–72: Our discussion of the likely economic impact of B2B e-commerce was based on extensive research prepared for a semiannual report, "One to One Online: Best Practices of the Top One to One Web Sites," Peppers and Rogers Group/Marketing 1to1,

Inc., August 2000; "The Bazaar Nature of Exchanges," *Siebel Observer on the Web,* Special Edition, October 6, 2000; "U.S. Business-to-Business E-Commerce to Reach $4.8 Trillion in 2004: New BCG Research Reveals Rapid Growth in Online Ordering While Price Negotiations and Online Collaboration Still to Take Off," PR Newswire, September 7, 2000; and Forrester Research, "EMarketplaces Face the Law," report, October 2000.

Pages 272–77: We conducted a lengthy telephone interview on October 12, 2000, with John Cochran, chief executive officer of e-Greenbiz.com, to gather details about e-Greenbiz.com's business model, goals, and customer-centric strategies. Cochran's forthright description of a fledgling B2B exchange provided a clear picture of the challenges and opportunities facing online entrepreneurs.

Page 277: For a valuable discussion of the difficulties of setting up an online initiative, see Adam Feuerstein, "Wal-Mart to Build Private Net Marketplace," *Upside Today on the Web,* October 16, 2000.

Pages 277–80: To complete our description of e-Steel's online initiative, we conducted telephone interviews in March 2000 with Gene Moses, e-Steel's strategic services director, and Sherry Sigler, an e-Steel spokesperson. We also relied on articles by Clinton Wilder, "Construction Boom: Web Exchange Operators Are Building Marketplaces at a Frantic Pace," *Information Week.com,* March 27, 2000; and Connie Guglielmo, "Ransom: Customer Data," *Inter@ctive Week,* October 9, 2000, p. 88.

Page 280: Our description of and predictions about the future of horizontal B2B exchanges are based on our own experiences and perceptions. For a valuable discussion of the rapidly changing landscape of B2B exchanges, see John Foley, Beth Bacheldor, and Bob Wallace, "E-Markets Are Expanding: Online Exchanges Add More Services and Interconnections," *Information Week.com,* February 28, 2000.

Page 282: A vertical portal's inherent conflict of interest arises from having sellers pay, which leads to the inevitable preferential treatment of the highest-paying sellers versus objective recommendations on behalf of the buyers.

Page 283: Our interview with Mary Whelan, vice president of Lucent's e-business initiative, appeared originally in an article by Tom Shimko, "Any Portal in a Storm," *Inside 1to1 on the Web*, August 10, 2000, http://www.1to1.com.

Pages 283–85: The statistics we cite in our discussion of corporate vortals were drawn from two reports, Varda Lief, Bruce D. Temkin, Kathryn McCarthy, Jeremy Sharrard, and Tobias O. Brown, "Net Marketplaces Grow Up," Forrester Research, Inc., December 1999; and Glenn Ramsdell, "The Real Business of B2B," McKinsey & Company, September 29, 2000, http://www.zdnet.com/ecommerce; and from Bill Millar's article "To Be B-to-B Virtually," cited above.

Page 284: The interview with John Carroll, general manager of EverythingAircraft, appeared originally in an article by Tom Shimko, "To Vortal or Not to Vortal," *Inside 1to1 on the Web*, August 17, 2000, http://www.1to1.com.

Page 290: Our discussion of "destination status" was based on a March 27, 2000, telephone interview we conducted with Dave Ritter, VerticalNet's chief technology officer. He provided many valuable insights about current and future B2B exchange strategies.

Page 291: Our discussion about the value of becoming a trusted provider of technology information was gleaned largely from a March 17, 2000, telephone interview we conducted with Michael Hakkert, Cisco's senior manager of corporate communications.

Page 292: The information about GE Plastics' Polymerland Web site was contained in Claudia H. Deutsch, "G.E.'s Management Methods Are Put to Work on the Web," *The New York Times on the Web*, June 12, 2000.

Pages 292–94: Our suggestions for including a collaborative design feature among the value-added services offered by a one-to-one B2B exchange were based on internal discussions at Peppers and

Rogers Group. For a brief, but useful discussion of collaborative services, see Theo Mullen, "A Shared Supply Chain: Semiconductor Firm Builds Collaboration into Its Design Process," *InternetWeek*, October 23, 2000, pp. 35–36.

Pages 292–94: Our discussion of end-to-end e-commerce integration was based on a telephone interview we conducted on April 10, 2000, with Larry Blazevich, vice president and chief information officer of Sigma-Aldrich. He also provided us with highly useful information about managing and maintaining a knowledge database.

Recommended Reading

Books

Amram, Martha, and Nalin Kulatilaka. *Real Options: Managing Strategic Investment in an Uncertain World*. Boston: Harvard Business School Press, 1998.

Combining theory with real-world case studies, *Real Options* explains how to find opportunity in risk and uncertainty and how to incorporate these results into investment strategy. This approach is particularly relevant when considering customer-centric sales or marketing strategies, which can be difficult to cost-justify using traditional methods.

Christensen, Clayton M. *The Innovator's Dilemma: When New Technologies Cause Great Firms to Fail*. Boston: Harvard Business School Press, 1997.

This book explores the idea that some successful companies can fail by listening *too* closely to their customers. Christensen argues that there is a difference between what customers say they want and what they need or can actually use, especially when innovative technologies are involved. *The Innovator's Dilemma* explores strategies for using "disruptive innovations" to benefit enterprises and warns firms about the long-term risks of focusing exclusively on products or services that offer the highest immediate profits.

Colletti, Jerome A., Mary S. Fiss, and Wally Wood. *Compensating New Sales Roles: How to Design Rewards That Work in Today's Selling Environment*. New York: AMACOM, 1999.

The authors argue convincingly that a primary goal of any customer-centric enterprise should be to increase the value of its customers. To achieve this, however, the sales force must do more than simply sell; it must be focused on meeting customer needs. *Compensating New Sales Roles* provides guidelines and strategies for reinventing the traditional sales force and for rewarding customer-centric behaviors on a logical, consistent basis.

Dell, Michael. *Direct from Dell: Strategies That Revolutionized an Industry*. New York: HarperBusiness, 1999.

Michael Dell traces the success of Dell Computer Corporation, from its humble beginnings in a college dorm room to the present. The book's most important lesson, however, is that a customer-focused sales strategy can achieve impressive results when supported by an aggressive approach to supply chain management.

Dyson, Esther. *Release 2.0: A Design for Living in the Digital Age*. New York: Broadway Books, 1997.

Dyson offers a sweeping view of how new digital technologies can be expected to change economies and organizations as well as our social lives. She looks at an array of issues—everything from education to privacy to e-commerce.

Gilmore, James H., and B. Joseph Pine, eds. *Markets of One: Creating Customer-Unique Value Through Mass Customization*. Boston: Harvard Business Review, 2000.

This collection of ten *Harvard Business Review* articles chronicles the evolution of business competition from mass markets to markets of one—in other words, from creating standardized value through mass production to creating customer-unique value through mass customization. *Markets of One* offers the best of the leading thinkers on the topic, exploring both the promise and the pitfalls of mass customization. Practical applications are presented along with case studies.

Kelly, Kevin. *New Rules for the New Economy: 10 Radical Strategies for a Connected World.* New York: Viking/Penguin, 1998.

Kelly offers a good explanation of the economic value of interconnectivity. In the new economic order, Kelly argues, success flows primarily from understanding networks. In a traditional economy, value is created by scarcity. In a networked global economy, however, value is created by abundance, Kelly says.

Kotter, John P. *Leading Change.* Boston: Harvard Business School Press, 1996.

A practical resource that details eight crucial steps to successfully negotiating corporate change and explains why it is necessary to maintain the energy and goals of these steps at all times, not just in times of crisis. Kotter also explains how and why even the best plans can be derailed.

———. *John P. Kotter on What Leaders Really Do.* Boston: Harvard Business Review, 1999.

In this collection of his *Harvard Business Review* articles, Kotter defines the new roles of leaders and managers in the rapidly evolving business environment. One clear lesson is that traditional, chain-of-command corporate hierarchies cannot keep pace with the ever-quickening rate of social and technological change.

Kuglin, Fred A. *Customer-Centered Supply Chain Management: A Link-by-Link Guide.* New York: AMACOM, 1998.

An excellent "how-to" resource that maps out strategies on how to plan and implement customer-focused supply chain management solutions.

Molenaar, Cor. *Interactive Marketing*. Hampshire, United Kingdom: Gower Publishing, 1996.

Molenaar offers expert commentary about the impact of IT on the way goods and services are offered to, and ordered by, the customer. The author, now an independent management consultant, has made a special study of the application of IT to marketing, and this book was a bestseller in its original Dutch edition, when Molenaar was still a senior executive in Ogilvy & Mather's Netherlands operation. With the aid of practical examples and case studies, it explains why customer dialogue is the key to business success and how technology can provide the means. The possibilities include not simply access to unprecedented marketing opportunities but, for example, the chance to specify new products to satisfy customers' needs—and ways of involving the customer directly in the production process. Molenaar's newest book, *E-Marketing: The End of Mass Marketing*, will be published in English in the summer of 2001.

Moore, Geoffrey A. *Crossing the Chasm: Marketing and Selling High-Tech Products to Mainstream Customers*. New York: HarperBusiness, 1995.

Required reading material in many business schools, *Crossing the Chasm* introduces the idea that in high-tech markets the greatest peril for many firms occurs at the moment of transition from an early market dominated by a few *visionary* customers to a mainstream market dominated by large blocks of *pragmatic* customers. *Crossing the Chasm* provides practical solutions for making the transition and creating a long-term marketing strategy.

————. *Inside the Tornado: Marketing Strategies from Silicon Valley's Cutting Edge*. New York: HarperBusiness, 1999.

Picking up where *Crossing the Chasm* leaves off, *Inside the Tornado* offers useful guidelines for capitalizing on opportunities found beyond the "chasm." Using examples from companies such as Microsoft and Intel, Moore explains the three life cycle stages of the mainstream market, analyzing each stage's effect on competition, organizational leadership, and other contemporary business issues.

————. *Living on the Fault Line: Managing for Shareholder Value in the Age of the Internet*. New York: HarperBusiness, 2000.

Moore outlines practical advice for managing shareholder value in a market dominated by the Internet and fast-growth technology companies. Moore insists that management rethink the concept of "core value" and argues that managing for shareholder value should be considered synonymous with managing for competitive advantage. Under these conditions, the ability to outsource effectively becomes a strategic weapon.

Newell, Frederick. *Loyalty.com: Customer Relationship Management in the New Era of Internet Marketing*. New York: McGraw-Hill Professional Publishing, 2000.

Loyalty.com shows companies how to shift their focus from impersonal database marketing to true customer relationship management (CRM) to outline a program for lasting customer relationships. The book includes case studies and real-world examples and provides e-commerce marketing strategies for both B2C and B2B success. *Loyalty.com* is packed with analysis tools and measurement techniques for holding customers in an increasingly fragmented marketplace.

Norton, R. D. *The Geography of the New Economy*. Morgantown, WV: Regional Research Institute, WVU, 2000. http://www.rri.wvu.edu/WebBook/Norton.

An excellent online resource that explains the components of the new economy, charts the evolution of IT and the roles of early adopters, and contemplates which U.S. cities will be ready for the next round of innovation and why.

Peppers, Don. *Life's a Pitch: Then You Buy*. New York: Currency/Doubleday, 1995.

This readable and entertaining collection of anecdotes is based on Don's personal experience trying to win new clients in the advertising business. Ideal for anyone selling in a B2B situation—new ways to prospect, new ideas for pitching, new methods for differentiating your company from your competitors.

Peppers, Don, and Martha Rogers, Ph.D. *The One to One Future: Building Relationships One Customer at a Time.* New York: Currency/Doubleday, 1993.

The One to One Future revolutionized marketing when it was first published. Then considered a radical rethinking of marketing basics, this best-selling book has become today's bible for marketers.

————. *Enterprise One to One: Tools for Competing in the Interactive Age.* New York: Currency/Doubleday, 1997.

Enterprise One to One has taken its place alongside *The One to One Future* as a marketing classic that teaches readers to sell more products to fewer customers using one-to-one marketing. In this brave new world, where microchip technology is making it possible for businesses to know their customers better than ever before, there is incredible opportunity to build unbreakable customer relationships.

————. *The One to One Fieldbook: The Complete Toolkit for Implementing a 1to1 Marketing Program,* with Bob Dorf. New York: Currency/Doubleday, 1999.

The One to One Fieldbook is a practical guide to implementing the one-to-one marketing principles that Peppers and Rogers made famous throughout corporate America in their best-selling books, *The One to One Future* and *Enterprise One to One.* The *Fieldbook* is the first hands-on manual for implementing customer relationship management programs, featuring step-by-step guidance on how to initiate, evaluate, and upgrade one-to-one initiatives.

————. *The One to One Manager: Real-World Lessons in Customer Relationship Management.* New York: Currency/Doubleday, 1999.

In *The One to One Manager*, Peppers and Rogers go behind the scenes to report on the challenges and solutions discovered by managers leading one-to-one efforts at organizations such as Xerox, General Electric, Oracle, First Union, Hewlett-Packard, USAA, Levi Strauss, and British Airways. Filled with in-depth interviews with executives on the front lines of the one-to-one revolution, and based on more than two dozen case histories from companies around the world, this book examines the actual day-to-day issues involved in setting up and running one-to-one initiatives.

Peters, Tom. *The Circle of Innovation: You Can't Shrink Your Way to Greatness.* New York: Random House, Inc., 1999.

Circle of Innovation encapsulates the author's often-radical ideas on how to survive in a world where business is in a constant state of change. Peters is a thought-provoking guide through companywide transformations.

Pine, B. Joseph II. *Mass Customization: The New Frontier in Business Competition.* Boston: Harvard Business School Press, 1992.

As mass customization guru Joseph Pine demonstrates in this powerful book, the era of mass production is quickly coming to an end. In its place will emerge an era of cost-effective personalization on a grand scale. Pine shows how companies such as Motorola and McGraw-Hill have embraced "mass customization" in order to tailor their products and services. Mass customization, he explains, combines the personalized benefits of the preindustrial craft economy with low costs associated with mass production—often resulting in an overall cost *reduction* over standardization.

Pine, B. Joseph II, and James H. Gilmore. *Every Business a Stage: Why Customers Now Want Experiences.* Boston: Harvard Business School Press, 1999.

In this compelling book, Pine and Gilmore argue that the economy has moved into a new phase—one that revolves around staging experiences as opposed to simply selling products and services. They cite Disney, Planet Hollywood, and the Las Vegas casinos as pioneers in this economic transition. Experience providers, the authors contend, will develop coherent themes, leave lasting impressions, eliminate "negative cues," sell memorabilia (to remind the "guest" of the experience), and actively engage all senses.

Porter, Michael E. *Competitive Strategy: Techniques for Analyzing Industries and Competitors*. New York: The Free Press, 1980.

A valuable and well-structured resource, *Competitive Strategy* details, from economic theory to the practical application, how industries develop and how your company can play a distinctive role among its competitors.

————. *Competitive Advantage: Creative and Sustaining Superior Performance*. New York: The Free Press, 1985.

The follow-up to *Competitive Strategy*, *Competitive Advantage* focuses intently on the framework, from distributors to manufacturers, of an enterprise, and pioneers the concept of the value chain.

Reichheld, Frederick F. *The Loyalty Effect: The Hidden Force Behind Growth, Profits and Lasting Value*. Boston: Harvard Business School Press, 1996.

Reichheld argues effectively that loyalty is not dead. In fact, he says, loyalty can be significantly more profitable than perpetual churn. Companies that focus on retaining customers, employees, and investors will be more successful in the long run than companies that focus on short-term gains and ignore the positive impact of loyalty.

Schwartz, Peter. *The Art of the Long View: Planning for the Future in an Uncertain World*. New York: Currency/Doubleday, 1991.

Schwartz builds a convincing case for the use of scenario-based planning as a tool for preparing an enterprise to anticipate and prepare for a variety of possible outcomes when considering business strategies.

Siebel, Thomas M., and Michael S. Malone. *Virtual Selling: Going Beyond the Automated Sales Force to Achieve Total Sales Quality.* New York: The Free Press, 1996.

From the Silicon Valley entrepreneur who created Siebel Systems, this book makes a powerful case for enhancing the salesperson's role and facilitating a more collaborative relationship with the customer.

Trigeorgis, Lenos. *Real Options: Managerial Flexibility and Strategy in Resource Allocation.* Cambridge: MIT Press, 1996.

A comprehensive reference for the application of corporate resource allocation. This book also offers investment alternatives, melding option theory, and practical insights.

Underhill, Paco. *Why We Buy: The Science of Shopping.* New York: Simon & Schuster, 1999.

Often humorous, *Why We Buy* describes the science of shopping, a discipline created by Underhill, and its impact on the relationships among marketers, retailers, and increasingly knowledgeable consumers.

Wiersema, Fred. *Customer Intimacy: Pick Your Partners, Shape Your Culture, Win Together.* Santa Monica: Knowledge Exchange, 1996.

With powerful examples such as Airborne Express, Nike, and Staples, Wiersema discusses the strategies and techniques that have been employed to build lasting customer relationships. The book shows you how to provide complete solutions to customers' needs; create a partnering rather than vendor relationship; and differentiate your customers.

Wunderman, Lester. *Being Direct.* New York: Random House, 1997.

This book describes Wunderman's personal evolution as he helped to lay the foundations of the now pervasive direct marketing industry, and includes fascinating stories about his company's pioneering work with companies such as American Express and the Columbia Record Club.

Reports, Studies, and White Papers

Andersen Consulting. "Leveraging Customer Relationship Management in the High Tech Industry for Improved Financial Performance."

This study advises tech companies to respond to customer expectations for more speed and value-added services by developing better CRM capabilities.

Dobbs, John H. "Competition's New Battleground: The Integrated Value Chain." Cambridge Technology Partners, 1998.

This white paper provides a detailed and useful definition of the integrated value chain concept. It also looks ahead to what it calls the New Business Ecosystem, in which business partners collaborate under a single brand to reach customers via the Internet.

Philips, Charles, and Mary Meeker. "The B2B Internet Report: Collaborative Commerce." Report, Morgan Stanley Dean Witter & Co., 2000.

A comprehensive report that focuses on the trends created from B2B e-marketplaces, specifically market transparency, lower procurement costs, demand and supply chain management, customer intimacy specialized hubs, partnering, and what will and will not draw investors. Appendixes include company profiles and a B2B-specific glossary.

Newspaper and Magazine Articles

Banham, Ross. "The B2B Bazaar: Market Leader VerticalNet Expands the Universe of Online Trading Communities." *Executive Edge*, April–May 2000, pp. 33–37.

An in-depth account of VerticalNet's plan to stay on top of a business where vertical portals are expected either to vanish or to consolidate in the near future.

"The Big 10." *Forbes ASAP*, April 3, 2000, pp. 92–96.

A Top 10 list of the fastest-growing high-tech firms (companies with fiscal year revenues of $2 billion or more) that not only details how each firm achieves success but analyzes each firm's ability to "maintain its current growth rate for the foreseeable future."

Blattberg, Robert C., and John Deighton. "Manage Marketing by the Customer Equity Test." *Harvard Business Review*, July–August 1996, pp. 136–44.

Blattberg and Deighton urge that new products and customer service initiatives not be judged by asking questions such as "Will these products be profitable?" Instead they urge managers and executives to ask, "Will these products grow our customer equity?" The article describes how an organization can compute the optimal level of spending on customer-centric initiatives. The authors note that when managers strive to grow customer equity, they inevitably put the customer at the forefront of their strategic thinking.

Bousquin, Joe. "Eastman Chemical Scrapes Rust (Belt) and Takes B2B Plunge." *The Street.com*, March 9, 2000. http://www.thestreet.com.

A good description of Eastman Chemical's unexpected emergence as a leader in the world of e-commerce. Because Eastman is considered typical of the "old economy," its plunge into B2B e-commerce took many by surprise.

Campbell, Malcolm. "The New Sales Force: Swimming Against the Tide Is Out, Channels Are In." *Selling Power*, July–August 1999, p. 49.

Campbell discusses the potential value of a well-developed channel management strategy and explains why more companies view channel management as a competitive edge.

Chabrow, Eric. "Buying a Piece of E-Business: Eastman Invests in Partners." *Information Week*, March 6, 2000. http://www.information-week.com.

> The article discusses Eastman Chemical's investment in several Web ventures and predicts how such investments will help Eastman maintain a leadership role in B2B e-commerce.

Coy, Peter. "Exploiting Uncertainty: The 'Real-Options' Revolution in Decision-Making." *Business Week Online*, June 7, 1999. http://www.businessweek.com.

> A detailed look at a twenty-year-old concept coming into vogue again, this article explains why "real-options" theory is valid in today's unpredictable technology markets.

Dalton, Greg. "Easier Said than Done." *The Industry Standard*, April 10, 2000, p. 59.

> As companies race to create B2B exchanges, it is still unproven whether multiple partners "can have a harmonious business relationship while operating at Net speed." A useful discussion of the challenges facing B2B players in the Age of Interactivity.

Davis, Jeffery. "The Net Impact: The Brief History of the Major Market Sectors That Lit Up the Net Economy and Where They Lead Next." *Business 2.0 on the Web*, January 2000. http://www.business20.com.

> A useful series of articles that divides e-commerce into six unique market sectors (Net Access, Consumer Retail, Financial Services, Media and Entertainment, Business Services, and Supply Chain), explains how each sector developed, and predicts how they're likely to evolve in the near future.

Dell, Adam. "Claiming Space on the Value Chain." *Business 2.0 on the Web*, July 1999. http://www.business20.com.

> Adam Dell argues that vertical and horizontal analysis of value chains can help investors and start-ups focus on the most valuable links.

———. "Meeting Supplier Demand." *Business 2.0 on the Web*, March 2000. http://www.business20.com.

   As B2Bs demand more from hubs, supply chain management solutions emerge to bring functionality to exchanges that only provide transactional offerings.

Dini, Justin. "IBM, Nortel, Toshiba, Others to Start Tech B-to-B Marketplace." *The New York Times on the Web*, June 7, 2000. http://www.nytimes.com.

   IBM, Nortel Networks, Toshiba, and others create a B2B marketplace that caters to the computer, electronics, and telecommunications markets.

Donahue, Sean. "Supply Traffic Control: How i2 Keeps Sun's Global in Its Backyard." *Business 2.0 on the Web*, February 2000. http://www.business20.com.

   A detailed discussion of how supply chain management strategies have the potential to make or break competitors in rapidly evolving e-commerce markets.

Feder, Barnaby J. "For This Supplier, the Sum of Its Parts Adds Up to Success." *The New York Times on the Web*, September 22, 1999. http://www.nytimes.com.

   Even as e-commerce reshapes the world of commerce, a reputation for expertise and reliability may help keep old-line industries successful.

Fisher, Lawrence M. "Oracle to Build Market Site for Sears and French Chain." *The New York Times on the Web*, February 29, 2000. http://www.nytimes.com.

   Oracle's strategy in the B2B arena will focus on specialized products and services for vertical markets.

Gilder, George. "The End Is Drawing Nigh." *Forbes ASAP*, April 3, 2000, pp. 171–72.

   Communication as a technological force has surpassed the capabilities of computers. In the coming years, the most significant companies will be those who combine bandwidth and storage.

Gilmore, James H., and B. Joseph Pine II. "The Four Faces of Mass Customization." *Harvard Business Review*, January–February 1997, pp. 91–101.

    The authors outline the mass customization process in clear and concise terms. They discuss four distinctive approaches to mass customization: *collaborative, adaptive, cosmetic,* and *transparent.*

Hansell, Saul. "So Far, Big Brother Isn't Big Business; At Web's Rear Window, Marketers in No Rush to Mine Private Data." *The New York Times on the Web*, May 7, 2000. http://www.nytimes.com.

    Despite "corporate America's attempts to get more personal with its customers, most standard data-gathering systems used are ineffective." At the same time, the valuable customer information gathered at many Web sites doesn't rate a second glance from marketers.

Landry, Julie. "Big Three Automakers Face Big B2B Challenges." *Red Herring on the Web*, February 29, 2000. http://www.redherring.com.

    The challenge for the planned automobile manufacturers' exchange is "consolidating a tangled, often fractious network of suppliers." Yet the automakers see future benefits such as lowered inventory costs and customer-friendly options such as build-to-order cars and trucks.

Lewis, William J. "Forging the Value Chain." *Intelligent Enterprise Magazine on the Web*, January 20, 2000. http://www.intelligententerprise.com.

    Lewis discusses how data warehousing strategies can play a significant support role in each link of an integrated value chain.

Lyons, Daniel. "Michael Dell's Second Act." *Forbes Magazine*, April 17, 2000, p. 208.

    As Dell's online sales of PCs fall, Michael Dell makes plans to stanch the leakage by moving into other areas, such as servers, storage systems, and moving across verticals, as well as maintaining its presence in the world of low-cost PCs.

Markoff, John. "Plan Aims to Foster Electronic Commerce Between Businesses." *The New York Times on the Web*, September 5, 2000. http://www.nytimes.com.

IBM, Microsoft, and Ariba make plans to create an online catalogue of products and services to further automate transactions.

McWilliams, Gary. "Dell, Publishing Expansion Plan, Bundles Web Services with PCs." *The Wall Street Journal on the Web*, July 27, 1999. http://www.wsj.com.

Dell announces plans to bundle Internet access services with hardware for home office and small-business customers.

———. "Dell Shifts Strategy to Make Servers Its No. 1 Priority." *The Wall Street Journal*, April 6, 2000, Technology Journal, p. B6.

As Dell Computer Corporation's personal computer sales fall, the company changes its focus to the more profitable server-computer market.

———. "Dell Computer Posts 21% Rise in Earnings, Topping Estimates." *The Wall Street Journal on the Web*, May 12, 2000. http://www.wsj.com.

Dell's sale of servers and workstations and a lower component cost boost the company's bottom line.

Morrow, David J. "The Markets: Market Place; Three Drug Companies Are Moving to Dump Their Agricultural Units as Worldwide Sales Decline." *The New York Times on the Web*, January 29, 1999. http://www.nytimes.com.

The American Home Products Corporation, Novartis AG, and the AstraZeneca Group are all trying to sell their agricultural divisions as market troubles beset Europe and Southeast Asia.

Pine, B. Joseph II, Don Peppers, and Martha Rogers, Ph.D. "Do You Want to Keep Your Customers Forever?" *Harvard Business Review*, March–April 1995, pp. 103–14.

This article introduces the concept of a Learning Relationship, as well as the concept of a Learning Broker. With case studies on Andersen Windows, Individual Inc., and Peapod, it explains the intimate link between interaction, learning, and mass customization.

Pine, B. Joseph II, and James H. Gilmore. "Welcome to the Experience Economy." *Harvard Business Review*, July–August 1998, pp. 97–105.

Beyond goods, products, and services lie "experiences" and "transformations" as a force in the economy. Pine and Gilmore argue that companies must sell a compelling and memorable set of experiences if they hope to sustain their customer relationships.

Raynovich, R. Scott. "The Business of the Internet IS Business." *Red Herring on the Web*, January 19, 2000. http://www.redherring.com.

Practical advice for investors on what to look for in a successful B2B: more expertise, more management connections, and products that are "easily moved or described over digital channels."

Reynolds, Roy R. "Dell Introduces New DellHost Capabilities." *Dow Jones Newswires*, May 15, 2000. http://www.wsj.com.

Dell expands DellHost services to include next-business-day setup for PowerEdge servers and lower prices for Web hosting.

Roth, Daniel. "Dell's Big New Act." *Fortune on the Web*, December 6, 1999. http://www.fortune.com.

In addition to providing a good overview of Dell's e-commerce initiatives, this article also discusses Eastman Chemical's entry into the field with a Web service that echoes Dell's Premier Dell.com. Like Premier Dell.com, Eastman's Web service enables top corporate customers to track orders, review purchase histories, and receive technical support on customized Web pages.

Sawhney, Mohanbir, and Steve Kaplan. "Let's Get Vertical." *Business 2.0 on the Web*, September 1999. http://www.business20.com.

A detailed look at some newly formed B2B exchanges, with explanations of how they work and what they need to be successful.

Schenker, Jennifer L., and Tony Glover. "The Trillion-Dollar Secret Beneath the Hype: The Internet Is Fostering a Silent Revolution Through Online Exchanges That Allow Fast and Efficient Trading Among Corporate IT Systems." *Time Digital*, February 28, 2000, p. 10.

A useful look at how companies like Bayer and Swisscom are lowering procurement costs by moving their B2B transactions to the Web.

Schlesinger, Jacob. "Puzzled Investors Seek the Real Economy As the Idea of Old vs. New Loses Potency." *The Wall Street Journal on the Web*, March 22, 2000. http://www.wsj.com.

An interesting look at how companies from the "old economy" are utilizing technologies provided by companies associated with the "new economy." The transformation of these "old economy" firms is creating something Schlesinger dubs "the real economy."

Sinha, Indrajit. "Cost Transparency: The Net's Real Threat to Prices and Brands." *Harvard Business Review*, March–April 2000, pp. 43–50.

A solid, detailed explanation of how cost transparency aids buyers, but remains a disadvantage to manufacturers and retailers.

Smith, David. "The B2B Revolution." *The Times* (London), March 5, 2000, Sunday ed., News International section.

This article discusses the potential impact of business-to-business e-commerce on the industrial economy of the United Kingdom.

Sorkin, Andrew Ross. "International Business; AstraZeneca and Novartis to Shed Agricultural Units." *The New York Times on the Web*, December 3, 1999. http://www.nytimes.com.

This article provides detailed information on the plan by AstraZeneca PLC and Novartis AG to merge their agribusiness divisions and spin the joint venture off into a new company.

Stirland, Sarah Lai. "Putting B2B Under the Microscope." *Red Herring on the Web*, March 1, 2000.

Stirland argues that the traditional measures used to evaluate a company's performance are ineffectual in the new B2B Internet marketplace.

Strout, Erin. "1999 Best Sales Force, Dell." *Sales and Marketing on the Web*, July 1999.

This article provides a good description of how Dell's Web services help its sales force remain competitive while providing improved customer service to Dell clients.

Surowiecki, James. "Why Salesmen Never Die." *The New Yorker*, July 17, 2000, p. 30.

A useful article that restates a valid point: Despite advances in technology that make it possible to move more sales-related services to the Web, customers still yearn for personal relationships cultivated by good salespeople.

Tedeschi, Bob. "E-Commerce Report: A Mad Dash to Create Electronic Marketplaces for Business-to-Business Transactions." *The New York Times on the Web*, January 24, 2000. http://www.nytimes.com.

Tedeschi looks at how B2B exchanges are striving to remain competitive by offering more services to customers.

Vallejo, Maria P. "Dell Computer Unveils VC Direct Program." *Dow Jones Newswires on the Web*, August 29, 2000. http://www.wsj.com.

An interesting look at how Dell's VC Direct program leverages technology to help venture capitalists and the companies they've invested in.

Voedisch, Lynn. "For Beta or For Worse." *The Industry Standard*, May 8, 2000, pp. 239–42.

Voedisch urges caution for any enterprise considering the use of new and unproven software. Firms may risk exhausting employee resources and endangering their operating systems by using technology that isn't ready for general release.

Warbach, Kevin. "E-merging Markets." *Release 1.0, Esther Dyson's Monthly Report*, September 1999.

A brief description of the emerging B2B market, including a useful discussion of vertical portals.

Index

Page numbers in *italics* refer to illustrations.

Index

The Authors

Globally respected thought leaders, futurists, and management consultants, DON PEPPERS and MARTHA ROGERS, Ph.D., are the authors of four business best-sellers, *The One to One Future*, *The One to One Fieldbook* (co-authored with Bob Dorf), *Enterprise One to One*, and *The One to One Manager*. Their company, Peppers and Rogers Group, is the world's preeminent customer relationship management consulting firm, with offices on six continents and a number of Fortune 500 clients in both the B2B and B2C arenas. Before teaming up with Dr. Rogers, Don Peppers was a celebrated Madison Avenue rainmaker and the CEO of a major direct marketing agency. Rogers is Professor of the Practice at the Fuqua School of Business at Duke University and a member of the Dean's Advisory Council at Indiana University.